WHEN TH

WHEN THIS IS OVER

Reflections on an Unequal Pandemic

Edited by
Amy Cortvriend, Lucy Easthope, Jenny Edkins
and Kandida Purnell

Foreword by Sue Black

Afterword by Gary Younge

First published in Great Britain in 2023 by

Policy Press, an imprint of
Bristol University Press
University of Bristol
1-9 Old Park Hill
Bristol
BS2 8BB
UK
t: +44 (0)117 374 6645
e: bup-info@bristol.ac.uk

Details of international sales and distribution partners are available at
policy.bristoluniversitypress.co.uk

© Bristol University Press 2023

British Library Cataloguing in Publication Data
A catalogue record for this book is available from the British Library

ISBN 978-1-4473-6806-9 paperback
ISBN 978-1-4473-6807-6 ePub
ISBN 978-1-4473-6808-3 ePdf

The right of Amy Cortvriend, Lucy Easthope, Jenny Edkins and Kandida Purnell to
be identified as editors of this work has been asserted by them in accordance with the
Copyright, Designs and Patents Act 1988.

Cover design: blu inc
Front cover image: Stocksy/Luis Velasco

Bristol University Press and Policy Press use
environmentally responsible print partners.

Printed in Padstow by TJ Books

To the pandemic's dead, those who loved
them and those who cared for them, and
to those who continue to suffer and grieve.

Contents

Foreword   x
Sue Black

═══ 'When this is over' by Jennifer Mustapha   1

Introduction: A record, an accounting and a memorial   4
Amy Cortvriend, Lucy Easthope, Jenny Edkins
and Kandida Purnell

PART I: In this together?

═══ 'Home and away' by Sue Bryant   23

1   Pandemic deaths and the possibility of politics   24
     Jenny Edkins

═══ 'May 8th, 2020' by Marvin Thompson   42

2   Black, Asian and Global Majority experiences: 43
     a conversation
     Safina Islam, Jo Robson, Amna Abdul-Latif,
     Yvonne Edouke Riley, Sandhya Sharma and Circle Steele

═══ 'Illustrating grief: Lumière Tarot' by Dipali Anumol   75

3   Bodies with COVID-19   77
     Kandida Purnell

═══ 'Post-Covid thoughts' by Michael Rosen   102

4   Grieving and collective loss in assisted living   103
     Hannah Rumble and Karen West

PART II: Policing in an emergency

▬▬▬ *'Unlawful gathering' by Gracie Mae Bradley*   121

5   Protest and policing in a pandemic   123
Paul Famosaya

▬▬▬ *'Dying declaration' by Anjana Nair*   137

6   Legal education after COVID-19   139
Patricia Tuitt

▬▬▬ *'I have a wall in front of all my windows' by Manca Bajec*   154

7   Border harms in a pandemic   160
Amy Cortvriend

PART III: Caring for the dead

▬▬▬ *'Reckoning with grief' by Mark Brown*   179

8   Lessons from a mortuary   184
Lara-Rose Iredale

▬▬▬ *'My impending adventure, a story for another day'*   201
by Irene Naikaali Ssentongo

9   Funerals, cemeteries and crematoria: different   202
community experiences
Avril Maddrell, Danielle House and Farjana Islam

PART IV: Commemorating lives lost

▬▬▬ *'Photo story' by Led By Donkeys*   221

10   Walking the wall: COVID-19 and the politics of memory   232
Mark Honigsbaum

▬▬▬ *'Pandemic Easter' by Herbert Woodward Martin*   251

11   A wall of pain and love   252
Fran Hall

Contents

PART V: What comes next

━━ *'Go ahead, tell me' by Rita Coleman*   265

12   Emergency planning is dead   266
     Matthew Hogan

━━ *'Waiting to exhale' by Mehreen Hamdany*   276

13   Moving on   279
     Lucy Easthope

Afterword   291
Gary Younge

Notes on contributors   301
References   306
Index   335

Foreword

Sue Black

Much of my work has focused on uncovering the hidden stories of lost lives, whether as a result of suspicious circumstances, mass fatality events or atrocities of war. Without exception, each story has conveyed and confirmed both the fragility of life and the pain of loss. Therefore, this anthology of the COVID-19 pandemic resonated strongly with me.

COVID-19 was an inescapable global disaster, consumed 24 hours a day, on a multitude of repetitive media channels. There was no place to hide. Yet, despite our apparent familiarity, we seem to struggle to find the words and the means to express how something so unique to our generation impacted us all so profoundly. There is a gap in the ceremonies of honour and remembrance that we have developed in our *memento mori* culture over the generations that doesn't quite fit this scenario. Despite the magnitude of the experience and the scale of the loss, coping with the pandemic was alien to our prior lived experience, and so we had no carefully layered and practised memory on which to build a reflective meaningful response. In a mass fatality event the world stops, even if only for a brief moment, and all too often it is swiftly overtaken in the news by the next storyline. But the pandemic impacted us all and its presence persisted. It changed our established life patterns, challenged our well-rehearsed expectations, and for many it raised questions on what is truly important in our lives. It brought out the good in many, and the worst in others.

We learned swiftly that things were not going to be the same for quite some time, but we didn't know how long and so we had to adapt swiftly. Collectively, the world took tentative steps forward into largely unchartered territories, making decisions, good and bad, that would live with us all, perhaps for a lifetime. Yet somewhat ironically, we also knew instinctively that normal life had to keep going, and so we continued to raise our families, run our businesses, pay our bills, shop, cook, consume endless hours of electronic entertainment and just get on with it. It wasn't a 'wartime mentality'; it was something different, perhaps because the enemy was largely invisible and its tactics fundamentally unknown. The normality of life persisted, but in a totally abnormal style.

This volume provides us with an opportunity to pause, reflect and remember, and I was deeply touched by the personal testimonies, poetry and notes. Images can support words but they are also powerful solo performers, and the photographic record and illustrations will bear testimony through time to the lived experience. This is a collection drawn together with heart, spirit and purpose, and describes and depicts the pandemic in all its rawness through moving accounts gathered from across the country and from a diverse range of perspectives. Whether the photographs of the National Covid Memorial Wall or Dipali Anumol's hauntingly iconic Tarot cards, the reader cannot fail to be touched by the honesty conveyed in every piece. Some pieces are beautifully creative, and others depict the unfiltered accounts of the reality of work on the front line, for both health workers and emergency planners.

Poetry has a special place in the power of conveying sentiment, and the rawness of Gracie Mae Bradley's account of pandemic disruptions and injustices legitimised by the Coronavirus Act of 2020 will endure. Reality is conveyed in all its stark nakedness by Michael Rosen's moving tribute to the NHS, in whose hands his life balanced 'like a clothesline' when he became a critical COVID-19 case during the pandemic's first wave.

But it is not only the living that require support, and I know only too well the challenges of caring for the dead. Such work often passes without comment, almost as if society was afraid to name it and recognise it. Death is not a failure and something of shame; it is a reality. It is the mark of a civilised society that this duty is performed with trust and dignity, away from public eyes, and was perhaps the one part of the pandemic that we did not see up close in the UK, perhaps for fear of causing greater alarm. As a result, there was little public debate around death, its management and our expectations. Had we been permitted that freedom, it may have allowed many to better understand the scale of the tragedy and individualise the 'numbers' with which we were bombarded and even 'numbed' by, as Kandida Purnell discusses in 'Bodies with COVID-19'. Lara-Rose Iredale taught us of 'Lessons from a mortuary', and took this vital work out of the shadows and into the public spotlight. This work honours their commitment and dedication to a job that few could imagine undertaking on a daily basis.

A final strength of this volume is the comfort and ease with which it approaches conflict, and its ability to juxtapose gently opposing perspectives. The book honours the ambiguity we experienced, and recognises the need to grieve while looking forward to better times with the understanding that it may not yet be totally over. It is simply the time to pause and take stock, but not necessarily to celebrate.

There are so many big questions following the experiences of the pandemic. Do we consign the memories to history and just move on? Do we prepare ourselves for the next onslaught? Do we use this as a time to change our lives? How do we honour the lives lost? The answers are often individual and personal, but perhaps the most fitting beacon of hope to emerge from this adversity would be a collective determination to be better, to do better, and to think better.

WHEN THIS IS OVER

Jennifer Mustapha

Some will overcompensate.
Theirs will be
a need to make up
for time wasted, waiting.
For them this time will mean
a fervid rush
into each other's homes and arms.

I know that I
will likely find myself
unmoored
after more than a year of being free
of the fear that I am missing out.
That I will get left behind.
That the jokes won't be for me
because *you had to be there, of course.*

This is bittersweet
because new fears took up that space.
Fears of jagged breath
and being alone in terrible ways.
But really, how is that so different
from the anxieties that came before?

What if I told you
that all along
I have feared other people?

Their faces. Their hot breath.
Their demands and desires.

Fear that
I would get caught up
in diseases for which there is
no cure.
The race for better lives
bigger houses
newer things
smaller bodies
running by on the scroll
of even smaller minds.

But I'm not a misanthrope,
exactly.
I hold low expectations
but hopes that are higher.
They surprise me, these optimisms.
More than once I have been told
that I 'like people',
because apparently, this is notable.

But is this still true?
How does one recover from
knowing
that comings and goings
were rebukes of what it means
to care?

That movements rose and fell
in ways that never seemed to matter
when the bodies trapped

by emergencies
and risk mitigation
and fear of the unknown
were Black,
brown and bruised?

When this is over,
we tell ourselves
that we will un-mask
and stand closer
like before –
as if we weren't always
wearing masks
and standing alone,
our pools of light
already drifting
further and further
apart and away
from what it means
to love.

We tell ourselves
that this ends
that *if* this ends
that *when* this ends
there will be new beginnings,
as if we weren't already
in the process
of our own slow undoing.

Introduction: A record, an accounting and a memorial

*Amy Cortvriend, Lucy Easthope, Jenny Edkins
and Kandida Purnell*

In the poem that heads this collection – and the poem that gave the volume its title – Jennifer Mustapha articulates her ambiguity about any return to what counted as normal in pre-pandemic times. While some people, she says, will 'need to make up/for time wasted' with a 'fervid rush/into each other's homes and arms', she, in contrast, will find herself 'unmoored'. She points to how she cannot forget that those who were most 'trapped' were 'Black,/brown and bruised' and reminds us that, although 'when this is over,/we tell ourselves/that we will un-mask', we were always anyway masked and 'standing alone'.

Some of us will choose to forget the pandemic years – understandably. Others may not have that choice. If we do look back, we may find it difficult to remember what it was like. This volume, with its collection of accounts from different positions, records stories, often first hand, sometimes heart-breaking, from that time. It puts on record the unpalatable inequalities revealed and exacerbated by what happened, and looks forward to what happens next. In doing so, this volume acts as a record, an accounting, and a memorial.

When This Is Over is the result of an encounter of four women: a criminologist (Amy Cortvriend), an emergency planner (Lucy Easthope), a politics professor (Jenny Edkins) and an international political sociologist (Kandida Purnell). Meeting online for our initial discussions about the pandemic in March 2021, we decided to focus on the UK – where all four of us live – and to narrow down to the local, a move that we thought would enable us to dig down into the details of what was going on. To begin with, our focus was on the role of the politics of commemoration in the process of recovery, but our scope soon widened. To understand what the work of commemoration meant it was necessary to explore other areas, such as the policing of the pandemic and caring for the dead, as well as the role of emergency planning.

It soon became very clear that our main questions could not be divorced from the question of inequality. In that context, our own position, as four white women – admittedly of differing seniority, from different regions, with different backgrounds, and differently placed in relation to the pandemic – was an issue. For this reason, we are particularly grateful to those who participated, who, together, make this volume a reflection of a wide range of raced, classed and gendered pandemic experience, well beyond what we were able to bring as editors. The creative contributions and the personal stories presented in the chapters demonstrate the ambiguity and impossibility of imposed categories, and many of the chapters show that those groups often forgotten in the narrative – the communities that contributed to Chapters 2 and 9, and the assisted living residents whose accounts we read in Chapter 4, for example – are far from being passive victims of an unequal pandemic. Other chapters, such as Chapter 7, highlight how the inequalities pervasive during that time were structural.

When this is over

Pandemics don't end; rather they fade into the background. There will therefore be no date on which this will finally be 'over', meaning we can all move on and go 'back' to 'normal'. However, even if we could, if the pandemic has taught us anything it is that the experience and its impacts were so vastly different for different people in the UK – depending on socioeconomic position, age, job, race, class, gender, and a myriad of other factors discussed in this volume – that for some there is no 'normal' to go back to. However, for others, their lives, families and health remain intact, and so it will be easier for them to resume things. Indeed, we have lived and died throughout this pandemic in a deeply unequal society: some people were particularly exposed, including older age groups and people experiencing racism, while emergency regulations and policing led to a singling out of racialised groups, and caring for the dead proved challenging for specific religious minorities.

Of course, due to such profound societal inequity, the pandemic will not fade away for us simultaneously. This is especially apparent at the global level due to the 'vaccine apartheid' (Bajaj et al, 2022), meaning the arrival of vaccines is yet to come to wide portions of the global population while here in the UK some of us are more able to begin to start 'living with the virus'. In this way and many more there remains intense ambiguity and contest around if and when the pandemic can and should be declared as 'over' and, of course, declaring it so is unavoidably political. However, this volume is aimed at bringing together and amplifying critical responses to the COVID-19 pandemic – as it continues to claim and disrupt lives – especially as the UK continues to move towards its UK COVID-19 public inquiry. Indeed, as the UK and wider world attempts to move past the pandemic, *When This Is Over: Reflections on an Unequal Pandemic* provides an account of and takes stock of the inequalities and injustices engendered and exacerbated through this period. These socioeconomic and health inequalities are the very things that, from our perspective, require not 'getting over' but rather learning how to overcome and implementing change accordingly. However, in such taking stock and in light of the inquiry, this volume highlights tensions in the UK's COVID-19 response by asking: *What are the injustices of the COVID-19 pandemic? Who counts as one of the COVID-19 dead? What are the stakes of commemoration during COVID-19? How can we contribute to both recovery and justice?* And *how do we prepare for the next pandemic?*

The volume highlights the variety of ways our contributors – from academics to activists, poets, artists and practitioners – have responded to the inequalities of the pandemic. Not only do we look back through the pandemic in hindsight, but we also look forward to examine possibilities of commemoration and practical ideas and political vision aimed at planning for future pandemics and disasters, helped by contributions from practitioners and planners active as advisers or health workers. We amplify the less publicly heard voices of the pandemic, so often unheard groups and the disproportionately bereaved feed into the public discourse. We place original poetry from Michael Rosen, Marvin

Thompson and others alongside a first-hand Twitter response from a bereaved family member, artwork created in response to experiences of the pandemic, a photo story from activist group Led By Donkeys, and academic chapters.

We have chosen to concentrate on the UK. We pay attention to the specifics of deprivation, mass death and commemoration, emphasising issues of race, gender and class, and doing so with a political voice to make practical suggestions as to ways to appropriately respond to and commemorate the COVID-19 pandemic, and prepare for the next one. The volume is arranged in five themed parts: Part I: In this together?; Part II: Policing in an emergency; Part III: Caring for the dead; Part IV: Commemorating lives lost; and Part V: What comes next.

Part I: In this together?

The contributions included in Part I begin to take stock of inequalities pre-existing, exacerbated and embodied by the COVID-19 pandemic by evaluating the extent to which we really were *in this together*. The arterial dividing lines of inequality identified and discussed at most length in this volume are race, class and gender, and through this part we provide a record of diverse everyday pandemic experiences – of men and women, of the young and old, of the working, middle and upper class, and of white people alongside people experiencing racism. The written works and analyses presented use multidisciplinary lenses from social, political, cultural, and feminist and postcolonial theory. They are presented alongside artistic reflections and illustrations: contributions that together work to delineate and explain the disparities and outcomes of pandemic governance in the UK, and to draw out how and the extent to which contemporary class, gender, racial prejudices and structural inequalities impacted experiences of the pandemic as well as how these materialised as the UK's disproportionate body count.

The illustration by Sue Bryant – a Registered General Nurse – that opens this part perfectly captures the disjuncture between 'home' and 'away' during the pandemic. The largely unseen and unvisited NHS wards where medics struggled to help the ill and dying, and the emotional and physical exhaustion felt by those staff in their 'time off', when they faced the unreality of the public narrative, is shown powerfully in this image.

The first chapter in this part, by Jenny Edkins, focuses on the question of how and why traumatic deaths, like those that took place during the pandemic when grieving was heavily constrained and people were not able to sit with dying relatives, not only led to a demand for proper recognition of those lost and a national memorial, but also to political action. There was a disconnect between many people's experiences of pandemic death and the responses of the government, and Edkins argues that people's experiences, uneven though they were, share something that could, and did, lead to a political response. The chapter discusses the way people responded to the revelations that those supposedly leading the country through the pandemic had not been respecting their own regulations – and were, in fact, laughing at the rest of us for obeying them. We were not 'in this together', as we had been told repeatedly. Edkins asks whether such responses to traumatic loss provide an opening for a different politics that could carry forward into the years to come.

Asking 'should we wear May poppies for the disproportionate deaths/of Britons of Colour, Covid bereft?', Marvin Thompson's poem 'May 8th, 2020' immediately brings the inequalities of the pandemic into focus along with the life and death stakes and violent undertones of pandemic times by evoking 'race riots' and 'plantation', and drawing on British collective memory of 'Victory in Europe' and the 20th-century mass death event of the Second World War. Following Thompson's poem is a chapter from Safina Islam and community co-authors from the University of Manchester-based Ahmed Iqbal Ullah RACE (Race Archives and Community Engagement) Centre. Their Manchester archive includes hundreds of books on the history of race, migration and ethnicity, and contains a wide range of documents, leaflets, posters, photographs and ephemera donated by communities across Greater Manchester and, in line with the Centre's mission, the chapter contributed to this volume is presented in the form of a conversation exploring the rich intersectional stories of the collections donated during the pandemic as a means to ensure that Black, Asian and Global Majority experiences are documented. Islam and community co-authors' conversation also tells of how grass-roots community groups and individual activists were able to respond to their communities through the pandemic as they suffered disproportionately.

Following Islam's chapter is Dipali Anumol's vivid and evocative selection of Tarot cards – 'Illustrating grief: Lumière Tarot'. The cards contributed to this volume by Anumol depict characters including 'the caregiver', 'the resilient', 'the hopeful' and 'the grieving', and in this way name the new and often extra roles and facets of identity that we took on and were weighed down by through the pandemic. Vivid and iconic in style these cards speak to how we have changed and been changed irreversibly as a result of the pandemic, and remind us how there is no going 'back' to our former selves and society as we and it was 'before'. In this way Anumol's cards help us to recognise and reconcile our new selves as we emerge from the pandemic and survey the individual and collective damage.

Following Anumol's Tarot cards, Kandida Purnell provides auto-ethnographic reflections and social-political analysis of the UK's pandemic to help begin to unravel the profoundly raced, gendered and classed body politics and body count of the UK's COVID-19 pandemic. Towards this, in her chapter Purnell traces differently pressured and more exposed or sheltered pathways through the pandemic, and reflects on her own particular pandemic vantage point and relative privilege that enables her to shed light on the attitudes and behaviours of those in her vicinity able to take advantage of the pandemic for their own self-improvement. Crucially, written from and about life and death in a commuter town in the wealthy English county of Surrey, this chapter considers the degrees of social-emotional as well as viral circulation and containment that social-political hierarchies afforded members and segments of the UK population through 2020 and 2021. Here Purnell describes how societal discord and losing touch – both physically and affectively – led to the containment of grief within parts of the population, resulting in the heightening of 'atmospheric walls', which, she argues, continue to segregate and therefore set sections of society further apart from one another, echoing Jennifer Mustapha's reminder at the start of the volume that 'our pools of light' were 'already drifting/further and further/apart'. After doing this, Purnell's chapter moves on to discuss the particularly gendered nature of the UK's pandemic response, highlighting how misguided and toxically macho ideas about bodies came to (mis)inform UK pandemic policy. Here, Purnell takes the case of former UK Prime Minister Boris Johnson's 'fight' with the virus to emphasise how dangerous bodily assumptions rhetorically reverberated around the British body politic during the pandemic, and came to infuse 'common sense' around individuals catching and becoming ill with COVID-19 in ways that were not medically sound, but rather promoted the blaming and shaming of particular bodies catching and dying 'with COVID-19'.

Purnell's chapter is followed by Michael Rosen's 'Post-Covid thoughts', an original poem and tribute to the NHS that saved Rosen's life after he became gravely ill with COVID-19 in early 2020. Finally, as academics and experts in social policy, ageing, death and bereavement, Hannah Rumble and Karen West's chapter highlights the impact of COVID-19 on assisted living residents via rich diarists' accounts gathered from ExtraCare residents and written during the spring and summer of 2020. Crucially, in themselves, these allow us to bear witness to the collective losses and grief of an ageing population that rarely makes the headlines, making this chapter's empirical contribution a much needed remedy to the fact that older people's lives and voices are already often excluded from disaster narratives and grief politics. However, this chapter also astutely highlights the challenges raised by the institutional contexts wherein those in assisted living are deemed less important than those living beyond institutional walls in the so-called 'wider community'. Indeed, Rumble and West explain that older residents in assisted living housing in England were not only subjected to isolated, ambiguously marked deaths, but their lives were increasingly cut off from the lives of the larger UK population during the pandemic; discriminated by their age, the vagaries of the residential provider and their co-residential, rather than familial, grieving unit, they nevertheless act to ameliorate their situation and resist imposed disconnection.

Part II: Policing in an emergency

Part II of this volume considers how already existing inequalities have been magnified during the pandemic in the realms of law, crime and immigration. During the pandemic, the killing of George Floyd in the USA brought to the forefront the racialised inequalities and institutional racism in policing in the UK. The part begins with Gracie Mae Bradley's poem 'Unlawful gathering', which reflects on Sarah Everard's murder and the vigil held to show support for Sarah and for women in general. The poem draws from perceptions of women as victims and people who need to be looked after while also showing their strength and solidarity in response to the policing of the vigil in the context of pandemic lockdown rules. Drawing on similar themes, Paul Famosaya's chapter discusses the policing of protests during the pandemic, drawing from the examples of anti-lockdown protests, the Sarah Everard vigil and Black Lives Matter (BLM) protests. This chapter argues for a negotiated management approach to policing to improve police–protester relations during such events.

Anjana Nair's poem – 'Dying declaration' – written about India, but equally applicable to the UK, is a reflection on anger and forgiveness. The poem draws out the divisions forged through the pandemic, divisions between the masked and unmasked, criticism of governments and politicians who did not care and did not prepare. This is particularly poignant in light of the revelations that Boris Johnson and other politicians attended parties in lockdown while many others were facing the deaths of relatives or friends or their own illness. The poem expresses the anger many felt.

The second chapter of this part by Patricia Tuitt discusses the problems of the conflation of law and guidance. It considers inequalities such as those of citizens and non-citizens, drawing from the Windrush scandal to highlight the consequences of the conflation of law and guidance. Tuitt argues that all citizens during pandemic lockdowns were subject to unregulated force, albeit to a much lesser extent than victims of the Windrush scandal. The chapter identifies lessons learned from the law during the COVID-19 pandemic, in particular with regards to the disproportionate impacts on marginalised groups. It concludes by suggesting that the use of *unregulated* force by state officials, the police and others in authority, such as university managements, which was experienced acutely by Windrush descendants and more broadly by the population at large during the pandemic, is a serious threat to the rule of law, which relies on the legitimate, *regulated* force of law. Those seeking to be lawyers need specific training in these dangers and how to contest them.

Manca Bajec's extract from her monodrama, 'I have a wall in front of all my windows', is a play reflecting on solitude during the pandemic. It draws from the interactions between two main characters, one of which is a metaphoric wall representing the imagination of the main character. The title of Bajec's play forms a perfect segue to Amy Cortvriend's chapter that refers to the case of Badreddin Abdallah Adam Bosh, an asylum seeker living in a hotel room during the pandemic who had a physical wall in front of his window. Badreddin's mental health declined after arriving in the UK and being housed in a hotel, and this ultimately led to him attacking several people in the hotel and consequently being shot dead by the police. The case frames this chapter that discusses the forced evictions and accommodating asylum seekers in hotels, shared accommodation and disused army barracks during the pandemic. This negatively impacted on the mental health of asylum seekers during a time where there were additional barriers to support, such as digital inequalities and no access to any income to fund travel expenses and the like. In concluding this part of the volume, the chapter further evidences inequalities between citizens and non-citizens of the UK during the pandemic, emphasising the powerlessness of the latter group.

Part III: Caring for the dead

In this part we turn our attention to a matter that is often outside the range of the public gaze but that the pandemic brought to the fore: caring for the dead. The care others demand of us – and that we feel called to give – does not cease when they die. It extends from the initial treatment of and respect for their dead body, through announcing the death, posting on social media, making arrangements for burial or cremation and an accompanying funeral or wake, to the setting of a memorial stone, perhaps, or the naming of a tree or a park bench in honour of that person, a scattering of ashes, maybe, and indeed the whole process of mourning, condolence and the sharing of memories. This care can extend for years, even generations, as graves are tended, anniversaries of the death marked and stories recounted. The person who has died still has a place in social and family life. Family or friends can continue their Facebook page or Twitter account. Their personal possessions survive and are distributed among the living, sold or given away, and their wishes continue to be respected – and talked about – beyond the grave.

For many, the form care of the dead takes is detailed in religious traditions. A particular ritual of cleansing the body, an early burial, the role of specific family members – all these may be laid down in detail. For others, cultural or family practices determine what is appropriate, to a greater or lesser degree. There are certain processes that are defined by legal requirements: death certification, authorisation of cremation, the holding of an inquest, an autopsy, obtaining probate. Cemetery owners, often the local authority, may dictate the duration of funerals, the size and shape of headstone allowed, and opening times for access to cemetery grounds; churches can do the same for graveyards. Funeral directors prepare the body, organise viewing times in their chapels of rest, and offer a limited range of services, although those bereaved have choices and their preferences will be respected. There is a whole bureaucracy to be dealt with when someone dies.

As John Troyer, director of the Centre for Death and Society at the University of Bath, and the son of US funeral directors, describes in his moving account of his sister's death, no amount of familiarity with these processes and practices can prepare you for the emotional impact of a personal loss (Troyer, 2020). During the pandemic, even the understanding or familiarity most of us might have had from watching when people we knew were bereaved, or from previous bereavements of our own, was upended as practices and procedures were suddenly and drastically altered. And funeral directors, along with others involved professionally in caring for the dead, had to adapt rapidly to the different and challenging circumstances.

In this part, we are privileged to have two chapters that give an insight into how the necessary adaptations worked – or didn't

– in those changed circumstances: one, a personal account from a mortuary technician, the other, an account of interviews with funeral directors, cemetery and crematoria professionals and chaplains.

In Chapter 8, Anatomical Pathology Technologist (APT) Lara-Rose Iredale gives a revealing, personal account of how she and her fellow professionals coped under the pressure of the pandemic, and how they continued to offer the best care possible under the circumstances. They experienced both an enormous increase in demand as deaths rose, but also a need to adapt how they worked to comply with COVID-19 restrictions. These challenges had to be dealt with in a situation where those they worked for did not understand fully what changes were needed. She emphasises how important it is for planners and those in charge of services to listen to those with the practical and professional experience to know what should be done. Importantly, her account reveals the stress and emotional impact of working through the pandemic.

Chapter 9 by Avril Maddrell, Danielle House and Farjana Islam draws on interviews with funerary workers in Dundee conducted as part of a research project, ongoing before the pandemic, designed to look into how inclusive cemeteries and crematoria are in several European countries, and extends Farjana Islam's doctoral work on bereavement in Bangladeshi-Muslim communities. It gives us insights into the impact on cemetery and crematoria staff, who attempted to cope with the changed situation brought about by the pandemic as they struggled to continue to provide the best services they could, and on bereaved family members faced with the increased difficulty of continuing to care for their deceased in ways appropriate to their religious beliefs.

Part III opens with 'Reckoning with grief', images of two Twitter threads posted by Mark Brown in April 2022, and includes the imaginative poem 'My impending adventure, a story for another day' by Irene Naikaali Ssentongo, written from the point of view of someone dying from COVID-19. The Twitter threads raise the big questions about how the pandemic was handled, and talk about not only how this affected people like Brown, who lost relatives, but also its impact on a society that proved unable to react wisely. He points out how in his view we didn't listen enough to those most seriously harmed, and tells us that 'pandemic grief is weird because your bereavement is part of a story in which everyone else has been taking part'.

Part IV: Commemorating lives lost

Commemoration is a contentious and politically sensitive process after conflict or disaster. In some cases – and the Irish famine is an example here – it can be a very long time before any form of memorial is contemplated, as the hurt runs deep. There is a tension between those who wish to remember and those who would rather move on and forget the trauma. It is often the case that after war a state, in many instances the instigator of a conflict, will promote talk of heroism and sacrifice to give 'meaning' to the lives lost, and will produce memorials that glorify the dead and the nation-state on whose behalf they supposedly gave their lives. There are those who resist such narratives and instead insist on remembering the failures of leadership that led to the casualties, and campaign against war in all its forms. In the First World War, the phrase 'lions led by donkeys' was a popular description of British troops – the lions – and their generals – the donkeys – used to highlight such failures.

Commemoration after pandemics is no different. There was very little by way of memorials or commemoration after the 1918–19 influenza pandemic, despite a huge death toll, as Mark Honigsbaum discusses in his chapter in Part IV. This may have been to do with the way that the pandemic coincided with the end of the First World War, but that doesn't seem to entirely account for the absence of memorialisation globally (Beiner, 2022a). It is not difficult to articulate a narrative of heroism in a battle against a virus – a 'hidden enemy', as British leaders called it – and the first moments of silence in England in 2020 were framed in that way, as Jenny Edkins reminds us in Chapter 1. Speaking of the response to COVID-19 in military terms as a 'fight' and describing those involved as 'on the front line' lends itself to such forms of commemoration, and to a justification for otherwise unjustifiable deaths: those health workers, often from racialised groups, who contracted and died of COVID-19 because of a lack of PPE (personal protective equipment), or key workers who were similarly unprotected.

There have been numerous small memorials to COVID-19 dead in the UK – for example, the Westerleigh Group, which describes itself as 'the leading developer and operator of crematoria and cemeteries in the UK', has installed memorials in its crematoria. These take the standardised form of a black obelisk or pyramid embossed with images designed by local people, often school children (Westerleigh Group, 2020). There have also been proposals for official national memorials, and one in Scotland in Glasgow's Pollock Park, constructed under the auspices of the charity greenspace scotland (2021), was unveiled in May 2022. That same month, members of the public brought messages to a memorial called 'Sanctuary', designed by Californian artist David Best and built in Bedworth, Warwickshire, which was set on fire to provide 'a cathartic release' (Lister, 2022).

The two chapters in Part IV focus on another memorial, the National Covid Memorial Wall, situated on the Embankment opposite the Houses of Parliament. The part begins with a 'Photo story' by Led By Donkeys, the activist group that was instrumental in helping the Covid-19 Bereaved Families for Justice organise the volunteer action that created the National Covid Memorial Wall. The images show the volunteers, many of them people bereaved by COVID-19, painting small red hearts – 150,000 of them – on a half a kilometre stretch of wall as other people pass by.

Mark Honigsbaum's chapter gives a detailed account of the work behind the Memorial Wall, and sets it in the context of the politics of memory more broadly. He discusses the lack of commemoration of the 'Spanish flu' and commemoration of the AIDS pandemic, and reminds us that the politics of memory is not static, but ever shifting. Remembering is both a personal and political process, and involves a struggle over meaning. The forms that memory takes change, too. Memory work is particularly important in instances of mass death when public commemorations are restricted, and Honigsbaum quotes Judith Butler's comment that private or digital commemorations in the face of the pandemic 'cannot assuage the cry that wants the world to bear witness to the loss' (Butler and Yancy, 2020).

The most moving parts of the chapter recount interviews Honigsbaum conducted with bereaved family members during his visits to the wall: people who came to the wall to name one of the hearts in commemoration of their relative. One woman had waited for the anniversary of her partner's death to travel down from Hull by train to leave a dedication, choosing a heart roughly a quarter of the way along the wall to reflect the time her partner died.

The second chapter in Part IV is by Fran Hall, a member of the Friends of the Wall, a group that visits the wall regularly to ensure that the painted hearts are not allowed to disappear, to be reabsorbed into the stone. Hall was involved with the wall from the very beginning, and she tells the story of its creation from an insider perspective. As one of those bereaved by COVID-19, the wall for her is 'an anchor for the anger, the injustice, the impotence of a people who feel their government have failed them'. It is a place where the bereaved can come together, not only to remember, but also to meet others who have been through the same experience, comfort each other, and discuss what political action they might take to make their feelings known.

In his poem 'Pandemic Easter', librettist and acclaimed poet Herbert Woodward Martin, author of two volumes of poetry published during the pandemic, *The Shape of Regret* and *Sometimes, Say My Name*, reflects on the empty cathedral and the absent body, gives voice to the agony of loss and remembering, and asks 'what breaths shall we take to survive?'

Part V: What comes next

The final part is all about what comes next, and focuses on chapters from those emergency planners charged with looking to the future in very grounded terms. One of this volume's editors, Lucy Easthope, is different from the other editors in that, as an emergency planner, she spent a sizeable chunk of her pre-pandemic work planning for a pandemic, and very much expected to see one in her lifetime. For years Easthope attended meetings and designed training exercises and talked about life in and around a pandemic. She gave talks on how it would be unfair and unequal and would scythe through areas of the country already experiencing massive disparity in opportunity and resource. For her, there have been very few surprises, but as this volume captures, there has been frustration and pain at the scale of the inequality. Crucially, part of her role as an emergency planner is always to look into the future as well as the past.

The COVID-19 pandemic is not a beginning or an end; it is a marker on a map, and it will become shortened to bookended dates. Its sharp edges will be blunted by other world crises. And our descendants will go again and then again. In the first chapter of Part V Matthew Hogan's rallying call reminds us that the emergency planners are always looking ahead and always scanning the stars. As he says, none of us can know exactly what the future looks like, but it's certain that there will continue to be disasters, emergencies and extreme events. Our future looks set to be riskier by virtue of a changing climate, demographic shifts and complex global economics. But there is comfort to be had in knowing that people like Easthope and Hogan will never stop campaigning for us to be ready for next time. Hogan finally pleads for emergency planning to be given the credence and weight that it deserves. In Easthope's piece that follows, she forecasts the limitations of any public inquiry into what went wrong, but ends again on a note of hope. She reminds us that there is the glimmer of possibility that we may yet see a more equal society emerge from the COVID-19 ashes.

The poems in this final part – by Rita Coleman and Mehreen Hamdany – are both united in their blistering evocation of the realities of the first two pandemic years. Coleman's poem speaks about the vast gulf of experience separating us due to and through the pandemic, and reads as an outpouring of sheer pain. Hamdany focuses on the seemingly easy and often taken for granted act of simply taking a breath and 'waiting to exhale'. Indeed, this reflex action became magnified in the pandemic coming to dominate the lives and deaths of many. There is particular resonance, of course, with the death at the hands of the US police of George Floyd and so many others whose last words were often 'I can't breathe', and as Suhaiymah Manzoor-Khan (2020) points out, 'Breathlessness is not a momentary condition'. Often it is only staccato verse that allows the roar of the past years to fully emerge. It may be a human trait and political necessity for the tragedy to be softened, but these poems sit loudly to remind and ground us one last time. 'Go ahead, tell me one more time that we're all in this together ...' Coleman goads, and in doing so brings this volume full circle.

Conclusion

The pivotal question of inequality animates this volume. In each part we have seen how the pandemic affected different people – different groups and different individuals – in radically different ways. For the rich and superrich – those living in 'million-pound towns' in leafy suburbs and the 'home counties' surrounding London, for example, able to escape to a second home, and generally more coddled by their privilege from COVID-19 – what happened did not play out in the same way as it did for some of those in residential care or in British-Bangladeshi communities, for example. The impact of the restrictions on funerals depended on how important swift burial and the participation of community members was. Interactions with the police enforcing emergency COVID-19 regulations were very different for racialised groups, already the frequent recipients of unjustified police attention, and those in positions of power. And those delivering takeaways, working supermarket checkouts or keeping public transport running experienced greater risks than those making use of such services.

This has led to what Gary Younge calls, in his Afterword to the volume, 'a teachable moment'. As he says, 'The pandemic has ... introduced a crisis that has given us the opportunity to take stock of the conditions in which we live and the consequences those conditions have engendered. It laid bare our inequalities, vulnerabilities and precarities.'

He notes that 'for all the trauma, COVID-19 has gifted us with an opportunity to rethink the way we do things', and many of the contributions in the volume show that a rethinking is underway. Younge warns that this rethinking is not a given. There will be temptations, indeed even an impetus, to return to the status quo. To get 'caught up' once more in what Jennifer Mustapha, in the poem at the start of the volume, calls 'diseases for which there is/no cure./The race for better lives/bigger houses/newer things'.

One of the aims of this volume, and maybe our main motivation as editors, is to collect and preserve reflections from a time when memories of what happened are still fresh, reflections that may serve to reinforce the need for change and carry the 'teachable moment' forward into the future.

Acknowledgements

First of all, our thanks go to all the contributors for their work and for their patience with us as we put the volume together. It would have been nothing without their generosity and insight. It was a pleasure working with each and every one of them – we thoroughly enjoyed reading their material and learned a lot. We hope that they are as pleased with the final result as we are. Special thanks go to contributor and poet Jennifer Mustapha for lending us the title of her poem 'When this is over' for the title of the volume.

We are hugely grateful to Stephen Wenham for his belief in the value of this book from the start, to the Policy Press's anonymous reviewers for their enthusiasm, encouragement and constructive input, to the designers for the amazing cover, and to the entire team including Zoe Forbes, Kathryn King, Inga Boardman, Vaarunika Dharmapala, Dawn Rushen, Margarete Lythgoe, Sharon Redmayne and Marie Doherty, who saw this book seamlessly through to publication.

A number of the poems in the volume appeared on a website produced as part of the Arts and Humanities Research Council (AHRC)-funded project, 'Poets Respond to COVID-19: Collaborative UK and International Poetry Project',[1] and we are grateful to Professor Anthony Caleshu, University of Plymouth, and Dr Rory Waterman, Nottingham Trent University, for putting us in touch with the poets concerned: Rita Coleman, Mehreen Hamdany, Herbert Woodward Martin, Anjana Nair and Irene Naikaali Ssentongo. We thank those poets in turn for allowing us to publish their work here. Two other poets have generously allowed us to include poems that had appeared elsewhere: Jennifer Mustapha's 'When this is over' appeared in *The New Quarterly*, Fall, 2021, pp 21–2; Marvin Thompson's 'May 8th, 2020' was his poem for the 2021 National Poetry Day, coordinated by the Forward Arts Foundation. Thompson's poem appeared in English and Welsh on their website (https://nationalpoetryday.co.uk/poem/may-8th-2020) and was placed on a billboard in Cardiff. Michael Rosen's and Gracie Mae Bradley's poems were produced specially for the volume, as were Manca Bajec's play, the Tarot cards by Dipali Anumol, the illustration by Sue Bryant, and the photo essay by Led By Donkeys. Mark Brown kindly allowed us to reproduce two of his Twitter threads from April 2022.

Note

[1] See https://gtr.ukri.org/projects?ref=AH%2FV006835%2F1

PART I

In this together?

HOME AND AWAY

Sue Bryant

1

Pandemic deaths and the possibility of politics

Jenny Edkins

In mid-April 2020 I couldn't seem to stop watching the Downing Street press conference. Every day we were told how many people had 'sadly' died. No names, just the numbers. When the UK passed what seemed then the significant milestone of 10,000 deaths, it did change – briefly – from 'sadly' to 'tragically'. 'Horrifically' might have come nearer the mark, given the manner of many of the deaths. And each day, whoever was presenting reminded themselves, under the guise of reminding us, that behind each of those numbers was a real person, with a family and friends.

They didn't mention that these were families and friends who could not grieve in the usual way: no vigil at the bedside, no last words, no viewing the body, no proper funeral, no visitors with condolences, no inquest to determine the circumstances of the death. A Twitter thread, some Facebook posts, perhaps, but the deceased were effectively disappeared. Into mass graves too sometimes, it seems (Percival, 2020).

They didn't mention, in those early days, that these deaths were not distributed evenly across the population, but were concentrated among certain groups: those who experience racism or poverty, the elderly and those in care homes, and those compelled to continue working away from home. Nor did they mention the impact of the measures they introduced on those for whom home was not a place of safety, or for those living alone, or for children.

The revelations in the UK nearly two years later, culminating in January 2022, that a series of parties, at least one attended by the then prime minister, took place in Number 10 and other Whitehall venues at a time when such gatherings were seemingly prohibited under COVID-19 restrictions prompted an outpouring of anger among the British public (Manhire, 2022). The opinion poll ratings of the governing Conservative Party fell dramatically. On 18 January 2022 the Politico Poll of Polls showed Labour on 41 per cent and the Conservatives on 32 per cent, an almost exact reversal of the position six months earlier (Politico, 2022). People were furious that while they had followed what they had been told were the rules, often at considerable personal cost, those responsible for making the rules had not.

The anger was greatest among those who had not been able to visit relatives in care homes, not been able to sit by the dying in hospital, and not been able to comfort each other at funerals. Stories were told in the press and on social media of such traumatic experiences (Covid-19 Bereaved Families for Justice, 2022b). People spoke out.

In this chapter I ask how pandemic deaths are experienced by those left behind, and how this experience can lead to political action. I explore what I see as the 'disappeared deaths' of those who died during the COVID-19 pandemic, and examine how these were ambiguous, traumatic losses, because the usual rituals of last goodbyes and mourning and the usual procedures for accounting for a death were absent, and because of the terrible manner of many of the deaths.

I look at some of the political responses we have seen so far from survivors and the bereaved, whether in the form of memorials or campaigns or just speaking out. What sort of experience are we talking about, and what is or could be the political outcome, in the immediate and the longer term?

Deaths during the COVID-19 pandemic

During a pandemic, the last relatives see of someone may be when they are carried off in an ambulance. Connections are broken and stories are lost: the stories of how people died, and the life stories that would be told at funerals and wakes. Mourning is hard.

And the pandemic dead are not just those who died of or with COVID-19, but all who died during or because of the pandemic: restrictions on funerals and hospital or care home visits were in place for everyone.

I have written in the past about the aftermath of wars, famines and genocides: the role of memorials, the tracing services set up to track down missing people, enforced disappearances, and forms of political protest (Edkins, 2003, 2011). It struck me early on that there were similarities between deaths during the pandemic and what happens when people go missing, whether as a result of enforced disappearances, refugee deaths at sea, those lost in war, or otherwise. When people are disappeared, relatives have to live with not knowing what has happened: there is no body to bury, the death is never acknowledged, and mourning is suspended. During the pandemic, when the last people saw of their relative was them being carried off in the back of an ambulance, it reminded me of enforced disappearances, with political dissidents bundled into the back of police vans, never to be seen again.

These thoughts crystallised for me when I read an article by Johanna Mannergren Selimovic (2020). She puts her finger precisely on something very specific to the pandemic. Despite the way it impacts differently on different people, she says, it is 'an embodied, emotional experience that plays out in intimate spheres for all of us'. The loss we suffer is 'an intimate loss': 'the disappearance of embodied interaction in our lives'. She then makes what for me is a crucial link. 'Intimate loss', she says, 'is also an "ambiguous loss"' (Mannergren Selimovic, 2020). Pauline Boss's (1999) term 'ambiguous loss' can be used to describe the experience when someone goes missing or is disappeared: no one knows whether the person is dead, or whether they may walk through the door at any moment. Such 'ambiguity' can happen in other cases too: with those whose relatives suffer from dementia, for example, or with the families migrants leave behind (Boss, 1999).

The experiences of bereavement during the pandemic and the experiences of the families of those disappeared or missing share similarities: the loss of a body to mourn is the fate of relatives left behind when someone is disappeared, and the pandemic means people are deprived of the chance to be there when relatives suffer, die and are buried. Both can be described as an 'ambiguous loss'.

Importantly, both can also be seen as a traumatic loss, not only because of the ambiguity, but because those left behind feel betrayed by those who should help them, whether it be the health services adhering rigidly to COVID-19 rules during the pandemic, or the police and the authorities denying responsibility in the case of enforced disappearance. In the pandemic, those who are lauded as key workers perhaps feel the betrayal more acutely than others. Their portrayal as heroes is belied by the paucity of their pay and used to legitimise their deaths as sacrifice. When the state or its proxies disappear people, those same agencies are supposed to investigate what has happened and why the person has not come home. But they turn their backs when relatives come asking for help. Sometimes they even imply that the missing person walked out, that they left of their own free will (Edkins, 2011: 175).

Trauma tends to be thought of as involving coming face to face with threatening and overwhelming force or violence. A traumatic event is generally seen as a threat to the person themselves, but often it can involve witnessing the horrific deaths of others (Edkins, 2003). It is an experience of utter helplessness: the person can do nothing. But, in an important sense, to be traumatic an event has to involve a betrayal of trust:

> What we call trauma takes place when the very powers that we are convinced will protect us and give us security become our tormentors: when the community of which we considered ourselves members turns against us or when our family is no longer a source of refuge but a site of danger. (Edkins, 2003: 4)

People no longer know who they are because the context that provided a sense of self has been compromised. The rug has been pulled from under them. Of course that context was always fragile in any case, and any sense of closure or security a fantasy, but people are adept at forgetting their vulnerability. That vulnerability is revealed when a traumatic event happens.

There are two common responses. The first is to try to reinstate that impossible sense of security: to medicalise the trauma, to seek 'closure' or to frame the event in a heroic narrative; to treat the trauma as something exceptional, unnecessary, avoidable with better care and more attention. Such a response attempts a return to the status quo, to whatever counted as 'normal' before the event. It is a response that tends to suit those in charge, as it reinstates existing power structures and hierarchies. It regards those experiencing trauma as in need of medical treatment, not a political voice.

When military personnel returned from the Vietnam War devastated by their experience and the atrocities they had been involved in, they were offered treatment that required them to identify a single 'moment' of trauma, and given a diagnosis and identity as PTSD (post-traumatic stress disorder) sufferers. Being required to give an account of what had happened in Vietnam to therapists who had not 'been there' was in itself traumatising, and veterans' feelings of shame, guilt and anger were denied. They were deprived of a political voice, any political action seen as an acting-out of their symptoms (Edkins, 2003: 47–50).

A second response is often found among the people who have experienced trauma. They have been forced to face the reality of vulnerability, and have seen the way the powers that be can betray them and those they love. They don't want to forget. On the contrary, they want to tell the world what they have come to know and to fight for accountability and political change. They can recognise the impossibility of wholeness and security, see through the fantasy of 'closure', and glimpse the possibility of living otherwise.

Many of the poets writing during or in the aftermath of the First World War expressed these feelings in their work. Wilfred Owen, in his poem 'Dulce et Decorum Est', with its unflinching description of death from poison gas, calls the idea that those who were killed in the trenches gave their lives in sacrifice 'the old Lie' (Owen, 1920). And local memorials to that war in Britain often took the form of community halls or trusts to provide funds for future young people to travel the world, rather than stone monuments.

In the case of enforced disappearances, one of the worst aspects for the families is the refusal by the state or police authorities to acknowledge a death or disappearance, or to investigate at all. The fact of the death is 'disappeared'. In the pandemic it seemed to me that in some parallel sense the deaths that occurred during that time were being 'disappeared' too – into debates over statistics. As Jacqueline Wernimont points out, numbers 'risk hampering our abilities to mourn the dead, repair our communities, and grow' (Wernimont, 2022).

The difficulty of counting COVID-19 deaths is acknowledged (Adam, 2022), but the regular changes in counting methods used in the UK did not inspire confidence (Griffin, 2020). For example, at the beginning, figures of deaths in care homes and in the community at large were only reported with a lag of two weeks or so by the UK Office for National Statistics (ONS). They weren't added to the curves on the slides in the Downing Street press conferences. These people didn't even count as a number, let alone a name. At that time the slides still, as Tom Newton Dunn (2020) pointed out at the press conference on 14 April 2020, compared the UK's figures (people who died in hospital after testing positive for the virus) with those of France, which included community and care home deaths. Comparing ONS figures for deaths over those April weeks in 2020 with the average over the same period in 2015–19 revealed excess deaths well into the thousands.

But that wasn't the worst of it. A report from a whistleblower involved in registering deaths shared by Ciaran Jenkins at Channel 4 News gave an account of doctors not recording COVID-19 on death certificates even when they believed it to be the probable cause, opting instead for 'lower respiratory tract infection' or 'pneumonia' – and thus ensuring these deaths would not be included in the ONS figures (Jenkins, 2020a). Reportedly, when the official was recording a death that was down as Alzheimer's and they queried this with the doctor, they got the response 'Yes, I just put that because we didn't go out to see him. It was probably Covid, but we put Alzheimer's because he's over 80' (quoted in Jenkins, 2020b).

The emergency legislation passed in such an apparent rush at the end of March 2020 had clauses with the aim, according to the Department of Health and Social Care (2020a), of 'managing the deceased in a dignified way'. What these clauses did was relax the requirement for the death certificate to be completed by a doctor who had attended the patient, remove the need for referral to the coroner where there was no attending doctor, and allow cremation without the usual double certification. Necessary as those moves might have been, as Lara-Rose Iredale's account in this volume demonstrates (Chapter 8), they meant that in many cases the circumstances surrounding the death would never be fully investigated, and relatives would be left to deal with not knowing what had happened.

In a leaflet containing members' reflections on their own experiences produced by Disaster Action, a charity founded by survivors and those bereaved by disasters, this need to know what happened is clear: 'I am obsessing about how he died. Where was he exactly, did he suffer, did he know he was dying, what was it like for him?' The leaflet also reflects two other notable aspects of trauma: the loss of the scaffolding built to survive life ('A part of me had died and I needed to grieve') and the need to share with those who understand ('What was needed was someone to talk to who had been in the accident') (Disaster Action, 2022).

The deaths that took place from COVID-19 were particularly horrific to witness and, even for people at several removes like me, to contemplate. In the beginning, medical teams were struggling with a new disease that they didn't know how to treat, and with numbers of patients that stretched an already threadbare health service. For a large part, the horror was screened from public view, but when cameras were allowed into the wards, first in Italy, and eventually in the UK, the appalling way that people were suffering was fully apparent.

Over and above the manner of many of these deaths, there was the trauma of enforced isolation. For those who witnessed people 'die as a biohazard ... cut off without and beyond the touch of family and friends', the horror was 'simply unimaginable' (Purnell, 2021a: 138). Lucy Easthope (quoted in Dodsworth, 2020) says:

> We've done something incredibly traumatising to the families that is potentially bigger than the bereavement itself. In any disaster you should still allow people to see the dead. It is a gross inhumanity of bad planning that people couldn't visit the sick, view the deceased's

bodies, or attend funerals. Had we had a more liberal PPE stockpile we could have done this. PPE is about accessing your loved ones and dead ones, it is not just about medical professionals.

This doesn't just impact the bereaved. Ruth Coward, who was unable to visit her mother in her care home, says that 'no amount of phoning, video calling or waving through the window' helped, and she describes herself as 'heavy with the grief of helplessness and powerlessness and, what is worse, it is a grief that, when expressed, has been rebuffed and denied numerous times' (Coward, 2021: 52).

There were those who were going to die anyway, from another illness – a 'pre-existing condition' – where the conditions of their death were 'radically altered'. As Martin Clarke puts it:

> The bringing forward of these deaths by days, weeks or months was not some mere inconvenience but the robbing of precious final moments of intimacy and dignity. ... Just as an end to the pandemic feels difficult to imagine, so too does finding a way of commemorating its indelible effects. (Clarke, 2021: 116–17)

Then there were those who died during the pandemic but neither with nor of COVID-19, like Laura Patterson's father. His death 'won't feature in any Covid-related statistics' but 'the ache and tragedy remain': 'our loss is the same, with an inability to mourn and grieve as we would want, no chance to fully celebrate the life lost and no loved ones to comfort us as we cry' (Patterson, 2021: 136).

For many of those experiencing racism, bereavement and funerals during the pandemic could be challenging in other ways, as described in Chapter 2 in this volume by Safina Islam and community contributors. There are parallels once again with enforced disappearances. When people are missing or disappeared, some are 'doubly disappeared': those who are discriminated against – Indigenous people or those without papers, for example – are already 'disappeared' or invisible. In the pandemic, those who experience racism or poverty or both were more likely to die than their white or wealthy counterparts (Mitha et al, 2020), and the bereaved with religious beliefs that did not align with majority practices could find their needs unmet, as Avril Maddrell, Danielle House and Farjana Islam discuss in Chapter 9 in this volume.

The Black Lives Matter protests following the murder of George Floyd in the USA in May 2020 made the question of racism visible for once and prompted widespread discussions. In a powerful piece published in June that year, Jacqueline Sanchez Taylor points out that for people who experience racism the pandemic feels very different, because, like Covid,

> Racism interrupts. ... It gate crashes your day, stops you in your steps, makes you enter a world you would not choose to go to. Racism comes in unpredictable, random patterns and is unsolicited. It just happens. ... And you don't always know how to respond to this random, unwanted, upsetting thing that has suddenly interrupted you. (Sanchez Taylor, 2020)

White people don't generally suffer such regular interruptions, but COVID-19 changed that. As Sanchez Taylor writes, 'It has interrupted *all* lives, even those of the most privileged', which means that conversations on racism are taking place 'when everyone's lives are already interrupted and disrupted ... and this is opening new spaces for talking and thinking' (Sanchez Taylor, 2020).

COVID-19 cases were worst in areas of poverty and deprivation. Pandemic deaths revealed and magnified existing inequalities of wealth in the UK. Those required to work, or those who couldn't afford not to, were most exposed to infection. In the midst of our attempts to flatten the curve of COVID-19 deaths through social distancing or staying at home, Naeem Inayatullah points out that there are those whose 'relative lack of means requires engaging in risks that could leave them infected and dead', and asks, 'Don't we need to flatten the death rate that results from our differential valuation of human beings? In a curved universe, everyone is both in front of us and behind us, and always within our reach' (Inayatullah, 2020: xli).

Disasters, and the trauma they produce, are often relatively circumscribed. A train crash, a ferry sinking, a football stadium disaster, a fire in a high rise, even a tsunami – in such disasters, those affected can form a close-knit group, relying on each other for support and understanding afterwards. What happens is sudden, seemingly over fast. COVID-19 produced a disaster of a different kind. It was felt by entire populations to some degree – more so, of course, along the fault lines of racism and poverty (Gamlin et al, 2021; Otele et al, 2021; Purnell, 2021a). And it crept up on people. In the UK at the beginning, a world away now, Sir Patrick Vallance, government chief scientific adviser, spoke of 20,000 dead as being a 'good' outcome (Vallance, 2020). By the time of writing this chapter, the total deaths officially attributed to COVID-19 in the UK stood at more than 200,000, not including excess deaths from other causes during the pandemic.

Significantly, it is not only the bereaved and those directly impacted in other ways who experience intimate, ambiguous, traumatic loss. The implications of Mannergren Selimovic's work are broader than that. As she points out, 'ambiguous loss includes losses that have no definite endings, no protocol and no predicted path towards closure as imaginations of the future are blocked' (Mannergren Selimovic, 2020). We are all potentially implicated. The world is uncanny: it looks the same, but everything important has changed and 'attention to the intimate and ambiguous loss in the everyday ... can give us a memory politics that is also a transformative politics' (Mannergren Selimovic, 2020). I begin to unpack this possibility in the next section.

The political impact of pandemic deaths

The common response to trauma for those trying to help is to promote recovery, healing or closure: to medicalise and get rid of the trauma. But those who have experienced trauma may well want to hold on to the anger, hold on to the sense of injustice, and try to right the wrong they've suffered. We saw this after the Hillsborough Stadium disaster, where relatives campaigned for decades; we are seeing it after the Grenfell Tower fire, where people take to the streets of North Kensington in silence to call for justice.

Perhaps we can see the beginnings of this in the aftermath of the pandemic: in the National Covid Memorial Wall opposite the Houses of Parliament in London, and in the way bereaved people came forward to tell their stories in the face of revelations about the Downing Street parties.

After the 1918–19 pandemic, memorials and commemorations were rare (Beiner, 2022a). But by 28 April 2020 the UK was already into full commemoration mode for the COVID-19 pandemic. A minute's silence was held at 11 am to remember all those key workers who had lost their lives while, to use the government's terminology, 'working on the front line' (BBC News, 2020b). The problems of using wartime terminology when talking about the pandemic have been widely remarked on, but during the commemoration, this way of speaking became blatant. Key workers – NHS staff, taxi drivers, refuse collectors, supermarket checkout operators and so many more – were referred to as having 'sacrificed' their lives.

Talking of heroism and sacrifice is an abhorrent enough way of speaking of war dead, with so many unexamined assumptions (Owen, 1920; Edkins, 2003: 101–2); it is an appalling way of talking about those who have lost their lives while at work under conditions that defy the long-fought-for provisions for health and safety. Did Uber driver Rajesh Jayaseelan, who died on 11 April 2020, sacrifice his life when he hid his illness for fear of being thrown out by his landlord (Booth, 2020)? As an NHS intensive care nurse said to BBC's *Panorama*, 'Calling us heroes just makes it okay when we die' (Bilton, 2020: 17:45).

These attempts at national memorialisation reflect countless other instances where, after war or disaster, the state has stepped in in some form or other to impose stories of national glory, sacrifice and heroism: to co-opt suffering and chaos, to bring 'closure' and to shore up the status quo (Winter, 1995; Edkins, 2003). But memorials and commemorations are always contested. Counter-memorials spring up to challenge the narrative, and the debates around built memorials are highly contentious and political – and often more significant than the final edifice of marble and stone (Young, 1993).

Traumatic events in particular resist narrative telling. Some memorials attempt what I have called an 'encircling' or 'marking' of the trauma: they enjoin us not to forget what happened, while reminding us that traumatic events are not something that can be remembered in the usual way (Edkins, 2003). As Maurice Blanchot has put it, 'Know what has happened, do not forget, and at the same time never will you know' (Blanchot, 1995: 82). Memorials that attempt this marking of trauma without incorporating it into a narrative perhaps include the Vietnam Veterans Memorial in Washington DC, the Cenotaph in Whitehall in London and the Memorial to the Murdered Jews of Europe in Berlin.

The National Covid Memorial Wall, discussed in depth and very movingly in Mark Honigsbaum's and Fran Hall's chapters in this volume (Chapters 10 and 11 respectively), is perhaps another example. The wall is a collaboration between Covid-19 Bereaved Families for Justice (https://covidfamiliesforjustice.org), people who came together to share their experiences of bereavement during the pandemic and campaign for justice, and the activist and art installation group Led By Donkeys. It stretches along the Embankment beneath St Thomas' Hospital – one of the main locations treating COVID-19 patients in London in the early days of the pandemic – and immediately opposite the Houses of Parliament.

On 29 March 2021, 11 months after the minute's silence in April 2020, members of Covid-19 Bereaved Families for Justice were joined by hundreds of volunteers to begin painting 150,000 red hearts on the wall, one for each person who had died. When the initial phase was completed on 8 April 2021, there were 150,837 hearts, matching the figure released by the ONS that day (National Covid Memorial Wall, 2022). Like the Cenotaph, which was initially a temporary memorial built for a march past on the first anniversary of the 1918 Armistice, there are demands that the wall be made permanent.

At the end of November 2021, some eight months after the completion of the wall, reports began to surface of parties held in Number 10 in contravention of the regulations at the time prohibiting gatherings. On 7 December 2021 ITV News released a video of a mock Downing Street press conference held on 22 December 2020. The video showed Allegra Stratton and other Downing Street staff laughing and joking as they discussed how they would respond to potential questions about a party held four days before.

The Stratton video led to an immediate shift in the opinion polls. The Labour and Conservative Parties had been more or less neck and neck at 37 per cent immediately before then, but as soon as the video was broadcast, a significant lead began to open up for Labour. The lead increased further after the release in early January of an email from the prime minister's Principal Private Secretary Martin Reynolds inviting over a hundred Downing Street staff to 'bring your own booze' to a drinks event on 20 May 2020, during the first lockdown. An internal investigation to be conducted by civil servant Sue Gray was instigated, and a Metropolitan Police investigation eventually began too.

Accounts from members of the public expressing their anger at these revelations appeared across the media. People spoke about what they had been doing – or not doing – on the dates of the various parties. On 10 January 2022 Michael Rosen tweeted 'May 20 2020 Number 10 party. Damn, I missed it. I was in a coma. Just my luck' (Rosen, 2022). Replies in the thread are heart-breaking:

> Sue Carney: My Dad was admitted to hospital with COVID that day. As the ambulance arrived, Mum handed him the phone and we said goodbye. His last words to me were, 'God bless.' He died on 24th. We couldn't be with him. I will never forgive this government.

> Karen Schafheutle: On 20 May 2020, I was in Germany, having borrowed money to enable my son to have urgent surgery for a massive neck tumour. His op had been postponed indefinitely in the UK bec of the pandemic the govt failed to contain. But sure, they needed a party bec things had been 'busy'.

> Remembering Ruby: We were mourning the death of our 18 year old daughter who died 5 days earlier of leukaemia; on our own, in our house, unable to hold a meaningful funeral. She couldn't say goodbye

to her friends or grandparents in person; they saw her for the last time on Zoom.

Louise Waples: My son's 10th birthday. His friends came and sang Happy Birthday to him from the end of our drive before we ushered them away, worried people would judge us for 'gathering' then they had a Zoom sleepover. May sound trivial I know, but 10 years old. I'm so angry.

Tim Grant: On May 20th 2020 we hadn't seen her our daughter for 10 weeks as she was resident on a long stay mental health ward. On the 23rd we got to see her for a distanced, outside visit, in the rain. The rules said not to give her a hug, so we didn't.

Tracey Thompson to Michael Rosen: Your tweet is everything. I can't read all the replies because they're so heartbreaking. We're all still so raw from how awful things were & still are. It's shameful behaviour then & the cover up now.

And the reply to Tracey from Marie Jones: That's it isn't it? Even if you've not suffered a personal trauma, if you have a heart you cannot help being affected by so many other people's pain.

Meanwhile, it seemed that the prime minister and others were laughing at the public, as though people had been taken for fools. Sir Keir Starmer, leader of the opposition, summed up what the public had been through during the debate on the Sue Gray Report on 31 January 2022:

Over the last two years, the British public have been asked to make the most heart-wrenching sacrifices – a collective trauma endured by all, enjoyed by none. Funerals have been missed, dying relatives have been unvisited. Every family has been marred by what we have been through. And revelations about the Prime

Minister's behaviour have forced us all to rethink and relive those darkest moments. (Starmer, 2022)

Discussing voters' views following a focus group session reported on *Newsnight* on 26 January 2022 (BBC Two, 2022), Lewis Goodall comments, 'Perhaps the most interesting thing was this: the sense of anger because they felt the rules had been abused at a traumatic time but also a loathing to look back precisely because of that trauma. That the pandemic has been so searing that they wanted to look forward, to let it go' (Goodall, 2022).

That people nevertheless did speak out in anger points to the courage of those who went public, faced the trauma and told their stories despite everything. The mockery and disrespect was the final straw: 'It's not that they partied while you didn't, or that they broke the rules while you followed them, but that he laughed while you said goodbye on FaceTime, while you blew kisses through the care home window, while you didn't hug each other at funerals' (Manhire, 2022).

When the prime minister lied about the Downing Street parties during lockdown, using fire-hosing strategies of inconsistency and disregard for 'objective reality' ('there were no parties'/'it wasn't a party'/'I didn't realise it was a party' to the totally absurd 'he was ambushed by cake') that was one thing. But when people who had experienced the trauma of disappeared deaths and missed meetings with relatives saw him laughing at them, something else happened. People had believed in the rules. However, the rules had not protected them but had led many to ignore their moral compass and disregard their gut feeling about what they should do. Politicians, among others, had encouraged people to see the regulations as absolute, to be obeyed at all costs, contrary to the fact that, as Patricia Tuitt points out in Chapter 6, 'few, if any, laws are couched in absolute terms'.

Like truth commissions after conflicts or enforced disappearances, justice and commemoration after a pandemic demand an accounting, a full recognition of each life lost, an acknowledgement of those groups disproportionately impacted, and an answer to the questions of how and why. If an inquiry takes place, it will not produce justice. Justice, if it is possible, comes from facing the traumatic real, encircling and marking it. Inquiries are structured around objectivity and evidence, apportioning blame, instituting reform and suppressing revolution.

In that sense, fact-checking in terms of internal or police investigations or public inquiries is irrelevant: people already know all they need to know. The lies, the contradictions, the unreality confronts the traumatic real (Edkins, 2003: 12). And the real wins. The implication for politics when many in the population have experienced such trauma remains to be seen. As Lucy Easthope (2022c) says, 'we are all disaster survivors now'. Recovery need not mean forgetting.

Closing thoughts

People are angry at what has happened, at the traumatic betrayal of trust, and the anger can overcome the ambiguity and the grief and lead to political protest. In other countries, relatives of those disappeared by the state or its proxies demand the impossible: 'Alive you took them from us. We want them back alive!' They take to the streets to call for justice, holding images of their absent relatives aloft to insist on their presence and visibility.

This insistence on visibility is probably a large part, I would say, of what motivated relatives to create the National Covid Memorial Wall, a memorial that stares the decision makers in Parliament in the face, accusingly, standing not in a peaceful park where the bereaved can contemplate their loss in private, but in plain sight in the busy centre of the metropolis, with cyclists, runners and people on their way to work passing by every day. The wall also demands that each and every life be commemorated, and the choice of a stretch of wall that continues for many hundreds of metres and the use of small, hand-drawn hearts makes that possible, even with the vast numbers involved.

There is no narrative to the wall: it flows on unformed and unchanging. The hearts are not regimented but vary in size and shape. Family members are encouraged to add a name and dates to one of the hearts, claiming it for their relative in their own way. As Mannergren Selimovic (2021) points out, 'there is little space for the ambiguities and fine-tuned mechanisms of grief, dignity and co-existence in hegemonic accounts of the past, which often seem driven by an opposite ambition to close the ambivalence and mask presence of absence', but the former is what the wall seems to offer. It also offers a community of the grieving – a place to meet and speak with those who understand, and a place to talk politics.

Yuna Han, Katharine Millar and Martin Bayley argue that 'focusing on the particularities of the experience of death resulting from COVID-19', as I do in this chapter, can help 'understand the ways in which the pandemic is reordering our worlds' (Han et al, 2021: 17). As I have said, pandemic deaths seem to share elements of both ambiguous loss and, importantly, trauma. Of course this is experienced differently by those differently situated at the start. Trauma, as betrayal, occurs when one's expectations of the world and life are upended and 'the centre cannot hold' (Yeats, 1920). But people have different expectations in the first place. Everyone makes peace with their being in the world in a specific way, and an event that is traumatic for one person may not be so for another.

As Mannergren Selimovic (2020) says, 'the extraordinary is experienced in the ordinary, in the everyday. It is a realm that is often misunderstood as banal or unimportant and outside politics, but in fact the opposite is true.' It is through 'our private grief' that 'we can see and act upon our long-time failure to care'. Mark Howard, in an erudite analysis of the impact of the COVID-19 pandemic, makes a similar point:

> In making death visible [the pandemic] has also made visible who in our own societies has been rendered expendable and who must necessarily be exposed to death: the elderly, the homeless, racial minorities, immigrants, rural populations; those who are unproductive or whose productivity is so essential that their lives can be given up to the priority of economic continuity. (Howard, 2022: 2)

For Howard, 'the event of COVID-19 is a moment of revelation; by revealing what was already there in the past' – and, I would add, by exposing the untrustworthiness and mendacity of those that govern us, 'it has fostered a vicious debate over the present and future' (Howard, 2022: 2). Howard argues that 'trauma as grief can be the catalyst for widespread challenges to elitist injustice, of the hypocrisy on show with no attempt to conceal it' (2022: 12), and asks 'whether we can channel the trauma of death made visible into processes of memorialization that might catalyse revolutionary action' (2022: 1).

We can only guess what the political impact will be in years to come of the experience of traumatic and ambiguous loss among members of the UK public over the pandemic years. Will the trauma be suppressed, will people find closure in memorials and public inquiries, in promises of better responses to pandemics next time? I doubt it. Will people try to forget what happened, as it seems was the case after the 1918–19 pandemic? Maybe. Or will the experience of traumatic betrayal by those supposed to protect us reverberate in UK politics – and indeed, global politics – across the years, despite other 'stories' taking over in the media? Perhaps.

Acknowledgements

Many thanks to Owain Williams for inviting me to post on his COVID-19 Diaries blog, and convincing me I might have something to say about the pandemic. This chapter develops that blog post. Thanks also go to Johanna Mannergren Selimovic for her thought-provoking piece that not only inspired my thinking but also brought together the group of like-minded scholars who co-edited this volume. Finally, my gratitude to my co-editors for being such amazing partners in crime, and to the anonymous reviewers for their comments.

May 8th, 2020

Marvin Thompson

For Eric Wilson

Is May the month of bluebells, smiles or death?
Victory in Europe or womb blood
spilt before a son takes his first breath

on a plantation, a pregnant belly cleft?
My partner lays the fake grass – I'm a dud
at DIY. This May we fist-fight death

like Walter Tull, goalscorer, Lieutenant
who left ape chants for the Somme's trench songs. Mud
was dug for Eric – his sweet, soaring breath

was lost to Covid. He still knows the heft
of Dad's coffin. In Kingston, they were buds
that ran through May rain, V signs raised to death.

Race riots blazed Newport and Toxteth
yet Britain was my army father's love.
Should we wear May poppies for the disproportionate
     deaths

of Britons of Colour, Covid bereft?
My partner tells our eldest, 'Fam or blud,
not n...' Silence. Her warm and flowing breath
is the breath of children born to out-run death.

2

Black, Asian and Global Majority experiences: a conversation

Safina Islam, Jo Robson, Amna Abdul-Latif,
Yvonne Edouke Riley, Sandhya Sharma and Circle Steele

Introduction

Safina [Co-facilitator, Head, Ahmed Iqbal Ullah RACE Centre and Education Trust, and Chair of Ananna (Manchester Bangladeshi women's organisation)]:

In March 2022 – two years after the first UK lockdown – the organisations that played a role in the grass-roots response to the pandemic for Black, Asian, refugee and migrant communities in Greater Manchester gathered. This included the Ahmed Iqbal Ullah Race Archives and Community Engagement (RACE) Centre and Ahmed Iqbal Ullah Education Trust (AIUET), and this chapter is based on the conversations that took place between them. In particular, this chapter explores the context behind their initial responses to the pandemic, their experiences of inequalities during the pandemic, and what we can learn from this going forwards.

The Centre is a specialist library and archive collection that focuses on the study of race, identity, migration and community history. Our work focuses on documenting the history of UK race relations, as well as archiving the lived experiences of Global

Majority communities in Greater Manchester. Part of the University of Manchester, we provide access to our collections for research and academic collaboration. The Centre works closely with the AIUET, its sister organisation, a registered charity. Together, the Centre and Trust are one of a few national heritage organisations that actively collects, preserves and provides access to the stories of Global Majority[1] communities that are currently underrepresented in UK archives.

The range of communities that the Centre and Trust staff work with is a unique strength, one that helps to draw out both individual and collective lived experiences where communities choose what is important to them to record in their own words, rather than it being led by the heritage institution.

During the early stages of the COVID-19 pandemic, staff within the Centre and Trust acknowledged that there were many call-outs from collecting institutions to capture the experiences of the pandemic, but the majority of them were quite generic and not inclusive. We knew that they would be unlikely to lead to donations from the communities that we work with, the communities that were disproportionately impacted by the pandemic. There was also a focus on race and ethnicity rather than racism at a time when (systemic) racism was the real reason for the disproportionate impact of COVID-19 and the health inequalities experienced by Global Majority communities. Our fears about the inequity of stories collected, told and amplified during the pandemic led to the start of AIUET's COVID-19 collecting project – #allstoriesareinmportant[2] – which aimed to gather the experiences and stories of Global Majority community organisations, individuals and activists that were organising and responding to the unmet needs of their communities during the pandemic.

This chapter is a condensed version of two longer conversations that were conducted virtually on 22 April 2022 and 9 May 2022. The initial conversations were supplemented through subsequent email correspondence with individual participants to expand on or clarify specific points.

Initial responses to the pandemic

Safina: Can you talk a little about your initial response to the pandemic that you were involved in? What were you doing? What were you organising? What were you involved in?

Yvonne [CEO, Dynamic Support Greater Manchester]:
Just before the pandemic we were based in Ardwick, in the building we were sharing with the Salvation Army and other support organisations as well, like the Construction Academy. When the pandemic started, we were forced to close, to stop our activities, and to reflect to see what we can do and how we can carry on our activities. We notice that we cannot continue doing our classes or social activities which were involving people coming together because of the coronavirus. We didn't stop our food bank because people needed that help. We approached Manchester City Council and we became part of food Response Team in Manchester. Then you know the [food] delivery became big, we didn't have a space. We didn't have warehouse. I opened my garage at home to receive a delivery. The number of volunteers increased even. ... So even my neighbours came and give help, you know, to join to this, food bank. So yes, we responded in a good way, by helping the community. We didn't only have one side of Manchester; we were delivering food to people's home across Greater Manchester – Wigan, Rochdale and Oldham, everywhere, including the list of people that Manchester City Council were sending to me electronically. So yes, we fed more than 5,000 people, their families and children during the pandemic. So

it has enhanced our work, it has is allowed Dynamic Support to grow.

Jo [Co-facilitator, archivist for COVID-19 collecting project and freelance archivist for the AIUET]:

So I actually brought that subject [to our trainees group] of should we be collecting in a pandemic, and if so, how would we collect? What are the ethics of it? Should we be asking people to contribute at such a time? And then this opened out into a wider staff discussion and we ended up setting up the COVID-19 collecting project group. As part of that I think Safina had seen call-outs from several other organisations, one of which was Manchester-based, which their call-outs were just really very general. They weren't really inspiring for Global Majority communities to actually contribute towards, and again, with our archive, we're very much trying to ensure that these marginalised voices are being recorded and available. So we went ... we put together a team. We created call-outs in multiple different languages. We did quite a big piece of work looking at our permissions form and we got that online and I know a couple of you have actually gone through this process, because you've donated material to us. We got some funding and we had a member of staff come in and so that how I was involved in this area.

Safina:

So I had two initial responses to the pandemic in both day job and my voluntary sector work, particularly, with Ananna. My first response was around, and this was really early in February, before lockdown was really widely talked about in the UK, but other countries, such as China and Italy, had begun restrictions on their population. My first concern was for our service users and our really vulnerable community members and just thinking that we need to be a few steps ahead of whatever is being talked about or whatever is being planned. I think that was when I first realised that

I'm going to have to start mobilising and organising with our staff team and trustees because our service users, particularly our older and vulnerable women, are going to get left behind. I was already well versed in raising awareness of the fact that being of Bangladeshi heritage and being minoritised within an already marginalised group meant our service users experienced profound health inequities.

The other part of it was much more about in my day job, we'd been having discussions around how different experiences of the pandemic were going to be collected and recorded, and I've seen a few different call-outs from collecting institutions. I read them and there was one from a Greater Manchester institution and I remember there was one from a national institution and I just thought, communities I know who are vulnerable or marginalised aren't going to respond to those, so who's going to record their experience and tell that story? How is that going to be available for the future generations?

Circle [CEO, Wai Yin Society]:

I think, well, as soon as lockdown happened, we … we're worrying because we moved all the services to a mobile service unit. The Chinese older people's centre, people weren't coming in. They used to depend on our hot meals, our phone calls or welfare provision so immediately some of the support had to stop. Everything went digital and we had to make sure that for the community they're able to access support. When we checked in, made welfare calls, we found that not everybody had smartphones or Wi-Fi data. So immediately we got some funding from the Good Things Foundation that enabled us to secure some devices. So, having secured the devices, we also needed to show them how to communicate with each other and our team. Working remotely, we did that and then I heard somebody say 'Oh, I can see my granddaughter now', so they can show them how to answer the Zoom call, or use Wi–Fi to WhatsApp a picture.

The other more problematic issue was about mental health. An example of one of our service users standing outside the A&E, a woman of Chinese heritage who speaks only Mandarin. She didn't speak any English outside A&E; they had no idea what happened, her daughter needed to be sectioned for mental ill health.

The significant rise in hate crime experienced by our community, as soon as Covid started even before lockdown, because you know coronavirus came from Wuhan, so a lot of people always see you are Chinese ... already, people were shouting on the street to our users. They come into our centre to report the hate crime, that was escalating until the lockdown. We also got more complaints about women suffering domestic abuse and also faced hate crime by services. So, it's a lot of complex things happening at the same time, we [were] coping with the demand, with the team working remotely.

Amna [Manchester City Councillor, Associate Director for Youth Empowerment: Anne Frank Trust]:
There was a lot going on right at the start, but when we went into lockdown, everything stopped. Literally everything stopped, all of our community centres, all of the kind of the food banks and community spaces and all of where we would go to for that support had closed, and so there was kind of this silence and then I was asking, I was kind of trying to figure out who's doing what, and I knew from the community that I represent is that ... it's one of the most deprived in the city, although it's improved massively over the years. And it also has a large population of minoritised communities, different minoritised communities, many of whom work within the retail/hospitality sector. Many who worked in kind of jobs that weren't secure, freelancing or working where they wouldn't

be getting furloughed, or whatever, so there was lots of issues that I knew we were going to get lots of problems and lots of concerns that residents raised and would need support for. But we had nowhere where they would get that support because all of that supporting infrastructure had closed down.

And everyone seemed to be really scared, which obviously everyone was scared right at the beginning because we didn't know what it was and how we were going to manage and everyone had to be shut off in their own homes and so on, but nobody wanted to lead anything, take lead of what could be done at a more collective level and so somebody said to me, just put a Facebook group together.

The Mutual Aid Groups were kind of starting to take shape. Ardwick didn't have one and nor did Longsight and they work as a neighbourhood. So even though I didn't represent Longsight, they kind of worked as a joint neighbourhood group, I essentially just put up a Facebook group and then suddenly it just kind of went from there ... so we had our buzz health workers getting involved, our neighbourhood officers getting involved, local residents, groups and local charities and the churches, the mosques, etc all started to then participate in this group.

And so it started from that, from that Facebook group, and we were trying to assess what was needed and what we could do safely right at the beginning when we didn't really know what was going on and so food support was the main offer that we did, partly because that was the main thing that was coming up for residents. Whether it was residents who couldn't get out because they were vulnerable or had other vulnerable adults in their home or children, or, you know, single parents, families with disabled adults or children, etc that just couldn't go out and do their shopping and so they needed someone to either go and do their shopping or be provided food parcels because actually they had lost their main income etc and couldn't afford shopping.

And then one of the things that we started to pick up on very quickly is the fact that a lot of the foods that was being provided by the government and the local council was not really culturally appropriate, so we ended up having to really think about actually if we are going to be providing food for people, then we should make sure that it's something that they can make meal out off. So rather than sending them random tins of stuff that actually their kids and they wouldn't eat, was that we actually tried to think about it as a set meal. So we thought very carefully about what we were producing and we asked people what they were likely to eat and if they were given something that they wouldn't eat, then we would go and pick it up.

And so we ended up with this very big volunteer network within the first few months of the Mutual Aid Group setting up and we ended up setting up our own phone line and that was run all by volunteers, and we created kind of different projects that, depending on kind of the volunteers that we had ... so we had the mental health nurse, she created a group where she was specifically targeting the African community, where particularly she was working with women who were single mums who were really struggling, so she was doing kind of phone calls after work to just check in on their mental health. We had Eid parcels because we felt that people should be able to celebrate. You might be struggling but people should be celebrating and kids should get something nice for Eid.

Sandhya [VAWG specialist and previous co-director of Safety4Sisters]:
We were about to do this incredible street protest on, the anti-rape anthem around sexual harassment, sexual abuse, sexual assault and kind of inspired by our sisters in Chile ... all this alongside the regular work of Safety4Sisters delivering group voice-based activities, campaigning, protest, dance work, plus

incredible specialist advocacy work with some of the most vulnerable migrant women in our society.

So, we work with women who are homeless and destitute due to gender-based violence … already working with a deeply marginalised, deeply vulnerable group of women who have frayed networks and support networks, very little support and then are placed under hostile environment conditions. They are forced to live by a set of mechanisms, infrastructure, policy and procedures that frame their identity and their lives when they're in the UK, and that may mean that they're very transient and that may mean that they're continually moving, and of course, because of gender-based violence women are moving all the time, attempting to keep themselves and their children safe from violence … the pandemic just really exacerbated some of the really horrendous conditions, and it shone a light on the hostile environment and, in fact, what we found that women were living under several pandemics.

They had few resources and during lockdown they were also worried about their children accessing education. So if they had a phone, that is very precious, and a child might be using that phone for their online homework. There was an increase in poverty, but certainly some of that poverty was related to digital infrastructure, digital devices, data, et cetera. But again, it was food, we immediately thought about food. How do we get food, money, resources? All the things that we were doing before became more entrenched and immediate – how do we get them to women who were quite disparate?

The women that we worked with, Safety4Sisters worked with across the North West, and I mentioned transiency before, being very transient because the Home Office, for example, when you're asylum seeker, you may go through several different sites. Manchester Ardwick might be one place, but then you whipped off to, I don't know, Bury or Oldham. So, often we're working with women not in our immediate locality and quite distance away, with a growing sense of panic from the women which is 'We were already feeling really scared, scared from abusers, perpetrators and we're scared about our connection with the state and what the Home Office are gonna do.' Because any change, any significant change ... these women are very used to sort of trying to monitor the temperature of the Home Office and that is a very difficult thing to do. We're always thinking 'What is their policy?' But we never know, and that's the whole point to create instability.

The hostile environment doesn't allow us to know because it's ... if you keep people on their toes (you're more likely to keep them in a state of fear) and subject to that fear, which is the purpose to make it very hostile and uncomfortable. So women were growing in their sense of fear, what's going to happen. And so we were trying to deal with that the best we could online. Everything went online, we increased the group, we used to be one face-to-face group support and it turned into three groups online very quickly ... just it filled the gap, but it was not appropriate, it didn't deal with deep-seated trauma and we lost so much of our connectivity that we had created through the face-to-face work ... but we were compelled at the beginning to not lose contact with women and that was our biggest thing, to make sure that we had contact with the women, with our users, with the women first, and make sure they had services and connection with the organisation.

An unequal pandemic?

Safina: What does the term 'an unequal pandemic' mean to you? In the context that you were working in? And to the groups that you work with?

Yvonne: Unequal already means that something is wrong. That means the balance is not equal. So sometime, maybe higher or lower. So being a community organisation, being a charity as well, working with BME group, Yes, we face, a lot of inequality during the pandemic. Most on funding, but can I say care, we didn't have more funds. Because why, I don't know. Was it because of our size of, the charity size? Was it because we were small charity? Or was it because we're BME charity? I don't know, but we found ourselves let down sometime. I had to complain [and ask another umbrella organisation to step in] and contact other organisations in Greater Manchester to help us. If not, our people would have just been isolated or carry on dying in their own house without food without anything.

So why do bigger organisations, who doesn't even do the job that we are doing, get funding? When we are the bridge to these people, we touch them. We know their needs. We know what they want. You know, like cultural foods we created, we started doing the cultural food during the pandemic because our people were unable to eat what was being sent, I don't know. Anyway, they had their own type of foods that they were eating before the pandemic and then the pandemic just came. ... Inequality has already been existed even before the pandemic, but it's just gone worse during the pandemic; we saw people dying because of lack of care.

Circle: I mentioned before about the shielding letter? I remember government which it did issue all the shielding letter, and I did really ask for translation into Chinese, because they were five pages long. As, there's all the users in lockdown, we can't read their letters by them bringing it into the centre [as usual]. We did use mobile phones, and they took a picture and send it to us. We could read the letter and tell them over the phone and then ... there is still a lot of anxiety there and we work quickly to respond and talk to the GP. For those few people, we can contact them, explain it and what to do. Okay, well, very quick and at the same time because the situation happened so fast ... so that's the situation we are facing on top of the very practical information.

We set up the men's wellbeing group ... men willing to come to join the group. We have a counsellor, a men's counsellor, who's giving some resources. That gets fully booked, the men talk about all their anxiety, stress. A least they got space for them to start to work out it is which [will lower the violence] at home or whatever, so this one of the solutions. The other's cancer, men's cancer group. During the Covid we had more people died of cancer in our community, we set up an inclusive lived experience group to support.

Amna: At the start of the pandemic there was a lot of this kind of 'we're all in the same boat' crap that was going around and I was like, yeah, maybe we're ... obviously that everyone was in lockdown we were all experiencing that, but actually the massive inequalities that we were just seeing were huge ... the thing that I really saw was that existing inequalities in my community were just further exacerbated, as Sandhya said it, was just that things got worse.

I think it's partly because maybe because other people don't actually seem to understand inequalities unless it's really profound and in their face, and I think what the pandemic did, was that it showcased that actually there were huge, massive inequalities that exist in the UK and that marginalised communities like ours were being massively impacted, and so I think it needed that to show that there was ... the death rate of people in our communities was much higher, support with benefits who'd lost their jobs, who had a massive impact on their mental health, et cetera. We're just compounding them and that is because these things have existed before.

Safina: It's really interesting you've all given examples of the
            different layers about all the existing inequalities. It felt
            like to me, thinking about with Ananna and the work
            that we were doing, it felt like those kind of sticking
            plasters, the ones that don't stick very well, what
            policy makers, what NHS providers have been using
            for years to get some services to some of our women
            some of the time. And that's after lots of advocacy, lots
            of support and all those sticking plasters, all fell off, all
            at once, and it just showed the lack of thought, the
            lack of care, the lack of even thinking about sort of
            long-term public health responses that were needed
            that weren't done, but it's really interesting as well,
            thinking about privilege because that's another layer
            of inequality, isn't it? That access to platforms, access
            to decision makers and access to people who can
            really quickly make changes, and so you add some
            of that up, which meant you could harness funding
            resources but that still doesn't change necessarily those
            big structural inequalities. You can sort of be reactive
            in a more effective way because of where you were
            and who you knew.

Amna: One of the things that kept coming up all the time
            from all of that ... like from the Council and from
            the NHS and someone that we were working with,
            was that we responded very quickly. ... I think they
            struggled with that. They struggled with the pace and
            the fact that we were making decisions and getting
            things done very quickly. But we did think about that,
            we took time to process and so you know, like, for
            the food offer we had lots of people from different
            communities coming together and saying, well, the
            African community, 'What is your base? What do you
            need in your cupboard to make good meal?' And this
            is what they ... and then we got a list from that and
            for the Asian community, 'What do you need?' And
            then from the Arab community, 'What do you need?'
            'cause these are our core communities.

Sandhya: The pandemic of violence against women and girls, and the particular hostility and challenge for migrant women and those with no recourse to public funds. And if you just think about it in terms of these are the women that are denied housing, they're often denied access to the welfare state and some health benefits.

So many refuges had shut their doors, the few refuges that might have taken women with no recourse to public funds had shut their doors at that very initial stage anyway, and it was just really scary. These were going to be women left on the streets under a pandemic, so the inequality manifested itself in ways in which it always manifested itself, that the state does not have the capacity. They don't have the policies and procedures or the capacity to take in these women because national government legislation states that people have no recourse to public funds. Then you have what I call internal bordering at the civil society level because of the pervasive nature of the trickle-down effect of the hostile environment and the consistent ramping up of the terms like 'illegal and undocumented', 'outsider', 'undeserving'. So lots of civil society and domestic violence organisations also have in place policies of … don't take in women with no recourse to public funds because they don't get funding for it … it's really important to get women into health services but also into quality immigration advice services because they're either at the beginning, middle or end or combination of various different status in terms of stabilising their immigration and they need immediate assistance, and there's often a time frame attached to important applications to be in by.

And I think that really does tell you, where we're at in terms of looking at inequality and the sticking plasters, as you say. And it really … I think that showed what we're up against so clearly that even under pandemic conditions this was the response from our government, that they were not prepared to provide the most basic of support, if you think of Maslow's hierarchy of needs, the most basic of protection – shelter and food. No recourse doesn't necessarily mean you can't work, a lot of the women who couldn't get access to the welfare were working, but a lot of the women, because of their status as migrants, because of the violence, because of the constant upheavals that violence creates, were in cash-in-hand or low-paid economies, and, of course, a lot of that went [in lockdown] so they were left with no recourse to public funds and then lost any earnings they had and they were destitute and very isolated.

So I talked a little bit about the fact that there was there were no support services … a lot of their mental health support, because these are deeply traumatised women who have been through immense trauma, not just in terms of their experience of gender-based violence but also in terms of the migration process and the migration journeys, they are often deeply traumatic and complicated journeys and journeys of loss, journeys of trauma, journeys of a profound trauma that they may not have spoken about or were speaking about to counsellors, and, of course, when we … when women go out and meet and it's about breaking down of isolation. But it's also about dissipating the effects and the impact of trauma.

When you sit in your one room, and often they're in one room in shared accommodation, either in asylum, support accommodation or in B&Bs or in hostels. When you sit there and trauma comes in via Zoom it traumatises your space, the only safe space you might have, and although that may seem like a small thing in the grand scheme of things it was an important thing and it had a marked impact on women's mental health. It was the legislation that came, from national government that said, some people do not deserve or we will not provide protection and safety services for this group of women.

Disposable lives?

Safina: I wanted to explore this term that ... it's kind of a difficult one, but I kept coming back to it when we were trying to process the loss. ...

We had a lot of young men who died of COVID-19 during the pandemic, and it wasn't really being talked about in the media; they just kept talking about protecting the elderly, protecting the vulnerable, and it wasn't giving us any kind of strategies to help these men who were really ... actually working in frontline roles, bus drivers or taxi drivers. ... As well as sort of the disposableness of it all was just very apparent to us, both in terms of their lives, but also how their lives were ended and not allowed to have the things that both they would have wanted and the community needed to be able to process that grief. And I still think there's a lot of that unprocessed and unresolved grief and pain within a lot of the families and communities that that we work with that are still going to come out in the next few months and years.

Circle: I went to that meeting where they said they got some additional funding. A Greater Manchester commissioner told me, based on the ONS [Office for National Statistics] data, Chinese community not a priority. I was very angry ... with my tears inside the heart ... after fighting and fighting I got some resources. So something they have to reflect on, on the commissioning or their policy/practice and in healthcare services. But the loss and the grief I tell you, I'm. ... It's really hit hard.

We lost a volunteer who was so precious to us; he's our volunteer and very dedicated member; a few months ago he was cutting the grass for us outside. During lockdown, his wife, who is also our worker, and does the 'check and chat' for our service users everyday to make sure the other users are okay, but then her husband died and it was a big loss for us all.

I suggested to do a Zoom memorial which I've never done before and I did it for the first time, which is where people sing the songs and say goodbye and share a story online. Second time I need to conduct a memorial again because another member died. Then, the third one I attended was a mother and her son who went into hospital and they never come out, and that hit hard. For me, I am still very emotional when I reflect on that time – all the grieving and the loss. I mean, in the pandemic time, I think we will never forget with our community and the way I need to conduct the Zoom memorial, we never forgot that because the loss is huge. We need people to do culturally appropriate counselling, Chinese-speaking counselling. I find very hard at the end of the day because we get full take-up of the counselling service but then the provision is still not guaranteed at this moment, so it might end.

Amna: When I think about the disposable lives, it makes me think about privilege – of being able to be on furlough, to be able to stay at home, to be able not to think about your finances, because actually, you're still getting paid, you've still got, or you've got enough money to be able to function, or you can work from home, and so your income is continued, and that the lives of those people, predominately from my marginalised communities, is that they had to go out to work, that they didn't get a choice.

They didn't get a choice to stay at home because the jobs that they often do … you can't do them from home. I think about my sister who is a nursery manager at the time and who had to go in throughout the whole of Covid because there was no choice … if you're running a nursery, and lots of other people who just couldn't be on furlough. They couldn't manage, and if they lost their jobs, they couldn't afford to stay at home and so they had to find something else and most of those jobs required them to be present [and compromise their safety], the delivery drivers and those that work in the hospital and I think those are the lives that I often look at and see those are people who are disposable. The people who are poor, the people who can't actually manage, who will have to take any job because that's what's available at the time.

It's the government treating them as if their lives are disposable and not offering the right support, not offering the right, you know, equipment, as we found out in various reports that came out during the Covid pandemic about hospital staff not having the right equipment to even give them a chance of not contracting Covid or at least not dying from Covid ... but it's very much about those people that don't have.

I think that most of the grieving for our group was much more around the loss of contact with people, the fact that if they did lose a family member that they just couldn't see them or they hadn't been able to see them for such a long time. That funerals, they couldn't attend funerals, that there was that loss of connection was a big thing for our group because they just couldn't figure out the best, safest way to be able to connect with their family and people before they passed away.

Yvonne: I talk about the death of a vulnerable lady. She wasn't old, so because old is about from 55, let's say, but she wasn't that much old. She wasn't able to walk and she was, she has to be cared on her bed and her food was delivered she didn't have everything. Yeah, it's like when you say this possible. Yes, it's like you know someone that you, you don't take care, you [the carer] don't have the time of looking after that person. But you know, when we see that that young boy has family, has mother, has father, and the lady didn't have her children around her. She was living on her own. She was a disposable one for the government, I think, I don't know, what can I say? Because she died and they didn't talk anything about her death. She was neglected. ...

Not easy to tell you, the truth is not easy, it is not easy, because you devote yourself, you give yourself, you don't want to let go, you know, to let down your community people that you are supporting. They all look at you, they are looking at you, so I don't know. It's very difficult. People are suffering out there. You have to be next to them to see how people are suffering. Most women [because we work with women and girls], and now that we have a place at Aquarius community centre, we receive them every day, when they come they first cry, because, you know, sometimes when they come and I let them cry, I can't stop them because I notice that after crying, what they had in there, they let it, that stress first gone and then now you listen to them. But how can we help these women when we don't have means? …

Now that the pandemic is not over, but, you know, is at least relaxed a bit, I have young women as well who gave birth, who gave birth to their children but not having their partner with them in the theatre, and that affect them a lot. I have them in my group and they're still talking, they are young, but they're still talking about that today, which I don't think that it will easily pass them. It will remain in them. It's something that, you know, they will not easily forget about that. That will stay in their mental health. That will affect them mentally and then again even though it happened during the pandemic it's still there in their mind today. It's very difficult.

Today the ladies who lost their friends, those vulnerable women, African women who lost their friends during the pandemic. As I said, we lost. … We didn't only lost one, the one that I talked about was very apparent and, you know, is that just hits there, it was very bad, that's what I'm talking about. But we lost three other community members that we couldn't, they couldn't come assist and participate in the, you know, the how do you call it … traditionally, in Africa, when even here it's when we lost somebody,

61

we have to participate, we have to cook, we have to assist every night until the burial day, but we ... that didn't happen and it created fear, these women are still thinking about their friends till today and they're still ... it's still there, they are still sad about that, anxious, they are not happy at all. They are even ... they even fear to come out.

Where are we now?

Safina: I'm going to move on to thinking about where we are now and two years on, two years and a bit on from the first lockdown and restrictions.

Where are ... the women that you supported and those marginalised women, where are they now in terms of ... have they been able to get back to a place in the system or within their lives that they've been able to get back on track, to rebuild? Is it so much worse? Have they been completely knocked off the direction of travel? Give me insight into where we are today.

Sandhya: Remember that moment where we all stood and 'clapped for carers' and we had a moment, all be it very brief, but there was a moment of compassion that we felt for our fellow human, and I remember thinking I'm feeling this on a national level, then how quickly it has gone away is what I'm blown away by. It was so sad that it dissipated so quickly. I think people were moved because we moved away from this abstract concept of outsiders, others, illegal, and that is wrong to see another human person suffer, in that way, and we were seeing those people with masks ... but not just the NHS, the cleaners, the nursery managers, the people that had to face the day-to-day realities that they just couldn't stop, they had to carry on.

But that compassion, that empathy was brief, and I'm sad about that because then what we had at state level when responding to migrant women was not compassion in any form, as I mentioned before, the Domestic Abuse Bill and the Nationalities and Borders Bill, and seemingly the most pernicious, the most hostile, the most punitive and almost dystopian measures that the Home Office are now putting in place that. It's hard to imagine that we've been through two years of actually thinking about caring for not even our neighbour, but someone who's very different from us and that sense of empathy and that brief moment of compassion.

I'm deeply sad that we've come out of this with a government that actually wants to do more harm and think about new ways and more complex and challenging ways in which people have to navigate. I'm not filled with an optimism. But it has reminded me of the power of our work and the power of our voice, and I think that Safety4Sisters really sharpened its voice, our argument, her voice, her narrative, her spirit under the pandemic, despite having heavy casualties.

Safina: That's giving me a nice lead in because what I wanted to do is just bring Jo in actually and I was just thinking about what you were talking about, the power of her voice and making sure that … being reminded of that power and how it's used, and I just wondered, Jo, if you could just reflect on some of the collections that we took in and some of the … I suppose for me there's lots of power in recording those different experiences, but I just wondered if you could just give us a bit of an overview of some of the things that we took in that will enable us to be able to make sure those experiences are there for everybody to understand and remember.

Jo: Yeah, thanks Safina. I loved working on this collection,[3] and was so honoured to be able to be part of the team that was responsible for recording them, and I think it sort of picks a bit up on what Amna was saying earlier that the media was very keen on telling us that we were all in the same boat but ... and feeding us that continually, but actually we were all in the same storm, but we weren't on the same boat. Some people were on large luxury yachts and other people were just in the storm with nothing to hold on to at all.

So some of the collections that we've got ... there's some really personal ones, so there's a Chinese student who was in the UK at the time in February/March 2020, and part of their donation is information that they got from the Chinese embassy and they were being issued with Chinese herbal medicines and PPE and things, quite early in the pandemic, so there's a picture of them queuing up outside the embassy. There's a picture of the pack that they got. There's also another little personal donation from a lady who lost her job during lockdown and she really wanted to record her reflections on how much the job had meant to her and all it is [the donation] is the inside of the card where she'd written to her boss to return her key for a locker and kind of expressed how much the job and the building had meant to her.

Circle we've got some great stuff from you, so we've got that poem from one of your users that's a thank you and we've got some photographs of when you did some deliveries to ... I think they were ... was it dragon boat day and Chinese New Year, so we've got material relating to that. We also undertook a few outreach and engagement sessions ourselves, so a really nice one was where we've got some young people to reflect on the pandemic, and they've done little videos and posters and things like that.

And obviously the whole Black Lives Matter very much wove into the pandemic, so we've got some really striking photographs that came from several of the protests in Manchester. We made the decision as part of the COVID-19 to not try and separate the Black Lives Matter from the COVID-19 pandemic collecting. We actually felt that it was all kind of bound up together and couldn't really be separated, so we've got some really powerful photographs around those protests.

I think, the COVID-19 collection is very broad in what we've collected. When you were speaking about grief and losing people in the community that made me think, of there was a mosque and they organised with the hospital ... people were just being buried without the religious ceremony that went with it, so they organised it with the hospital, they went through training and we've got photographs of them in full PPE, doing that work ... it really shows how people put themselves out and put themselves in harm's way to undertake these things, so that was one that resonated I think.

So, yeah, these culturally, the services that are not culturally appropriate, and so I think, your story [Yvonne], of where you're taking the time to learn about who you're caring for and trying to make, that is really a theme that goes through quite a lot of our community stories that came in, and I think it's a real strength of smaller organisations that is not always recognised by funders.

Safina: The way people were trying to process what was happening or to deal with what was happening, being creative or using their creativity to try and record their experiences. I felt that was really powerful in some of the things we collected too.

I'm thinking about the present day still, and where we are now and whether there was any learning or good practice and whether it's been shared, or do we feel it's been shared? And I wonder, Amna, if I can come to you for that one?

Amna: There was a lot of learning. I think ... there was a lot of stuff that I think we picked up around what was not working in terms of the services ... that we just couldn't access, people couldn't access. Just the ability to actually respond quickly was huge and I think that was the biggest learning that I think the other big statutory bodies learned from us in terms of the way that we did things.

But I think one of the big things for me was about how do you keep communities and volunteers engaged and how do you keep them connected? And so that was quite a big part of my role was just getting them to actually talk to each other and then seeing what volunteers, what skills the volunteers were coming with, what were they interested in doing, and making sure that they had stuff to do. We wanted to make sure that the organisations, the ones that already existed before Covid, could be sustainable and could carry on and continue the work that they were doing, and so one of the community centres ... there's a big need in terms of food poverty in the local area that they support, and they became ... what they called themselves a community grocers so they charge a minimal fee per year for families to come and register and then they pick up food and stuff so that they would then sustain that support for people when the Mutual Aid Groups stopped doing their food parcels.

I remember one of our volunteers going off and I think he was buying lentils or something for a family and he was like 'There's too many.' He went to one of the Asian superstores that he was like 'There's loads of lentils, I don't know which to choose ...' and he was like taking pictures of all of the lentils that he could see and sending it to the group and then everyone was kind of educating him about what this lentil was and this one and this, and actually which one that was more used and more commonly used, and he wrote when he left, because he left the city because he got a job somewhere else, and he wrote about how much he enjoyed learning about all of this stuff, because he's just not ever been exposed to it.

So it's like, you know, that kind of learning, and we had fun and I think that was something that I think a lot of people kind of lost that connectivity with others and to be able to talk about things in a serious way because things were serious. But then to also enjoy each other's company and have fun, and we constantly talked about having a party as soon as this was all over and then it [lockdown] just kept dragging, a lot of the volunteers kept saying that they felt that they were part of something and that it was fun and that they had a role and they felt like they made a difference, and I think that was really important throughout.

What do policy makers and others need to hear?

Safina: So, building on from a lot of what Amna said, which I just think is really important in terms of the learning that happened because it was putting in all these different structures for people to connect and learn in a different way. What do you think that our policy makers, or even broader public sector workers, need to hear or understand about our experiences? What do you think they need to hear?

Circle: I think for me, it's the experience of learning during Covid for what I think is where we go forward and it's about the partnership and the collaboration. It's been so many partnership[s] with our partner within the city. For me, it's [not just been] Manchester, it's at the regional, national, and this solidarity to stand together and remember all. ... I know because now we are still on, you can imagine that during the Covid we have more, two times more the meeting here back to back ... up and down the country, but the solidarity building I see everybody try to help each other, even Amna just talking about, we try to offer anything we can help or support until the things change. I want this legacy are left behind for many years because we are. ... I'll never see so many organisations come

together and any funding bid that we can join up,
support each other, put in. But what I'm saying is
they offer the opportunity for social change, now
this is what I want, equality, inclusion coming out for
every level of our work, what the policy team needs
to know is, voluntary organisations should be playing
a very important role.

Sandhya: Well, the problem is I don't think they do hear, so what
I would like them to do is to read the reports, it's also
set out in the Safety4Sisters reports, and it was under
great pressure and under extreme stress that we wrote
those reports, and I do wish that policy makers would
attend to those, because everything that we could have
said as an organisation we were experiencing were
contained within them. I think that the constructs of
legal, illegal, illegality have enabled policy makers to
not attend to some of the most serious human rights
issues, particularly for the women Safety4Sisters work
with, and that has been a ruse and a way, a medium
through which, you know, policy makers have looked
the other way or said 'Well, we can't do support, we
can't support those women'. I think that the pandemic
has clearly showed that regardless of immigration
status no person should be left on the streets within
pandemic conditions and be homeless.

I think in terms of learning. … I think what we
have done is shown how actually really good politics,
and I don't mean in a big 'P', but really good ways of
working comes from a community perspective and
comes from the community, and I think, for a long
time, we've had this top-down approach towards
looking at vulnerability, squeezing those on welfare
benefits, making it far difficult for people with
disabilities, asylum seekers, the vulnerable.

Safina: I remember I got invited to so many panels
and so many roundtables, particularly about the
disproportionate impacts of COVID-19 on the

Bangladeshi community, with Bangladeshi women in particular, and they kept asking me what we should do and I kept repeating I don't have anything to say that is any different than what I've been saying for the last 10 years at least. But what is really important is the social capital that we have with the women that we work with, and the groups that we work with, because of that trust, because we've invested in those relationships because we've taken the time to understand where they're coming from that is really important to form the basis of any solutions. So where do you see the future?

Yvonne: The priority for the immediate short term, the priority is to enhance our organisation in a way that we have to delegate. ... I have to delegate posts, because we are growing. Before I was almost doing everything because ... as my board, the board members, most of them have their full-time job, and it's very difficult to commit with the charity work. The charity work for them, they have, they are volunteer, and while they have their bills to pay and so on they commit more on the paid role. So the short term here ... now my priority is to find people who can allow me, allow the charity to be, to look professional. So that is the first priority for now. Actually we are on holiday, Easter break, but we will start back. We will resume on the 25 April. So for me is to look to have professional people, even, who can give their time, maybe two hours or three hours paid per week, but being professional.

And secondly, we want funding, because we have more activity, we have the demand is there, the need is there, but we don't have means to support those needs. We came here in Aquarius, we've been seeing, how to call it ... the community, the community, our members, the number of members is growing, and the need is growing. Yes, so that's our priority. And again we want to see these demands to be resolved and we want to save our community, but by having some means, and we want to see as well as to work with other community to know … that is also another need for the charity, we want to join to work with other community around the area where we are based because and working together always strengthen the organisation.

How prepared are we for the next pandemic?

Safina: In summary, based on what we've said and discussed, how prepared do we feel for the next pandemic, and what would our priorities be to get prepared?

Amna: I mean, are we prepared? Were we ever prepared? I don't think we are. I don't think we would be. I think people were just too quick to try and move forward and get back to normality whatever that was that I don't think that learning that we are talking about is really there. I think things will start to just go back to how things have always been done, and I think that's problematic.

I think in, my opinion, I think the best things that worked was, when you know your community and your audience … and that's who you focused on, and if everyone just focused on kind of a small part of their community or groups of people that they understand that they support, that they connect with that, they can deliver too. I think that is the best way that I've seen function, and I think that's how you get people to connect and so on. But the infrastructure isn't there. That's the problem. Under this government, there isn't that in infrastructure. There isn't that investment in community groups, there is no investment in community itself. That's all being destroyed, and I think it's getting worse. It's not getting better under this government, and so it's. … So I don't think we'd be ready.

I think there would be a lot of learning that maybe we could take forward from what we've experienced, but I think as a society, and as it's kind of those big structures that really need, needed to have shifted, but I don't think they have. I don't think that they are going to, and I think in another pandemic we will end up in the same situation, trying to manage at a community level because our communities roll their sleeves up and just get on with it, because that's what we're used to doing. Unfortunately structures and those people in power and people with a lot of privilege don't have to, and that's the reality, and I think that's probably gonna be a continuation of what we see moving forward under what we currently have as a government ... and in the way that they've fragmented so much of all of our structures of support that are around us, unfortunately. That was really depressing to even say. ...

Circle: I'll say before I don't want another pandemic to happen, but it's some situation which just happen. I'll tell you even our centre, today, everybody we are still wearing masks. Different governments give up everything. So we are very cautious because of the experiences, so right from the beginning we use masks, but even now we still use it otherwise nobody want[s] to come into our centre. So, one thing I want to get back is interesting about the long-term sustainability, economic future. Manchester City building a lot of apartments ... a lot development. If they would donate one property to each volunteer organisation within the city. For example, I got one, Wai Yin got one, Ananna got one, you can use your rental income for some of the income generation from the private sector.

Sandhya: I don't think we're over the first pandemic, so I really do think we're still living with the repercussions, so in terms of the preparation for the next pandemic, well, it relies on not just the groups, but it relies on what national government does, and I don't feel that we've gone from 'Build Back Better' to 'The New Normal' to 'Levelling Up' and I think they're just buzzwords. They don't mean anything because it doesn't tackle the institutional forms of discrimination, oppression and inequality that were laid bare under this pandemic.

Now either we deal with them and go 'Yeah, we've really learned so much from that we must do better with that, we must think about how we address these' because you can't address COVID-19 until you address racism. You can't address COVID-19 until you've looked at violence against women and girls, asylum seekers, the most vulnerable, the most marginalised. So the learning has to be from a national level really in order for us to be able to be in any space in any way prepared for the next pandemic, because we'd still be saying the same things.

We shared something together. We shared that experience together, and that's the thing that I think gives us something if we ever were to go through the next pandemic, a sense of we can rely on each other as a community and there is – Margaret Thatcher famously said there's no such thing [as society] – but no, there is a community and it's thriving and it is compassionate and it has empathy, and for that I would say that there is a real hope that we would have preparedness and a shared sense of being able to deal with what happens next.

Reflections

Safina: Listening back to the roundtable discussions allowed me to reflect on how important it is to centre the voices of the communities that we work with. Too often in academia or the public sector we will frame and gatekeep narratives to suit the outcomes that we need and erase the words that don't sit comfortably. Too many of the policy decisions made during the pandemic reinforced racist, classist and ableist structures at a time when the awareness of deep-rooted inequity was supposedly at its highest.

The common theme of the importance of community-led organising and the speed and sensitivity with which the resulting services could be delivered demonstrates there is still much to be learned from the sector. However, little energy seems to be being invested into ensuring that learning is captured and built on to future-proof us from the next pandemic.

The discussions also illuminate the importance of local community intelligence and the social capital Global Majority-led organisations have at their disposal, but there are still not enough resources to secure the futures of many of these organisations.

We still need policy and decision makers to genuinely partner with organisations such as those that participated in this roundtable, and implement their solutions and recommendations rather than continuing in the endless cycle of superficial consultation resulting in piecemeal projectisation of what should be core-funded, long-term transformation work. There are so many examples of real activism and grass-roots leadership, visibility and presence based on dialogue and collaboration with those in need that resulted in meaningful responses. This at a time when many of us had the privilege of working from home or being furloughed with income and housing security.

The pandemic has shone a light on existing inequality, but it also enabled the resilience, courage and innovation of Global Majority communities to shine. These stories are captured in our collections at the AIU RACE Centre, and as we move out of crisis stage we aim to keep collecting these stories as the long-term impact unfolds.

We know the scale of the loss and pain in our communities is still not fully understood or accounted for, and while the country appears to be focused on getting back on track after reopening, there are still so many questions that have not been answered. There were so many preventable deaths that happened among our families, friends, colleagues and neighbours with so little 'care', another recurring theme in the roundtables. How do we begin to process and grieve for something as a community that we still can't comprehend the size of? The mental health cost feels so vast and unquantifiable currently. So many children and young people lost months of education due to digital poverty and actual poverty at a time when higher education has finally begun to meaningfully address issues such as the degree award gap, yet we will most likely see attainment gaps widen again if urgent and impactful interventions are not put in place now.

We were unequal before the pandemic, we were unequal during the pandemic, and there seems little change in the inequity Black, Asian and Global Majority communities are experiencing as we move into the post-pandemic era.

Notes

[1] We use the term 'Global Majority' to refer to Black, Asian, refugee and migrant communities unless it is a direct quote. We use this term rather than the term BAME (Black, Asian and minority ethnic) and similar terms (BME, minority ethnic), but recognise any umbrella term for groups that are so culturally and historically heterogeneous is problematic and remain open to debate on the language we use. African, Arab, Asian, Black, Brown, Latin, dual-heritage, Indigenous to the Global South, and/or, have been racialised, minoritised, as 'ethnic minorities' – globally these groups currently represent approximately 80 per cent of the world's population. As a term, 'Global Majority' decentres whiteness and removes the perception of otherness. It also reminds and perhaps challenges that white is not the majority (increasingly in many urban wards and cities across the UK) and the inaccuracy of the euphemism 'minority'.

[2] 'All stories are important' was the campaign that the AIUET ran for our COVID-19 collecting project: www.racearchive.org.uk/covid-19-collecting-project-and-resourcing-racial-justice

[3] Catalogue reference for the whole COVID-19 collection: GB3228.103.

ILLUSTRATING GRIEF: LUMIÈRE TAROT

Dipali Anumol

Lumière Tarot is a series of illustrations of roles we have played and continue to play during the COVID-19 pandemic. The impetus for the illustrations comes from working through complex feelings of grief, worry and helplessness of being far away from family and home. Illustration has always been a way for me to deal with mental health, and through Twitter, this project quickly became a collective effort as others began to suggest ideas for future cards. Ultimately the cards serve as conduits to remember, commemorate and grieve.

Here is a sample of the cards (the complete series can be found on Instagram @lumiere.doodles).

THE RESILIENT

THE HOPEFUL

THE GRIEVING

THE COMMUNITY

THE ACTIVIST

3

Bodies with COVID-19

Kandida Purnell

Over the years people have often told me that they prefer to 'stay out' of politics. However, as I explain in this chapter, any attempt to do so is futile because bodily health and life and death themselves are always and inescapably political. Thus, while some try and really believe that it is possible to 'stay out' of politics, politics does not stay out of them. Indeed, since the 1990s *corporeal turn* bodies have been considered by sociologists and cultural theorists as anything but natural,[1] leading me to rather regard them as contested sites of local–global politics (Purnell, 2021a). From my perspective it is therefore not possible to die from 'natural causes' because politics does not take place somewhere else; it rather happens in, through and to every body, all of the time – from cradle to grave. The poor, the differently abled, the 'vulnerable' and clinically extremely vulnerable (CEV), the unwell, the people who are ethnically and culturally diverse who experience racism, those denied abortions, and those who have had their body's sex, gender or other characteristics policed in the UK and around the world know this already. However, COVID-19's uneven death toll reveals local, national and global political incursions into bodies more clearly, and this chapter is accordingly devoted to introducing and explaining these even and especially while the vast socioeconomic and health inequalities discussed throughout this volume mean that not everybody has yet been able to see, know and feel the effects of body politics for themselves.

Before 2020, I had not stopped to think about the potential impacts of a pandemic on the UK and its population. As a social scientist – an international political sociologist, to be more precise – I had made it my business to look at, think about, dwell on and then write about explicitly violent political incursions into bodies occurring within the frame of war – what has been kept outside the lives and experiences of many of my generation in the UK, and what I could all too easily have shied away from. Choosing not to meant battlefield deaths and repatriation processes, torture, and practices of embodied resistance including hunger strikes became my grim areas of expertise as an early career academic (Purnell, 2015, 2018, 2021a, b, c). Despite, or perhaps due to this, when COVID-19 hit, I could not help but notice how more subtle and subtly violent political interventions meant some bodies were made able to reduce their likelihood of infection rather effectively while others had to keep going and keep going out – to work, for example – even and especially required to do so through the lockdowns and before being vaccinated due to having been designated 'key' workers. Indeed, these people would become 'key' towards enabling others to 'stay at home' and 'protect the NHS' in line with government policy. Thus, for me, the pandemic has shown undeniably that what happens to our bodies – not only our health and what we die of and how – but where we go and what we see, taste, smell and feel all owe to political decisions. Indeed, every time you trace the root of an everyday embodied experience, somewhere along the line you will find a decision made inside a parliament, government department or council office that has, in turn, informed the policy and practice of a local or big business, GP surgery, hospital, school, college, cafe, bar or restaurant, and which has finally informed or required your movements and activities.

In his speech announcing the first UK lockdown, the British public were instructed by the then Prime Minister (PM) Boris Johnson to 'not be going shopping except for essentials' and to 'use food delivery services where you can' (Johnson, 2020b: para 23), with the raced, classed and gendered results of this being embodied in the English, suburban, commuter town where I spent the pandemic, through an inverse relation between the easing and tightening of restrictions and the number of young men of African and Asian heritage appearing in Amazon vans hastily parked up throughout the day and pulling over on

Deliveroo scooters by night to drop off hot meals from takeaways, passing steaming bags of food carefully into homes on 'lockdown' or leaving them on the doorsteps of the even more cautious. My husband became one of these latter types, working from home and, at least for the first few months of the pandemic, ordering in regularly and leaving instructions for dinner time drop-offs via the relevant app. Then, after hearing the knock he'd shout 'Thank you!' and wait a few moments before carefully cracking open the front door to snatch the bags inside and finally giving them a wipe down with disinfectant before allowing me to tuck in. Indeed, the very ability to lock down at all was and remains a sign of privilege, with Gemma Ahearne (2021: 23) calling the very notion of a national lockdown a 'middle class illusion, where some of had less risk at the expense of those who have an intensified risk' (due to their jobs being unable to be 'moved online', for example). However, the embodiment of socioeconomic inequalities and their translation into unequal pandemic experiences not only applies in the demography of food and parcel delivery.

In this time of pandemic, some bodies have been told to 'shield' themselves from COVID-19 while others have been shielded. Some have been able and enabled to protect themselves and have been protected from COVID-19, by their wealth and more secluded positions within society, while others have remained more exposed. On infection, some bodies were then carefully nursed back to health – our own PM, for example, having a bed in St Thomas' Hospital 'prepared for him' (Sabbagh and Mason, 2020) days in advance of his COVID-19 admission in early April 2020 – while others died before the ambulance even arrived. Indeed, throughout this pandemic some bodies were made and left more vulnerable – abandoned and 'let die'[2] – while others were made disposable – used and used up accordingly, knowingly exposed to the power of death. Indeed, throughout this pandemic I have noticed that in life, and differently in death, some bodies count and are duly counted while others will be lost count of or discounted altogether, as we were gradually numbed by the numbers read out nightly as news and escalating the UK's COVID-19 death toll (Purnell, 2020c).

Before 2020, I had not stopped to think about the potential impacts on the UK, and I still know next to nothing of virology or epidemiology. However, in this chapter I will explain how, after over a decade of researching bodies in and at war, I was gradually turned towards the case of COVID-19 as I realised that the body politics of the pandemic were already familiar to me, and new questions began to rattle around my head. Most loudly in March 2020 these were, *who will comprise the COVID-19 body count?*

We know now that 'certain groups experienced disproportionate levels of exposure and deaths due to the virus. These included: older people, people from ethnic minority communities, disabled people and people working in certain occupations, including some keyworker roles' (Suleman et al, 2021: 14), and that 'these differences in mortality are largely explained by socio-demographic and economic factors and health' (ONS, 2022). Indeed, it is now wholly apparent that the COVID-19 death toll is profoundly classed and raced. However, back in March 2020 the bodies were yet to accumulate and provide this 'evidence'.

Early cases suggesting potential neglect and hinting at structural racism include that of Kayla Williams. Williams was a 36-year-old woman of African heritage and a Londoner – a mother of three married to a refuse collector – who died at home after a paramedic assessment and her husband being informed that 'the hospital won't take her, she is not a priority' (Laville, 2020). Only a year older than me,[3] and barely 30 miles away in Peckham, both Williams and I had early encounters with COVID-19, and her death therefore struck a particular chord personally while providing a startling contrast. Indeed, having come into contact with a confirmed COVID-19 case and become symptomatic myself, I had called 111 just six days earlier than Williams and could not understand how she was left to die at home while I declined an invitation to hospital for further examination in the same week.

Unpacking the UK's COVID-19 death toll further reveals that within the under-65s, death with COVID-19 was over four times more likely in the most deprived 10 per cent of areas in England; that occupation, living conditions and the ability to access financial support were also COVID-19 risk factors, with 'coverage of statutory sick pay and difficulty in accessing isolation payments reducing people's ability to self-isolate' (Suleman et al, 2021: 14), and that people's pre-existing physical and mental health 'made them more vulnerable to severe outcomes' (Suleman et al, 2021: 14). In short, COVID-19 in the UK changed nothing and only exacerbated existing health inequalities – speeding up already uneven death rates between populations of raced, classed and gendered bodies. However, this was not immediately apparent and would rather be slowly revealed through the weeks and months of 2020. Very early on, those in care homes were exposed to the risk of COVID-19 and allowed to die first, buying other bodies and, indeed, the UK's National Health Service (NHS) more time. Given the lack of investment in UK health and care services, and particularly in personal protective equipment (PPE) – the very purpose of which is bodily preservation – nurses and carers were quickly and noticeably exposed to COVID-19 and used up in service within a system failing to prevent their expiration. Indeed, the spring of 2020 accordingly saw a disproportionate number of NHS workers dying in service, and a sum of £60,000 being duly paid out by the government on each occasion.

In the following pages, I describe the dynamics of body politics materialising as the UK's disproportionate COVID-19 death toll. These are: (1) necropolitical logics, wherein bodies are assigned value according to raced, classed and gendered *uses*, meaning that the same demographics – the working class, people who experience racism and the 'vulnerable' – continue to pay the highest and longest term price for the pandemic while comprising a disproportionate amount of the UK's COVID-19 body count as well as continuing to make up a disproportionate number of 'indirect' pandemic deaths; and (2) I explain how a very British militarised–militarising machismo – crystallising in the metaphorically misguided belief that is possible to 'fight' the virus – came to further shape UK pandemic policy and individual and structural responses to COVID-19 and, in turn, further bloating and skewing the UK's COVID-19 body count along ableist and always already raced, classed and gendered demographic lines.

On 'taking it on the chin'

It is Thursday 5 March 2020, and PM Johnson is inside London's Television Centre, sitting on the *This Morning* sofa talking to presenters Phillip Schofield and Holly Willoughby and the viewing British public about the incoming coronavirus. To this day, and after 30 years of airing Monday to Friday, *This Morning* remains a highly popular daytime television programme, regularly drawing in over a million viewers. However, I am not one of them. I am on a train – commuting into and across London to take classes on international terrorism and counterterrorism and research methods at the university I am employed by as an Assistant Professor of International Relations. *This Morning* is not aimed at me but rather at the stay-at-home parents, carers and pensioners more likely to be home in the daytime (*before* the pandemic transformed a generation of corporate millennials into work from home-ers that is). On this particular March morning, the PM's appearance soon caught my eye as I scrolled through Twitter at the station, due to Johnson telling the British public that one response to the pandemic might involve the population having to 'take it [COVID-19] on the chin'. Indeed, the PM's comment triggered immediate uproar with the implication that we should just 'take it on the chin' (meaning 'accept unpleasant events without complaining'), sounding at best like lazy governance and at worst murderous.

In *Wilful Subjects* (2014a: 154) Sara Ahmed provides examples of people reduced to parts due to their deviance or perceived uselessness by referring to 'odd parts', singled out for sticking out like a 'sore thumb' or being 'mouthy' and accordingly 'reduced to the speaking part as being reduced to the wrong part', providing further examples of the *hand*maiden and *foot*man to demonstrate the historically classed and gendered demographics of the bodies reduced to their uses as parts of the 'service class' (Ahmed, 2014a: 111–12) to the social body. Thus, on hearing Johnson's 'chin' comment, I was truly chilled, thinking *who will become the chin? It won't be all of us*, but continuing on with my day nonetheless. *What do I know about pandemics?* I thought, pushing down my rising panic. *Nothing.*

As the weeks went by and the lockdowns began, the university switched to online teaching and I could not concentrate. I had a deadline approaching, for a book manuscript on the body politics of the Global War on Terror (GWoT) but, despite the isolation that I found somewhat familiar (Purnell, 2020a), I couldn't write it. The pandemic kept dragging me away, and over time I realised that my research into the body politics of extremely and obviously contested populations of bodies – soldiers and tortured prisoners of war – were, in fact, highly relevant towards understanding the body politics of the pandemic. And so I gave in, gave up on the book in May, and started again. By 1 September 2020 I had written 100,000 words for *Rethinking the Body in Global Politics: …in a Time of Pandemic* (Purnell, 2021a) – some of which is included and condensed here.

In my previous, pre-pandemic work I had been inspired by political philosopher Judith Butler's work on 'grievable' versus 'ungrievable' lives (Butler, 2004, 2009) to highlight and explore how the national (un)commemoration of soldiers and other casualties of war feeds into the 'contested grievability' of particular social groups, whereby 'bodies that count – dearly to some bodies – go uncounted by others' (Purnell, 2018: 156) and there is a tendency to 'reinforce a hierarchy of bodily (e)valuation and grievability based on intersectional class-, race-, and gender-based discriminations' (Purnell, 2021a: 161). Moreover, through these cases I found that the making of bodies ungrievable via mechanisms including national *un*commemoration and invisibilisation allows for certain policies and practices engendering precisely *more deaths* within certain populations to go on unchallenged within society. For example, in the of case soldiers killed in action during the GWoT (America's 'forever' war) I found that 'the suppression of feelings of grief has in this case facilitated a war without closure and end' (Purnell, 2021a: 43), and that *un*commemoration runs the risk of 'allowing other emotions and bodies to continue circulating, with deadly consequences' (Purnell, 2021b: 278).

Given what I had uncovered – about the links between bodily (in)visibilies and the contest and 'closure' of mass death events – in the case of COVID-19, when the UK Coronavirus Act came in on 25 March 2020[4] – limiting 'the possibility for a coroner to investigate a death', removing 'the need for a jury in the case of suspected COVID-19 coroner inquests' and 'removing the need for a second confirmatory medical certificate in order for a cremation to take place', when the government announced the opening of out-of-town NHS Nightingale Hospitals for the infected (NHS England, 2020), and when the Church of England banned church funeral services and announced that only immediate family could attend at gravesides with burials to be live-streamed to other relatives and friends (Sherwood, 2020), I wondered what kind of invisibilities would enable whose pandemic deaths to go unseen and unfelt through the pandemic, and what the knock-on emotional-political effects of this would be.

Reminding me of his 'take it on the chin' comment, on 25 May 2021 the UK's *Daily Mail* newspaper published claims that PM Johnson (cited in Walters, 2021) had weighed in on policy options during the second wave of the pandemic, exclaiming 'no more fucking lockdowns – let the bodies pile high in their thousands'. The reported remark again caused public outrage as Johnson depersonalised COVID-19 victims by referring to them as 'just' bodies. Then there was the making public of former Special Adviser to the PM Dominic Cummings' Whitehall whiteboard scrawling of the question *who do we not save?* Indeed, the UK's pandemic has been punctuated by the leaking out of such horrifying remarks by the ones governing us in a time of pandemic, and such remarks are all necropolitical in kind.

In short, necropolitics is a mode of governance oriented around death and concentrated on the production and division of populations into (a) those allowed, encouraged and even made to live and (b) populations of others allowed and even required to die. As a term coined by political theorist Achille Mbembe (2003: 39) to better capture 'contemporary forms of subjugation of life to the power of death', and finding the life-centred and affirming yet still popular biopolitical paradigm founded in the 1970s by sociologist Michel Foucault 'insufficient' for the purpose of accurately capturing and characterising the defining features of the primary mode of governance in the 21st century. As Mbembe (2020b: para 7) puts it:

> This [necropolitical] system always functioned on the basis of an apparatus of calculation; the idea that some are worth more than others. And who is without value can be discarded. The question is what we do with those whom we decide to be without value. This question of course always affects the same races, the same social classes, the same genders.

Mbembe especially emphasises the importance of race in the process of bodily (e)valuation determining ways of living and dying in the contemporary world by providing European colonial practices of slavery as the paradigmatic example through which to showcase the dreadful potential of the necropolitical mode of governance, underlining that 'it would be a mistake to believe that we have left behind the regime that began with the slave trade and flourished in plantation and extraction colonies' (Mbembe, 2013: 13). However, providing an extreme example of necropolitical control due to being 'kept alive but in a state of injury, in a phantom-like world of horrors and intense cruelty and profanity' (Mbembe, 2003: 21), the figure of the enslaved person also provides an extreme example of how it is possible for some to be reduced to the status of nothing more than fuel to be expended in the service of others and, of course, in the service of profit. As Mbembe (2018: para 13) explains:

> This living flesh has an economic value that can be, as suits the occasion, measured and quantified. A price can be attached to it. The matter produced from the brow sweat of slaves also has an active value insofar as the slave transforms nature, converts energy into matter, is itself at once a material, an energy-giving figure.

However, in his *Critique of Black Reason* (2013), Mbembe demonstrates how the principle of race has been used to gradually extend the category of expendable bodies, deemed suitable for being exposed to the power of death and used up in service, outwards, to encompass not only the enslaved but gradually all people of the former European colonies, and finally engulfing everybody. Thus, most recently, and writing on the necropolitics of the COVID-19 pandemic itself, Mbembe (2020a: para 7) has noted the complexity of present-day dividing practices, acknowledging that, while 'in theory, the coronavirus can kill everyone', some are able to 'escape or delay death'. Indeed, COVID-19 does not appear to be disrupting by reordering bodily hierarchies or relations of power between bodies. Rather, the disruption to patterns of life and death are being experienced as a speeding up of existing rates and ways of death and an accompanying closing down of the space between life and death for bodies all the way down what Dionne Brand (2020: para 1) has called the 'endoskeleton of the world'. Indeed, towards grasping the realities of contemporary necropolitics, I find Brand's use of a bodily metaphor most useful as (as I explain in this chapter) the parts comprising and literally supporting the global necropolitical order and its continued circulation – the *endoskeleton* – are, in fact, populations of bodies arranged hierarchically by value and used up in order to at once fuel other bodies and shield them from exposure to death.

Crucially, necropolitics depends on certain dynamics of (in) visibility being maintained in the public eye, whereby 'the (necropolitical) work of death is kept as far out of the public eye as possible, often pushed out to faraway lands and the bodies of others' (Purnell, 2021a: 68). In previous work I have referred to this as the 'visual necropolitical imperative' that works to help contemporary governments and states 'save face' during times of mass death and also keep necropolitical dynamics of death making intact by exactly minimising their view and, in turn, any contest. As I put it, 'the invisibilisation of the products of necropower (death and corpses) plays a fundamental role in the continuation of necropolitics itself' (Purnell, 2021a: 68–9).

To return to the question of the British 'chin' part, who and how they would 'take it', and illustrate how such theory 'flashed into flesh' through the UK's pandemic, I return to my own quite mundane life as it went on through the pandemic. To provide some detail on the specifics of the part of England within which I found myself locked down and sitting out the pandemic, it is a rather extreme part. For example, Chertsey (the town I live in) borders Virginia Water, the first 'million pound town' (Power, 2020) outside London, where house prices now average almost £1.5 million. During his enforced stay in Britain, General Augusto Pinochet chose a residence inside Virginia Water's private Wentworth Estate (Buncombe et al, 1998) – and became the next-door neighbour of one of the UK's most beloved television hosts, Bruce Forsyth (as local rumours had it). Other residents have included Sarah, Duchess of York, Sir Elton John, Sir Cliff Richard, Diana Dors and golfer Sir Nick Faldo, while Andy Murray is a member of the town's Wentworth Club – known for its tennis courts and the golf course where a friend of mine growing up once caddied for Sean Connery. My hometown, Chertsey, is rather more modest. Demographically, as part of the Runnymede borough, the people who live in Chertsey are predominantly UK-born (83.1 per cent), English-speaking (91.1 per cent) and Christian (63.4 per cent). Economically, it is a prosperous town, with an above-average level of employment (82.5 per cent compared to the 76 per cent national average), a mean house price of £510,001 coming in at nearly 60 per cent higher than the national average of £300,560, and only 12.9 per cent living in social housing compared to the 18.2 per cent national average. Finally, and with particular relevance to the pandemic and this volume, the people of Runnymede enjoy above-average levels of 'health and wellbeing' (with 51.3 per cent in 'very good' health compared to the national average of 47.6 per cent), and with males and females living on average to 80.6 and 84.3 years, respectively, compared to national averages of 79.6 and 83.2 years, respectively.[5]

Every day of the 2020 lockdowns I sat either in a foldaway deckchair on the pebble front drive of the block of flats where I rented a flat or, if it rained, reluctantly indoors on a makeshift desk overlooking the same spot out of the front window, while my husband toiled away on endless calls in the bedroom. Either way my view was the main road and the 24-hour service station opposite. Ambulances would drive past frequently as the road connects two local NHS trust hospitals – Ashford and St Peter's. At the height of the first wave one seemed to pass by every minute, and I wondered about who was inside.

When I was not sat working and watching, my movements were minimal and predictable. In lieu of the closed gym, my government-sanctioned hour-long 'daily exercise' sessions involved pacing laps around the riverside meadow just two minutes away, and during such peak first wave walks, I would look on in disbelief at scenes taking place as UK COVID-19 deaths reached over 1,000 per day, as they did for 22 days in a row from 2 to 23 April 2020 (Pyman, 2020). Swarms of people lined up daily through the hottest days of that spring's too frequent heat waves, sunbathing on deckchairs and mats brought from home and placed along the banks of the Thames, with families huddled in the sparse shade of an umbrella or gathered round speakers pumping out music while children zipped through the crowds, splashing down into the river to cool off, all while smoke from portable barbecues would sting my eyes as I looked on.

As time went by and particular and particularly large swathes of the UK population started dying 'with COVID-19', I realised that my question – about who was becoming the 'chin' that Johnson spoke of – remained pertinent. One thing was certain – it was not those I saw around me, enjoying the sunshine in the meadow opposite. It was not the ones I saw on Facebook and Instagram either – the middle-class furloughed now barbecuing daily to the point that they 'can't eat any more barbecued food',[6] desperately seeking hobbies to fill the days now emptied of commutes, pubs and holidays, and trying to replace in-person activities with online versions – from Zoom drinks, baby showers and birthday parties to online yoga and Pilates classes – I opted out of nearly it all, literally nauseated by the experience of attempting to socialise online (it brought on headaches and what felt like motion sickness) but also increasingly disturbed by the determination and indeed the ability for some to *go on* as normal at such a time.

I began to notice many 'using' the pandemic as an individualistic opportunity to self-improve – by embarking on a new exercise regime, doing a cleanse, giving something up or going on a diet – while others were suffering from a decline in their mental and physical health and dying 'indirectly' of COVID-19. We now know that in other demographics deaths from alcohol, for example, soared during the pandemic (ONS, 2021b). The self-improvers, however, were able to capitalise on and take advantage of the pandemic, and are a very particular kind of people. Not only was I 'friends' with some online, I used to encounter and be pressed up against them on the days I commuted on trains into and out of London. They are the man-spreaders on the tube and the loud work callers in the quiet coach, and during the pandemic they became what I found out to my great amusement are more widely known as 'MAMILs' (middle-aged men in lycra). I'd recognise their confident and nuanced home counties inflections (not too posh, not too common) anywhere, and watched how these profit-maximising, personal best-tracking, neo- and necro-liberal capitalist subjects became openly rebellious in the pandemic – flagrantly breaking social distancing and public meeting guidance without consequence as they cycled and jogged alongside one another in pairs and packs daily – seemingly using the time to 'train' … for something. They were also unwilling to deviate even an inch let alone two metres in order to make space for pandemic social distancing. Quite unlike the bodies Gracie Mae Bradley's poem in this volume is about (in Part II) – the ones 'unlawfully gathering' in March 2021 to remember Sarah Everard who – not outside the embodied inequalities described in this chapter – was kidnapped, raped and murdered by off-duty Metropolitan Police Constable and firearms officer Wayne Couzens after he lured her in, in uniform, under the pretence that she had flouted/broken COVID-19 rules/regulations. Those gathering to mourn Everard in public were abused for doing so by her murderer's colleagues while being told this was 'for their health' in reference to the same rules/regulations. Indeed, these women's restriction and criminalisation provides a stark contrast to the freedom and impunity with which the self-improvers around and sometimes surrounding me moved under the same rules. Once in early May I dared to challenge a group of no less than 20 MAMILs – asking them to give me and a trying-to-pass ambulance space on a narrow bridge in early May 2020, and in reply was ordered to 'calm the fuck down!' (Purnell, 2020b) before I returned to the flat shaking. Sometimes I'd overhear snippets of their conversations as they hurtled past me multitasking – they'd be chatting about work using corporate vocabulary that I thankfully couldn't make sense of. However, I still try to understand them and their behaviour – or at least how it so contrasted with that of other groups in society and even my own while we took up space in the same town. Indeed, I wonder what those policing the vigil for Sarah Everard do on their days off, and think of the ones fined for offences to the Coronavirus Act, including that committed by an 82-year-old woman by having a cup of tea in her communal garden with a single neighbour (Ahearne, 2022).

Of course, the MAMILs, those in my immediate vicinity, and the ones I 'follow' online – with their almost boastful pandemic era snaps and PBs (personal bests) – do not represent all of British society, but that is exactly my point. The particular, and in many ways practical, decisions of individuals and institutions – made to mitigate the pandemic and 'stop the spread' of COVID-19 – were producing a more extremely unequal social landscape nigh on cleansed of particular demographics, becoming dominated by some, and materially-corporeally supported by the use and using up of others. Within my own small family, it was the older women who disappeared during the pandemic – my widowed aunt lives alone and would not leave the house for 18 months after March 2020. She seems more easily manipulated by threats as our government and media inflate and deflate them – once terrified of immigrants, during the pandemic her fear has been displaced onto the new, yet 'invisible', enemy. Meanwhile, my mother's lung disease and CEV status made her more cautious. She keeps away from people, wears her mask and 'will not go back' to many activities, 'not ever' she tells me, with the list of activities now permanently off limits including her swimming and indoor exercise classes, eating inside restaurants and the in-person further education that she waited until retirement to pursue. Indeed, the pandemic has been seen and felt extremely unevenly as pandemic restrictions allowed and forbade particular populations from moving and circulating, and segments of the British public moved further out of sight and touch from one another for their own (yet still raced, classed and gendered) reasons. As Avril Maddrell (2020: 110) noticed early on, the pandemic quickly produced 'new geographies of death, and deathscapes ... in regions and communities unprepared for the effects and affects of a pandemic as well as those sadly familiar with historically high death rates'.

It was not until December 2021, over 170,000 national deaths later, and the onset of the Omicron wave – after being double-vaccinated and mostly 'boosted' by a third jab – that everyone *I know* 'got it'. However, by this time it was not the same. In terms of any collective experience and therefore memory of the pandemic it was too late, and as I have written elsewhere (Purnell, 2021a, b), the damage had been done by the heightening of *atmospheric* walls. These are defined and described by Sara Ahmed in her writing about pre-pandemic workplaces (2014b: para 1) as appearing and involv[ing] conscious decisions and collective will. People can 'in effect' turn their backs to form an atmospheric wall, a way of preventing some from staying. Or an atmospheric wall can be the effect of a habituation: someone who arrives would stand out, would not pass in or pass through, and the difference becomes uncomfortable by virtue of being a difference at all.

However, during the pandemic I noticed atmospheric walls came to emotionally segment the British population as we were moved out of sight and out of touch from one another by pandemic restrictions – no longer mixing with those outside our immediate social groups as the expendable yet 'key' working class kept circulating while the middle and upper classes – those that could afford to and whose non-essential (yet typically higher earning) jobs could be moved online – disappeared from tubes, trains and offices. As I have argued elsewhere, such atmospheric walls worked in the pre-vaccine Alpha and Delta waves 'to move individual and collective bodies out of touch while physically-affectively containing grief and some bodies – allowing other emotions and bodies to continue circulating with deadly consequences' (Purnell, 2021b: 277). Crucially, as the pandemic went on, such atmospheric walls worked to *contain* grief within the communities disproportionately dying during the pandemic with the knock-on effects of pushing an already deeply divided and unequal society further out of sight and touch, and thereby maintaining the visual, necropolitical imperative by keeping pandemic deaths from view.

Looking at the way COVID-19 has disproportionately worked its way around our social body, I'm of the opinion that such affective containment has further implications – of sharpening the emotional landscape of pandemic – and in doing so setting communities further apart from another, enabling some bodies to keep going, remain unaffected and to continue circulating while others feel the toll of the pandemic in private. In my mind it is these invisible walls that continue to divide us as we emerge from pandemic and begin to mix again, and in doing so lead to a lack of empathy between socioeconomic groups all vying for victimhood, as being forced out of touch results in a lack of affective reverberations at community, regional and national levels as we fail to grasp how the other feels.

Fighting the virus

The UK's Conservative government can often be heard speaking metaphorically about bodies. For example, in 2019 former Number 10 Special Adviser Dominic Cummings argued that the European reformist faction within the Tory party 'should be treated like a metastasizing tumor and excised from the UK body politic' (cited in Hossein-Pour, 2019), while during Brexit, former PM Johnson deployed metaphor to characterise Parliament as 'a blocked artery at the heart of the British body politic' (BBC Politics, 2019). These men are not medical professionals and yet speak knowingly of the body and its workings. In fact, they seem to share between them a common understanding of bodily health, and they dangerously mobilise this as they do the work of governance.

From the *arm* in army, to the public *eye* and the *head* of state, I have long been thinking about how politics is rhetorically and materially embodied. Thus, as we entered the time of COVID-19 (and further explaining why I was so alarmed by Johnson's 'chin' comment), as I watched the daily briefings and latest announcements, I could not help but notice our leadership's extremely gendered bodily assumptions coming to inform not only their own behaviour but also the UK's national COVID-19 response. Indeed, having described how the British body politic 'took it [COVID-19] on the chin' as necropolitically constructed, and underlined the profoundly classed and raced composition of that 'chin' part that 'took' and died of it, in this section I underline the role of gender and the profound gender*ing* of the UK's pandemic by moving from scrutiny of the 'chin' part to the intensely macho beliefs informing not only our leaders' attitudes, behaviour and rhetoric during the pandemic but also the policy and practice further producing our highly unequal COVID-19 death toll, as I argue that common knowledge about bodies – including that internalised by PM Johnson and used to explain not only his own 'battle' with COVID-19 but also to justify policies devised to 'fight' the virus – is of the severely outdated and unhealthy kind.

In January 2021 the UK's Office for National Statistics (ONS, 2021a) found that 'men continue to have higher rates of death than women, making up nearly two thirds of these deaths' (ONS, 2021a). Thus, on top of raced and classed, it appeared that the 'chin' part we were told to 'take it [COVID-19]' on, and that materialised as the UK's disproportionate death toll, would be gendered too. As an Assistant Professor of International Relations, I introduce the notion of *gender* (the socially-politically constructed characteristics that get attached to and acted out by bodies and things) by discussing the gend*ered* nature of international politics and conflict with students – how women have been historically excluded from everything, from parliaments to peace processes, and how war's gendered impacts materialise as women in wartime are more likely to become refugees and internally displaced persons, and therefore more vulnerable to trafficking and sexual violence, while men are more likely to be the ones fighting and being 'killed in action'. Indeed, as I remind my students, gender 'happens' to men too and not only in wartime, as the pandemic once again illustrates through its gendered death toll.

With a large, prominent, well-defined chin (to 'take it' on) being typically associated with masculinity and towards explaining the gendering of the UK's COVID-19 death toll – it is largely working-class and masculinised labour that cannot be done from home, forcing, for example, taxi drivers, labourers and other construction workers to continue circulating through the lockdowns along with the previously mentioned Amazon, Deliveroo and other gig economy workforces that are predominantly composed of men (Fletcher, 2021). However it is not only through the gendered death toll that the pandemic has been gendered. Returning to body politics, I have argued elsewhere (Purnell, 2021a) that our leaders' – often sexist and ableist – ultimately outdated ideas about bodies come to (mis)inform their policies with deadly consequences. Indeed, this was illustrated clearly during the pandemic as exaggeratedly masculinised knowledge about bodies – internalised by British elites and PM Johnson – has reverberated around the body politic and materialises as policy responses to COVID-19 that individualise and 'blame' particular bodies for 'failing' to stay 'strong' and protect the NHS to the very detriment of the health and thriving of the collective body politic.

Political leaders – from monarchs to presidents – have long been a focus of those (including myself) concerned with body politics and trying to understand the apparently 'mystic'[7] connection between the individual ruler's body and the collective *body politic* they preside over. Throughout this literature, these particularly visible, politically important and nationally symbolic bodies are understood to play a crucial role in reshaping and *gendering* national identity: the body politic itself. For example, in his study on masculinity and international politics, Robert Dean explains how President John F. Kennedy 'identified his own body with the state' (2002: 47) and 'cast himself as the embodiment of a national struggle against the Soviets' – going to great lengths to make his body at least *look* as masculine and vigorous as he wanted it and the USA to be. Kennedy did this by hiding physical disabilities and masking his debilitating pain with drugs. For example, prior to a 1961 summit meeting with the USSR's Nikita Khrushchev, Dean explains how 'Kennedy resorted to a drug-induced manly vigor by receiving, in addition to his regular procaine treatments, injections of "amphetamines, steroids, hormones, and animal organ cells" administered by his physician – Max ("Dr Feelgood") Jacobson'. It seems Kennedy could not escape a persistent sense of failure and was perpetually at war with his body as, 'paradoxically, his severe, crippling health problems made it impossible to act out fully the cultural script dictated by his own ideology of masculinity'. Inspired by this and other such literature, as I was turned to the case of COVID-19, I therefore took a great interest in Boris Johnson as I suspected that his bodily beliefs might have repercussions beyond his own health and appearance.

When they announced on Monday 6 April, that 'over the course of [Monday] afternoon, the condition of the prime minister has worsened and, on the advice of his medical team, he has been moved to the intensive care unit at the hospital', I felt immediately on edge. Compounding this, and contrary to what we now know about the highly disproportionate death toll, Johnson's malady was already being spun to scare, with former Secretary of State Michael Gove (cited in Milne, 2020) explaining 'the fact that both the prime minister and the health secretary have contracted the virus is a reminder that the virus does not discriminate'.

During those early days of the pandemic and as the PM lay in the intensive care unit, my mind would wander and dwell on his corporeal condition. *How is he feeling? Is he conscious still? Has he been ventilated yet?* However, details were not forthcoming. Rather, the updates from Number 10 were curt and daily:

> The Prime Minister's condition is stable and he remains in intensive care for close monitoring. He is in good spirits.

> The Prime Minister continues to make steady progress. He remains in intensive care.

As PM, it was not only my mind that Johnson's body had been playing on. When PM Johnson tested positive for COVID-19, during the morning of Friday 27 March, he had continued to work from home while self-isolating, explaining in his video announcement of his test result that 'I can continue to lead the national fight back against coronavirus' (Johnson, 2020c). Clearly attempting to do just that, hours before testing positive, PM Johnson had even been out on the steps of Number 10 Downing Street, flanking the front door with the Chancellor Rishi Sunak, and dressed in a suit and tie to partake in the weekly national 'clap for carers' at 8 pm.

In the days following the PM's hospital admission well wishes began to fly in. Now standing in for Johnson, Foreign Secretary Dominic Raab MP took it upon himself to reassure the nation, saying (cited in Schofield and Honeycombe-Foster, 2020: para 7) 'I'm confident he'll pull through because if there's one thing I know about this Prime Minister: he's a fighter.'

In Raab's metaphorical use of the term *fighter* to describe our COVID-19-stricken PM, Raab continues the metaphorical militarisation Johnson (2020c) had engaged in while he could, by describing the 'national fight back against coronavirus'. Indeed, such militarisation was by now coming to frame the British state-led response to the pandemic. In a rare speech given by Queen Elizabeth II on 2 April 2020, Her Majesty framed the pandemic with wartime nostalgia, by quoting a Second World War song by 'national treasure' Dame Vera Lynn – 'We'll meet again'. Vera Lynn herself died just two months later, and I thought at the time about how much she was venerated in the British press compared to the hundreds of daily COVID-19 victims who all too often disappeared without a trace after losing their *fight* with COVID-19. Indeed, in stark contrast to fallen heroes of war I had written about before (Purnell, 2018), the COVID-19 dead would be increasingly blamed for their own demise through the toxically masculine dichotomous logic and metaphorical militarisation calling for and applauding 'strong' and 'fit' 'fighters' over the weak, vulnerable, overweight, and ones with 'underlying conditions' as the pandemic went on.

The militarisation of the pandemic was by no means a British particularity, with Italian Prime Minister Giuseppe Conte invoking the Second World War when he used Winston Churchill's words to talk about Italy's 'darkest hour' and President Donald Trump describing himself as a 'wartime President' during the pandemic (Musu, 2020). Feminist international relations and critical military studies scholars (Enloe, 2020: para 8; Haddad, 2020; Van Rythoven, 2020) duly spoke out against the discursive and 'rose-tinted militarisation' of reposes to COVID-19. However, it seemed the British public would go on to internalise and embody the pandemic's framing as a particularly British experience of war. I remember vividly being struck while scrolling Facebook during the pandemic by a post made by a primary school teacher and old school friend[8] writing about working through the pandemic while also homeschooling:

> Being a homeschooling Mum has honestly been one of the hardest things I've EVER done! ... and being a teacher should have made things easier right. ... Keeping it real ... it's like being a landgirl, I'm just doing my bit for the country! Although at the moment, I'd rather be plowing [sic] fields or working in a factory! I'd also really like my kitchen back! Big shout out to other homeschools Mums, you're my hero and you need a medal. (Facebook, 25/02/2021)

Here, in seeing her role as a pandemic mother as to support the war effort on the *home front* as women of the 1940s did in the UK, this post demonstrates how the metaphorical appropriation of military masculinity into the British COVID-19 response works to move women to take on more unpaid labour during the pandemic.

In contrast to the metaphorical frame of war, but no less telling of the *kind* of body valued within the Johnson family, the PM's aged father then weighed in, citing Boris' character, rural upbringing and past active use of his body as an indication that he would be able to endure and recover from COVID-19, divulging (cited in Bhatia, 2020):

> Boris is not just a classicist but a countryman and that will give him a lot of strength at this time. He is not just 'rus in urbe' but 'rus in rus', meaning he is a countryman to boot. ... Ours was not a household that had dinner parties, we were not hunting, shooting. ... Boris was there, mucking in at all times. A part of the very person he is, optimistic, determined, resilient, came from this Exmoor valley.

Here, Johnson Senior links his son's body to the very land of England, suggesting that Boris's rural upbringing makes him more superiorly embodied than his urban counterparts and even those urbanites claiming to be of country stock – the *rus in urbe*. Indeed, Johnson Senior, along with the other above-listed well-wishers, share a devotion to a very particular strain of upper-class, English, exaggerated masculinity.

As I have explained, there *are* demographic trends in COVID-19 outcomes with more wealthy white British people disproportionately living through the pandemic. However, hard work, fighting and determination alone do absolutely nothing to affect one's chances of overcoming COVID-19. Inside St Thomas' Hospital, PM Johnson would have experienced first hand what it really means to 'fight' COVID-19 – a collective effort requiring the one suffering to give up any sense of control to those around them who work to keep them alive. On the realities of life inside a COVID-19 ward, Ricardo Nuila (2020: para 7), a doctor of internal medicine, has described exactly how patients are treated, and provides particular details on a procedure known as *proning*:

> A patient who is proned is flipped from her back to her belly while her breathing tube, IVs, and monitors are kept intact and attached. ... But carefully flipping an unconscious, paralyzed patient can require as many as six people – nurses, assistants, therapists, and sometimes doctors, each gowned in PPE – to coordinate their efforts, as though they are moving a large sculpture.

Despite this, British elites clung to the metaphorical frames of work, war and machismo throughout Johnson's hospitalisation. The PM himself did not give statements from hospital. However, looking back, Johnson's persistent hand shaking, with even hospitalised COVID-19 patients during spring 2020 – which continued even after the government's own Scientific Advisory Group for Emergencies (SAGE) issued guidance against the act – only reconfirms the PM's steadfast belief in at least keeping up appearances of masculine-coded strength. We can not know whether he felt truly comfortable shaking hands on these occasions, but only that he wanted to be seen doing it and indeed heard bragging about it afterwards, telling the press 'I can tell you I am shaking hands continuously, I was at a hospital the other night where there were actually a few coronavirus patients and I shook hands with everybody you'll be pleased to know' (cited in Mason, 2020: para 4). Moreover, in the lack of any statement from the ailing PM, others attempted to speak for him, with his biographer Sonia Purnell revealing that

> he has a weird attitude to illness. He was intolerant of anybody who was ill. Until now, he has had a very robust constitution. He has never been ill until now, and this will be a huge shock to him. His outlook on the world is that illness is for weak people. (cited in Mendick and Yorke, 2020)

Former secretary of state and current backbencher Sir Iain Duncan Smith (cited in O'Carroll, 2020) corroborates Purnell's character reference, saying: 'I know him very well so I am deeply saddened really that it should come to this. He has obviously worked like mad to try and get through this but it's not good enough so far.' Indeed, those claiming to know the PM project the same misguided bodily and indeed medical knowledge onto the PM. Troublingly, such character references appeared to be correct about the PM's views that remained steadfast even *after* his illness with COVID-19. Indeed, after being discharged from St Thomas' Hospital, Johnson's outdated ideas about what it means to be a strong, weak or more or less vulnerable body, and reflections on his own experience, began to more explicitly shape policy responses to COVID-19 and with them, the body politic itself, through the launch of the UK's 'Better Health' strategy, the promotion of which centres round Johnson's own bodily transformation. Indeed, in a post-hospitalisation interview with the *Mail on Sunday* Johnson claimed to be 'fit as a butcher's dog' (cited in Sibley, 2020), going so far as to ask the reporter 'Do you want me to do some press-ups to show you how fit I am?' before getting down on to his carpeted home office floor to *prove* that he was over the virus and back to full strength by doing some press-ups. Moreover, as the first wave receded, Johnson's personal experience and indeed body came to directly inform government policy, with Johnson explaining in an interview with BBC's Laura Kuenssberg that (cited in Shaw, 2020):

> One thing by the way that I think did make a difference and for me and for quite a few others is the issue of frankly being overweight ... and that's why we need to tackle our national struggle with obesity. ... If we're fitter and healthier and we lose weight we'll be better able to not only individually withstand the virus but we'll be better placed to protect our NHS and that's why we're bringing forward an obesity strategy. ... We will bounce back stronger than before.

With the PM emerging from a hospital COVID-19 ward unchanged and steadfast in his commitment to outdated and discriminatory logic, the COVID-19 pandemic has revealed the sheer persistence of outdated bodily understandings, clung on to within policy circles and circulating throughout the population as a means to mis-explain and *mansplain* a threat posed to human bodies with no immunity from COVID-19 irrespective of their exaggerated masculinity and muscle mass. Moreover, such bodily (mis)understandings are accompanied by a moral dimension wherein responsibility is individualised, meaning people can then be blamed for having failed to *stay strong* and *protect the NHS* by not 'using' it.

Some conclusions

As an emergency planner and co-editor of this volume, Lucy Easthope (2022a) exclaimed in January 2022, 'all deaths in the time of plague are deaths in the time of plague. All require respect, understanding and dignity.' And yet, my experience of 'post'-pandemic British society is one of an unending assault by a cacophony of often self-centred complaints delivered competitively and seemingly without empathy, while the same demographics – the working class, people who experience racism and the (made) 'vulnerable' – continue to pay the highest and longest term price for the pandemic while comprising a disproportionate amount of the UK's COVID-19 body count. From the ones missing the pub to the ones overwhelmed by the combination of work and homeschooling, to the ones closing and losing their businesses, to the ones suffering from delayed hospital treatments, and the ones becoming victim to increased domestic violence and child abuse. From the ones disabled by long Covid and the pandemic's bereaved, to the ones unable to raise their voice due to becoming either a COVID-19 or excess deaths statistic, this chapter has aimed at revealing the body politics of victimhood through this pandemic.

Having outlined the deadly raced, classed and gendered nature of the body politics shaping the unequal experience of the UK's COVID-19 pandemic as well as its disproportionate death toll, I have come to the end of this chapter – and this point in the pandemic – weary. However, I cannot help but consider what an alternative body politics might look like, and still hope that, in light of the inequalities becoming more visible through COVID-19 and aired in this volume, in a future pandemic and differently governed UK, an alternative response might see a complete rhetorical-political reorientation, placing the security of those at heightened risk of COVID-19 – including the working class, people who experience racism and the (made) 'vulnerable' – at the very centre, and reconstructing the NHS and care sectors as well-funded and decent employers ensuring safe working conditions in a time of national crisis as a means to *protect the workforce* and deliver safe care through the pandemic. Indeed, such a contrasting discourse and policy roll-out would reflect values of community and mutual support and recognise the inherent vulnerability of bodies rather than demonstrating the classism, bigotry and stubborn attachment to a toxic variety of old-fashioned and old Etonian masculinity that has guided the UK's COVID-19 experience and materialised as our shamefully skewed and bloated body count.

Notes

1. For example, the body has been rethought as a project (Shilling, 1993), a mirror (Baudrillard, 1998), a symbol (Synnott, 2002), a commodity (Scheper-Hughes and Wacquant, 2002) and an event (Budgeon, 2003).
2. Michel Foucault's the power 'to make live and to let die' (1976: 136) is the hallmark of modern governance.
3. I am a white English woman, and although I would describe myself as working class, I may sound and appear to be middle class due to my ability to code switch (Auer, 1998).
4. The full text of the Coronavirus Act can be found at: https://bills.parliament. uk/bills/2731
5. Runnymede Borough Council's 2020 'Runnymede Profile': www. runnymede.gov.uk/runnymede-borough-council/runnymede-borough-profile
6. This quote comes from a conversation that my husband had with his barber – about his other clients' experiences of lockdown.
7. Ernst Kantorowicz's *The King's Two Bodies* (1957: 6) traces a 'mystic' and common trend within medieval theological and English legal traditions identifying the monarch as simultaneously being a person with a fleshy 'body natural' and an embodiment of the realm as body politic, which, as the ultimate location of sovereignty, 'cannot be invalidated or frustrated by any disability in his natural body'.
8. This Facebook post is included with permission of the author.

POST-COVID THOUGHTS

Michael Rosen

I feel as if I'm like a clothesline strung between two poles. At one end, sits the NHS – or more specifically the care I received in the NHS and am still receiving. It expresses for me how we can and should think of each other: that we can combine to use our skills, training and knowledge to care for each other on the basis of need. In my experience, it was even more than this in that I was given the kind of attention that I can only compare to the kind of care we give our children. I feel in some ways that the NHS behaved towards me in my condition as if they were and are my parent. At the other pole sit all those responses and reflexes that regarded me as an over-70-year-old as dispensable, less entitled to survive or be cared for. Sometimes this was expressed indirectly, casually, flippantly – at other times it was expressed eugenically in terms of implementing herd immunity without vaccination. What is as horrifying as these sentiments themselves is the indifference towards them. I am horrified that people are not horrified by them! I wonder has a level of cynicism and hatred of people – the old, the 'vulnerable', the disabled, people with 'underlying health conditions' – that they (we!) could be written off so easily?

4

Grieving and collective loss in assisted living

Hannah Rumble and Karen West

Older people's lives and voices are already often excluded from bereavement narratives and grief politics. However, during the pandemic, we also saw how older people living, ageing and dying in residential collectives, such as residential and nursing homes, were deemed less important than those living beyond institutional walls in the so-called 'wider community'. The pandemic, and its attendant policies and social restrictions, has compounded the disadvantage and discrimination faced by many older people in a variety of other ways, none of which provoke anything like the sense of public concern that would be commensurate with their impact.

As an Amnesty International (2020) report noted, the decision to discharge older COVID-19 patients from hospital into care homes, and without adequate personal protective equipment (PPE) and with blanket notices not to attempt resuscitation (DNAR notices), represented 'one of the biggest and most devastating mistakes of the [UK] government's handling of the pandemic' and a violation of their human rights (Amnesty International, 2020). Subsequent restrictions of older people's access to NHS services and the banning of relatives' visits to care homes, together with their closure to public inspection, represented yet further violations of the human rights and dignity of care home residents (Amnesty International, 2020). This policy of hastily discharging older people from hospital back into care homes was judged to be unlawful by a High Court ruling in April

2022, but it took the determination of bereaved families to reach this conclusion.

The prolonged isolation of older people in care homes has, as the Amnesty International report also notes, had a devastating impact on their health: physical, emotional and mental. However, this experience is not just confined to care home residents. It is also true of community-dwelling older adults, albeit to a lesser extent. Research commissioned early on in the pandemic by the Centre for Ageing Better on the experiences of those aged between 50 and 70 showed that a sizeable minority (22 per cent) felt that, for a variety of reasons, their physical health had deteriorated during the pandemic, and particularly so among those whose homes did not meet their needs (Centre for Ageing Better, 2020). When it comes to mental health, over a third of those aged 50 to 70 felt that this had deteriorated during the pandemic. Again, pre-existing disadvantage seems to amplify this, with those living in rented accommodation, having poor financial prospects or already experiencing poor physical health and social isolation more likely to report deteriorating mental health (Centre for Ageing Better, 2020).

The pandemic also amplified ageist attitudes, some of which were actually supported by public health bodies. In the daily tally of COVID-19 deaths, age, and vulnerability in general ('underlying conditions'), mitigated the bad news about mortality, allowing the non-aged and the non-vulnerable to breathe a sigh of collective relief. In less official, and more vitriolic fashion, outpourings on social media meant we heard the meme of COVID-19 as overdue 'boomer remover' and of people spitting at older people in the street in an effort to accelerate the spread of infection among them. Against these negatively charged signifiers, we also heard of outpourings of community kindness and mutual aid directed at older members of the population. However, as uplifting and vital as these acts and sentiments were, they also served to reinforce the stereotype of vulnerability. For the vulnerable, acts of kindness and compassion were due, but those who 'selfishly' refused to enact this prescribed vulnerable status were met with contempt and scorn.

The most important sense in which older people were unequally impacted by COVID-19 was in the sheer concentration of death in the over-70s, and especially in the over-80s (Centre for Ageing Better, 2020). This was partly as a consequence of thoughtless discharge back into care homes, as discussed above. If deaths were concentrated in the older age groups, then it follows that the older age groups experienced especially high levels of spousal bereavement, or bereavement of a close friend, which forms the substantive topic of this chapter.

Assisted living and the grievability of older lives

Older people in England, living in assisted living housing (sometimes referred to as 'extra-care' housing or retirement communities), fared very much better than care home residents during COVID-19 (Dutton, 2021), but at the price of being cut off from the lives of the larger UK population during the pandemic. Not only have such residents been subjected to social isolation, but the quality of their lives and grieving were increasingly determined by the vagaries of their residential provider and co-residents, rather than self-directed or facilitated by close kin. Subsequently, the specific conditions of assisted living greatly influenced and affected the processes and behaviours by which people could grieve, communicate a death and acknowledge loss.

In this chapter we examine data from a short research project in which we asked residents in a number of assisted living villages across England, all run by the same organisation – the ExtraCare Charitable Trust (www.extracare.org.uk) – to keep diaries of their experiences during lockdown. What we find is a nuanced picture insofar as the stringent safeguarding measures put in place by the organisation gave rise to an acute sense of loss of liberty, independence and contact with family. However, at the same time, self-organising residents seized on the opportunity to take control of their collective grieving and memorialising in ways that they had not previously felt empowered or motivated to do. In the following pages we expand on and discuss our research findings after briefly explaining our research process.

The pandemic diaries project

The specific context from which the following discussion and illustrative diary quotes are drawn was a collaborative research project that began at the start of the pandemic carried out in partnership with the ExtraCare Charitable Trust (2022), together with researchers at the University of Bristol and Aston University. The work was financially supported by the Elizabeth Blackwell Institute at the University of Bristol, the Wellcome Trust Institutional Strategic Support Fund and Cruse Bereavement Care. The project was actually part of a much bigger five-year (2017–21) evaluation of a partnership between Cruse Bereavement Care and the ExtraCare Charitable Trust called the Bereavement Supporter Project (Cruse Bereavement Care, 2022), which was funded by the National Lottery Community Fund. Karen West, one of the authors of this chapter, led the evaluation.

The pandemic presented an additional opportunity for Cruse and the project team to document ExtraCare residents' experiences as the pandemic unfolded, and to capture what it was like for these potentially bereaved people, and the volunteers who supported them, in this type of co-residential housing, which combines private apartments, common facilities and onsite care, if needed. In particular, the project partners wanted to find out how these older residential communities were coping in order to ascertain how they could better serve their residents during the pandemic and into the future. Hence, we began a research project to capture people's experience of bereavement support, which we were both actively involved in when gathering and analysing the diary data. The project was carried out under the aegis of the University of Bristol's code of ethical conduct.

Subsequently, Cruse asked some of their volunteers to keep diaries, volunteers who themselves lived in ExtraCare settings, in order to document the impact of COVID-19 restrictions on grief between May and September 2020 (during and after the first period of lockdown). The diarists were already offering bereavement peer support to fellow residents in ExtraCare retirement villages prior to the pandemic. Luckily, eight diarists were able to keep written, typed or voice-recorded diaries

– whatever they were comfortable with – during this time. We received these diary entries on a regular basis throughout 2020, and it quickly became clear to us that these diarised accounts commemorated quietly unseen lives and deaths, and bore witness to the collective losses and grief of an ageing population that rarely makes the headlines. In the remainder of this chapter, we will present some of their insightful diary accounts to illustrate key issues arising from living and dying with COVID-19 that affected this community during 2020 (see also West et al, 2022).

Shared grief over multiple losses

The impact of COVID-19 on assisted living residents was made clear in a collective feeling of uncertainty, losing confidence and missing opportunities that, for some, may never come again. Diarists' accounts reflected on many kinds of losses that they were both acknowledging and grieving, not just those associated with death, which served as a reminder that the pandemic also involved a great deal of other kinds of losses that still need to be mourned: 'Grieving about not seeing family, not seeing friends. Grieving for the losses that aren't about death. All those little things make a lot of difference' (11 August 2020).

A commonality among all the residents in the ExtraCare villages is the fact that they all experienced identity changes as they moved from their own home, owned or rented, to a residential setting where they did not have complete autonomy and choice in their domestic 'home'. The ExtraCare diarists reflected on how lockdown had triggered, for some, a re-evaluation and sense of uncertainty about their decision to give up the autonomous space of home, and the additional support needs that this had given rise to. The opportunities for activities, free movement and face-to-face social interaction were eroded or disappeared during 'lockdown', and few were replaced virtually, so that the 'virus brought into effect a complete turnaround in many of our aims for living in a community setting' (27 August 2020).

The following diary entry powerfully demonstrates this sense of community life being placed on hold:

DIARY ENTRY
August 2020

Moving to our ExtraCare village brought a massive amount of change to all our residents in the last 3 years … there has been a shared community feeling of loss for 'what was life before ExtraCare' as no one here understood us as individuals, knew intimately, were aware of, our backgrounds or what our circumstances of living throughout life had been. This was a challenge to us all to make an effort to work at becoming a new community, making new friends and getting to know each other as we attempted to break new barriers of friendship making. … This virus brought into effect a complete turnaround in many of our aims for living in a community setting. A relatively recent 'new life' still being formed has compounded the loneliness for us and many have tried to develop other ways of engaging and holding together the very tenuous ties which were beginning to develop pre COVID. … The reasons that many of us chose to come to the village were suddenly negated and taken from us. Everything seems to have been put on hold … or 'a big STOP sign' introduced into our lives.

Or, as expressed more bluntly by another diarist: 'I wondered what was about to be taken away from us next' (21 May 2020). Even if residents were not directly facing bereavement due to COVID-19, many move to these communities precisely because they are bereaved and socially isolated. Without the distractions of normal village life, and without the usual physical contact with family and external friends, they were left with that grief. This was further compounded by the starkly institutional feel of the village management's safeguarding response to the pandemic.

As a regulated environment, full compliance with government guidelines was implemented in all the villages, and the combination of a new virus, government guidance and protecting residents and staff – many of whom were potentially vulnerable to the virus – required action contrary to ExtraCare's usual ethos. This meant that communal, social spaces followed social distancing guidelines, and the collective spaces that looked and felt like 'home' suddenly became 'no-go' areas, marked off with what resembled police barrier tape. Subsequently, there was a lot of 'loss talk' in the diaries, both individually and collectively articulated:

DIARY ENTRY
May 2020

The reality of the virus came home to me as a gathering of restrictions, from 23 March. Every day a notice came on the tablet in the hall, or a letter through the door. No non-residents were allowed in for activities. Then no one allowed in except delivery people, medical personnel, carers. The hairdresser's salon closed, exercise class instructors were barred, no meetings of Christian Fellowship group or choir. No family visits for Mothering Sunday. All outside exits/entrances locked shut except main entrance, where people had to sign in. No resident allowed to leave the site, not even for short walk to the park. Bistro only serving takeaways delivered to our own apartments. ... One of the bleakest signs of lockdown was the removal or stacking of all seating in the bistro, reception, lounge, even benches out of doors were removed. We were reminded of our own homes being stripped as we left to move to the village. ... We had all moved to the village with a hope, indeed a promise, of activities, social life and new friendships but now we shunned each other if we happened to pass on the stairs or corridors.

If safeguarding residents implied the suspension of normal community life, then new ways of bringing people together and maintaining community had to be found and run parallel to the measures in place to protect everyone. This generated some inspiring scenes, some very visible, like balcony exercise classes or a Thursday evening chorus of clapping for carers. Many other subtle forms of support came from one-to-one calls, doorstep talks or distanced walks for those who had been brought to breaking point by loneliness. It is to these that we now turn.

Recollectivising bereavement

Together with this limbo of daily life routines, there permeated the unspoken awareness of mortality and death. Even prior to the pandemic, discussing death openly in these communities was challenging:

DIARY ENTRY
August 2020

I don't think this village, residents or staff, have worked out how to deal with deaths. A few families have held wakes in the village hall, and sometimes the flowers from the coffin have been given and laid on a table by the front door, once or twice a notice has been put up at reception with a photo and date of funeral, but this has not happened for many months. I get the feeling that death is not a nice subject and should not be mentioned in a place where so many old people are living, or funeral flowers might put off people who are thinking of moving here.

Finding appropriate ways of acknowledging and communicating the death of other residents is a persistent challenge in ExtraCare villages, but this was compounded by COVID-19 where the usual word of mouth channels for communicating the death of residents among themselves became unavailable. Moreover, COVID-19 and 'lockdown' made it harder to identify when people were in need of bereavement support because there was no longer any one around to pick up information or receive referrals from staff.

For example, one audio diarist spoke of a member of her book club – that was no longer meeting because of lockdown – who had no idea that a fellow book club member had died:

DIARY ENTRY
June 2020

I said, Eleanor passed away and it just nearly floored him. He said: 'What you talking about?' I had to catch him up; update him you know. People have passed and you know it's a completely different thing! ... We're still grieving ... we haven't started grieving because not all of us can come together and say 'Oh Eleanor used to do this and Eleanor would have laughed about that', you know that sort of thing. ... That sort of conversation is still on hold. Our thoughts are completely different now!

Although not organisational policy, it appeared that staff were often of the view that death and illness were the private business of family members, whose decision it should be to inform residents, including those who may have formed strong bonds of friendship to the deceased. Residents often told us that they were not formally told by staff when another resident had died or had been admitted to hospital. Residents who are close friends sometimes attend funerals, as occasionally do members of staff, but there is little sense of these being 'communal event(s) for the social body' and an occasion for collective taking stock. However, two of our ExtraCare resident diarists also told us about more spontaneous acts of collective memorialising that occurred during lockdown, involving residents assembling on their balconies. In the example below, a funeral had been arranged for one of the residents by family members. It had not been possible for residents themselves to attend the funeral because of the lockdown. Residents therefore arranged to assemble in the car park and on their balconies to watch the hearse and cortège drive around and to recite eulogies and sing hymns. This, as our diarist stressed, was especially poignant because the daughter of the deceased resident was suffering the bereavement of three members of her family at the same time. In the diarist's words:

DIARY ENTRY
May 2020

We had a funeral on Wednesday. Well, the thing about it, that girl she lost not only her mum, she lost her father and she lost her grandfather. So what Mavis and Heather did was they printed out some songs. ... The staff came out to stand outside and by word of mouth I told some of the residents, ringing round saying to quite a few people that if they wanted to go down or stand on their balconies. They had a prayer and some songs and they talked about her for about 15 minutes and then the hearse came round and stopped a bit. It was very moving, very, very moving and personal.

We were surprised by the role that balconies can play in bringing together a community of mourners, and supporting individual and collective grief at a time when usual social customs and cultural rituals that support bereaved people were no longer available or possible: 'We said farewell to one of our residents yesterday ... many of us from our balconies as the hearse moved off to the very small, family funeral' (7 May 2020).

This, along with other spontaneous acts of collective memorialisation that we have heard about and experienced ourselves in regular neighbourhoods offer up potential new spaces of memorialisation (Hockey et al, 2010) and potentially new 'deathscapes' (Maddrell, 2016) that recognise the legitimate needs of those outside the family or locked in their own residential community to remember the deceased in their own way.

Emergence of peer support for bereaved residents

We found that residents were far from passive in the face of the safeguarding restrictions they have faced, and have found inventive ways to create spaces and practices of collective remembrance and memorialising. They have been equally inventive in developing alternative ways to support those who are vulnerable, isolated and bereaved.

The diarists wrote about how they or other residents organised 'chains' of telephone calls to those they knew who were especially vulnerable in their residential setting, ensuring that somebody contacted them at least once a week. These 'chains' of telephone calls were initiated to listen and support fellow residents during difficult times: 'We have set up a kind of neighbourly scheme for ensuring that over 60 people receive at least one phone call each week.' In the process, some residents were informally, but proactively, building support around those in their residential setting who were isolated, lonely, grieving, depressed or, more generally, struggling through a challenging year.

Nonetheless, what perhaps more than anything has characterised bereavement during COVID-19 is the absence of the kind of face-to-face support networks that those grieving might ordinarily draw on. One of the diarists gave the following account of one of her friends and neighbours, whose grieving had been directly and painfully affected by the summer lockdown restrictions in 2020. This experience, described in her own words, is especially poignant for its multigenerational impact that extends beyond the spatial confines of the ExtraCare Village:

DIARY ENTRY
May 2020

I have another resident (Eunice) I keep on phoning. ... The ambulance came on Monday I think. They didn't take her away, but she was in distress. I spoke to her and said, 'What was the matter?' Apparently, her grandson is in hospital very bad. He got the virus. She said, 'I want to see my daughter.' I said: 'You cannot see your daughter because of the problems and whatever, staying apart and so.' But she said: 'But I *need* to see my daughter.' I said, 'Why you need to because you are talking to her on the phone?' She said: 'I can't talk to her because I don't know what to say to her about my grandson.' You know he is very, very critical. I said: 'Even if you talk to her and cry?' She said: 'I don't know what to talk about, I just want to see her and hug her.'

This diarist's next audio diary entry for the following month sadly relayed:

DIARY ENTRY
June 2020

My friend Eunice, I told you her grandson was very ill [with the virus]. Well, he died. I did go round and see her. I didn't break the rules. She was in the bedroom and I was in the passage just talking to her. I spent quite a few hours with her, because she was absolutely down, absolutely, absolutely devastated.

This experience of the death of a young family member would be difficult to bear even in 'normal' times. In the socially restricted circumstances of the pandemic, the absence of physical contact for this family is quite clearly unbearable to the point where Eunice is herself almost hospitalised. Further into her conversation with the diarist, Eunice spoke of her frightened daughter making the journey to the assisted living village only to be turned away at the door because of COVID-19 restrictions, leaving us further to imagine the compounding sense of fear and destitution for both mother and daughter that this likely entailed. Eunice's grief was at least known about by this diarist, who continued to support her both by telephone and by being as physically present as social distancing measures allowed through her bereavement.

However, for many other older people experiencing such grief in a general community setting, there may not be such readily available acknowledgement and support.

The grief and opportunity to process for wider family

Thus far we have only reflected on the experiences of residents who are themselves grieving or supporting others through grief and bereavement, but the safeguarding restrictions had significant impacts on external family members of residents who had died during COVID-19. Here, again, our diarists have given us considerable insight into this grief experience.

We learned from the diarists that in normal times, family members would often liaise with other residents who had been close to the deceased over funeral planning and flat or apartment clearance, and revisit residents to reminisce about a family member. Again, the lockdown restrictions disrupted these ordinary ways of grieving and remembering.

The diary extract below concerns the daughters of a fellow ExtraCare resident with whom one of our diarists was the primary contact. The resident died and her funeral had taken place, but the daughters had not been able to gain access to her apartment for the duration of the first lockdown. In the diarist's words:

DIARY ENTRY
June 2020

They've got the apartment downstairs to go and clear out … they're going to go in there and relive the event. Mum isn't about! Do you know what I mean? Mind boggling really. We've buried her, but she must be about. Because there hasn't been that talking. The reality is that they are going to go into that apartment and see a lot of mum, her smell everything and all that and having to destroy it. I've buried her and now I'm throwing her things out.

What this diarist so poignantly reminds us is that the home of the deceased is an important site for sharing some last moments of intimate contact; a site where relatives and close friends might meet to sort through possessions, to ponder the arrangement of domestic space and in these arrangements to perhaps glean the life priorities of an erstwhile living being or, possibly even, as appears to be the case here, to take in the actual scene of death. Instead, during lockdown we find that grief is deferred, because in the denial of access to their mother's apartment these daughters have been denied the opportunity to talk ('there hasn't been that talking'). Distress arises from a disrupted sequencing of mourning tasks in which the burial of the physical body precedes contact with the last vestiges of living body – 'her smell' – followed eventually by the compulsion to destroy it all quickly so that new residents can take possession of the apartment.

Closing thoughts

Our diarists have given us valuable insights into life and grief in assisted living villages through the pandemic. The diary entries are windows on lives that were, by necessity, perhaps, quite sequestered during this time. First, the moving accounts of older people questioning what they thought was an empowering decision to sell their family home and move into an assisted living complex because of all that was taken away from them during lockdown by the housing provider's COVID-19 measures. These are accounts of lives lived and lives ended, unseen, and in isolation, during the pandemic. Quietly lived and ceased lives under COVID-19-compliant regimes that took more from this cohort of older people than simply a living body. Their lives are often regarded as disposable by an ageist society, and during the height of lockdown, their daily lives were rendered a crime scene, with all communal furniture removed or taped over with yellow and black striped tape. By virtue of their age, residents of assisted living communities found themselves living extraordinarily compliant lives as the restrictions on activities, free movement, available space and groceries became more stringent. And yet, despite this, and the injustices and inequalities they encountered because of their age and where they were living, some residents chose to create their own opportunities to grieve and support each other through living and dying during the pandemic.

Our diarists told us about the determined and inventive ways they had developed to mark the deaths of fellow residents and to remember them. Moreover, we speculated that these new spaces and practices may continue to empower residents to take ownership of their collective grief and to hold their place alongside family members as legitimate mourners. Grief scholarship has persistently emphasised the importance of navigating ongoing relationships with the deceased through memory (Hockey et al, 2001). Remembrance can happen through the medium of ongoing conversations about the deceased with those who knew them well (Walter, 1996), and through contact with the physical objects and the intimate spaces of home and shared environments (Hockey et al, 2010; Richardson, 2014). However, our diarists also speculated on the ways in which what has come to be known as COVID-bereavement may have lasting impacts on those affected in spite of the efforts of community members to recreate the networks of support that might more usually support the bereaved.

We learned of the harrowing account of three generations of one family literally torn apart by COVID-19 and the ensuing lockdown restrictions, which deprived them of the most basic of human needs – to be with each other. Forever recorded in the diary project, it becomes a 'text of grief' (Maddrell, 2016: 176), in which the older resident's physical response to the unfolding tragedy of her grandson's hospitalisation with COVID-19 and eventual death almost placed her in hospital too. We learned of a diarist's concern for the daughters grieving for their mother, but barred from the apartment in which she lived and died, and the objects that she touched and that still bore her smell. As Miller and Parrot (2009) have observed, there is no sequence to the tasks of distribution and divestment of objects about which one can generalise, but such tasks 'can help to create a long-term, processual relationship to the loss' (Miller and Parrot, 2009: 510). With what has come to be known as COVID-bereavement and the examples given by our diarists, the process would appear to be truncated with consequences we have yet to fully discern or understand.

As we noted in the introduction to this chapter, our diarists were, in some respects, better placed than many other older people during COVID-19, particularly in comparison to those in residential or care homes. They have not witnessed the same rate of death and physical suffering. However, in the rush to safeguard their health, it is evident that the emotional and spiritual side of older people's lives has been somewhat overlooked. The residents we have heard about were lucky to have the support of other active and inventive residents, but it is clear that much more could be learned from these experiences and other accounts that will doubtless emerge over time to develop more compassionate ways of safeguarding bereaved people in residential settings in the event of a future lockdown. Lest we forget the words of one of the diarists: 'Some of us haven't started grieving because we haven't come together yet … that conversation is still on hold.'

PART II

Policing in an emergency

UNLAWFUL GATHERING

Gracie Mae Bradley

there is no poetry
in the men who corralled us on the common
to press down our sorrow
and spring-dusk rage

no lyric in their fluorescent creep
their intimidation
and metal arrests

this is for your health, they spat
(no safe distance for transgressors)
we will be fining people
and you need to leave now

there is nothing redeemable
in the rank neatness of that night
the power that took a homegoing woman's life
redeployed against her public grieving

when the hollow state is punishment
only the grotesque remains

let her speak
we are here to blossom, poetry

in the chorus of tar-hot demand
in bodies warm and close and care-ful
uncowed by the crush of order

listen
the lyric in the naming as the light comes down
police are the perpetrators
shame on you

listen
in the embers of our questions
who do you protect?

and we move through those
who'd shade our edges
isolated incident
women and flowers

it's our incandescence they wilt in now
and law after law still cannot dim

March 2022

5

Protest and policing in a pandemic

Paul Famosaya

Introduction

The events of the COVID-19 pandemic have altered the operations of social systems across the world, and emerging studies are demonstrating how these events have shaped the operations of the UK criminal justice system (Carr, 2021; Rossner et al, 2021). Within the policing arena, some UK studies have indicated the heavy-handedness of the police (Harris et al, 2022; Inkpen et al, 2022), while others (Stott et al, 2021) have shown how the police's involvement in enforcing strict adherence to restriction rules has further damaged the public's perception of the police and its legitimacy.

This chapter takes the cases of the anti-lockdown protests, the Clapham Common vigil and the Black Lives Matter (BLM) demonstrations which occurred during the COVID-19 pandemic to reflect on police engagements with activists during this time, and to provide readers with a concise description of police–protester interactions during the pandemic. The need to explore this relationship in the time of pandemic arises because pre-pandemic periods have shown how policing protests has become fragmented, and emerging evidence (Harris et al, 2022) demonstrates how protest policing during the pandemic has further intensified pre-existing tensions between the police and the policed.

While the policing of protests during the pandemic has caused further damage to police trust and legitimacy, police forces may benefit from exploring new means of engaging with protesters in times of serious emergency. Drawing on Stephen Reicher et al's (2007) 'Knowledge-based public order policing' guidelines, this chapter proposes that such an approach can de-escalate encounters in confrontational situations, and is capable of facilitating more positive interactions between the police and protesters through effective dialogue, negotiation and cooperation.

A brief history of protest policing

Historically, the mode of policing protests in the UK has been largely shaped by the politics of policing and the ideological standpoints of specific periods. Generally, the policing of political conflicts in the 1950s and 1960s was softer and more tolerant in nature. During the 1970s and 1980s, public order policing in the UK maintained a more aggressive style in its various engagements and tactics (Reiner, 1998), exemplifying a model of policing that was particularly heavy-handed and aggressive in nature. The miners' strike protest of the mid-1980s can be described as the defining moment during which this aggressive stance became more apparent (Joyce, 2009). However, Robert Reiner (1998: 36) indicated that 'since the 80s, both the practice and the perception of public order policing have moved to a pragmatic yet brittle acceptance of a style with greater coercive potential'. These fluctuations suggest that the processes and techniques through which protest policing in the UK is operationalised is ever-changing, and its approaches are unending.

Policing tactics in many countries typified intimidation and aggression in the past, and some scholars would claim that policing in the UK has failed to move away from such traditional engagements. In their analyses of protest policing, della Porta et al (1998: 5) identified a number of policing styles: violent versus soft policing; repressive versus tolerant; diffused versus selective; illegal versus legal; reactive versus preventive; confrontational versus consensual; rigid versus flexible; formal versus informal; and professional versus artisanal. While police organisations are at liberty to deploy any of these styles at different moments of a protest event, policing protests in the UK has always 'retained the capacity to respond to protest in a more vigorous manner if the need arose' (Joyce, 2009: 31). This idea is quite central to Joanna Gilmore's (2010: 21) argument in her analysis of the growing 'authoritarian style of protest policing in Britain'. Drawing attention to the events of the G20 protests, she argues that 'despite being "organised" and "declared", according to the typology idealised in the Chief Inspector's report, the police responded to these protests with violence on a scale that had not been seen in the UK for over a decade'. James Sheptycki (2000) has previously established that traditional policing practices often fail to recognise the strengths and impacts of sharing and assessing intelligence accurately, and that the inability of police agencies to recognise the strengths of 'advance dialogue' also contribute to the negative interactions between both parties (Gilmore, 2010).

Clearly, pre-pandemic policing of protests in the UK often records instances of violence and conflictual interactions between the police and protesters. Arguably, one of the reasons for this has to do with the difficulties in formalising effective negotiation and dialogue with protesters. It is important to recognise that one of the tenets of good policing rests on the premise of crime reduction – something that is achieved through the facilitation of intelligence gathering, constructive dialogue and the establishment of positive partnerships with the public. Furthermore, the benefits of instituting constructive dialogue and enhancing police legitimacy with citizens have also been established in previous studies (Famosaya, 2020; Farrow, 2020).

Therefore, with an attentive eye on three key protest events that were witnessed during the pandemic – the anti-lockdown protests, the Clapham Common vigil and the BLM demonstrations – this chapter explores how negative interactions contributed to the collapse of peaceful protests in the UK.

As a core contribution, Reicher et al's (2007) 'Knowledge-based public order policing' model is re-examined to suggest that if police agencies are aiming towards de-escalating encounters in confrontational situations, it is important that they enhance their interactional approaches with protesters. As Reicher et al (2007: 404) put it, 'If the police can interact with crowd members in ways that lead to a deteriorating relationship and increase conflict, they can equally interact in other ways that lead to improving relationships and reduce conflict.'

The idea of 'knowledge-based public order policing' rests on the premise of dialogue, partnership, intelligence sharing and procedural justice. Premised within four key principles, the first guideline focuses on the 'need to understand the social identities of crowd members', that police agencies must not treat crowd behaviours alike, and that through intelligence, the police must scrutinise the spectrum of behaviours in the crowd. The second element is very much interlinked with the first. Here, the focus is on the need for police agencies to identify and make the most of crowd aims. Reicher et al (2007) argue that crowd movement generally consists of those who may want to engage in violence during demonstrations, but that there are others who participate for legitimate reasons. In such situations, the police must be able to separate 'the wheat from the chaff' using the information available to them to distinguish the mobs from legitimate protesters. The aim here is 'to shape interactions between police and crowd in such a way as to lead peaceful crowd members categorise themselves along with the police and in opposition to violent factions rather than categorising themselves along with violent factions against the police' (Reicher et al, 2007: 410). The third guideline focuses on the centrality of communication with crowd members. This means that in order to ensure smooth demonstrations, police agencies must be able to establish a good relationship and foster positive interaction with the protesters. The fourth guideline focuses on the need to 'maintain a differentiated approach with the crowd' (Reicher et al, 2007: 410). One of the most crucial elements of policing is treating the public with respect, so in the face of violence it is important that police agencies act to ensure procedurally fair justice by not treating illegitimate protesters like others who are participating on a legitimate basis. Adopting this approach can help police agencies in lessening the likelihood of escalating violence during the policing of protests.

The anti-lockdown protest group

As the COVID-19 infection rate was rapidly spreading, the guidelines from research and the World Health Organization (WHO) suggested that ensuring strict personal hygiene, limiting public gathering, quarantining and staying at home were capable of limiting the spread of the virus. In an unprecedented fashion, governments across the world began to impose a series of restrictions aimed at curbing the spread of the virus. In the UK, working from home became the new norm, churches and mosques moved their prayers online, gym classes moved their sessions online, schools switched to online classes and 'house parties' moved online, with a number of social media platforms emerging to aid this new way of life.

As these changes were ongoing in the UK, a group of anti-lockdown protesters emerged. This group was largely opposed to the lockdown restrictions, calling for people to 'unite for freedom'. Although there is evidence to demonstrate that the restrictions imposed by the government helped in curbing the spread of the virus, the anti–lockdown protesters shared a different view. Centrally, the anti-lockdown ideology rests on the belief that the scientific nature of the virus was suspicious, and that the restrictions on freedoms imposed by the state had gone too far (House of Commons and House of Lords Joint Committee on Human Rights, 2021). 'Anti-lockdowners' therefore challenged the lockdown rules and were opposed to the use of masks; they claimed that the vaccines were mandated by 'bad science'; they insisted that the pandemic was in no way different from a common flu; that it was the government and some fraudulent epidemiologists who were perpetrating a conspiracy; and that it was the media that was simply gaslighting the situation (Gerbaudo, 2020; BBC Two, 2021).

In May 2020, 'anti-lockdowners' began their gatherings peacefully in London – with the idea of simply carrying placards and speaking to people about the damage that the restrictions were causing. Their message soon spread to other cities across the UK, with other members giving speeches about the forceful nature of the government and how tyrannical the government was becoming. However, some of these activities did not adhere to the government's advice at that time. As the police were already tasked to ensure strict compliance with the lockdown rules, any demonstration during this period was to be classified as unlawful – particularly if it flouted any of the lockdown rules.

As these protesters continued to spread their ideologies across different cities in the middle of the pandemic, what is evident from several reports is the aggressive nature the police adopted in responding to some of these protesters. For example, in one of the demonstrations held at Trafalgar Square in September 2020, a number of news media outlets (see Cockroft and Speare-Cole, 2020; Gayle et al, 2020; Global News, 2020) reported how the police had used force to engage with the protesters for not complying with their risk assessment. Some of the officers were filmed using batons against protesters and some were left bleeding with visible head injuries while the police officers attempted to stop their demonstrations. In another event that took place in central London in November 2020, there were videos showing both the police and protesters engaging in mutual violence (Sky News, 2020) after some police officers tried to disperse protesters for breaching COVID-19 regulations. In April 2021, another video (CGTN, 2021) emerged online showing 'thousands of anti-lockdown protesters' clashing with the police in Hyde Park, and around the time when some of the restriction rules were meant to be lifted in June 2021, other videos (*The Sun*, 2021) emerged showing both the police and protesters physically attacking each other, where clear exchanges of violence between both parties were recorded. Various video clips can be accessed online showing how these protests turned violent, and are clearly indicative of how the enforcement of adherence to the COVID-19 regulations further intensified a series of sociopolitical conflicts in time of pandemic.

Excessive force used by the police against protesters was also recorded in other demonstrations – particularly in those that challenged violence against women, as in the case I turn to below.

The Clapham Common vigil

The protest against the death of Sarah Everard was not excluded from such violence, and this can be classified as a period where police misconduct and the public's mistrust of the police became more evident. In March 2021, the UK public woke up to the news of the gruesome killing of a 33-year-old marketing executive by a police officer who had stopped her under the pretext that she was flouting COVID-19 regulations. Her death, which eventually contributed to the resignation of Metropolitan Police Commissioner Cressida Dick, clearly exemplifies the continuous and incessant violence against women and girls.

The series of events leading to the death of Sarah Everard, including the string of police scandals that were exposed during the pandemic, as well as the 'cultural collusion in the sharing of explicit material in a WhatsApp exchange' (Brown and Horvath, 2022: 1), all intensified the outrage and anger of the public against the police.

In the wake of this killing, a peaceful vigil had been planned by a group of organisers who wanted to take to the streets to channel their collective grief, to draw attention to violence against women, and to offer their condolences to the family of Sarah Everard. There were reports that the organisers of the event had contacted the Metropolitan Police to register their intention, but were refused because the vigil would simply be flouting the lockdown rules (see also Grace, 2021). Given the depth of the social discontent about the police already at that time, including the combination of failures that typify violence and scandals, many of the protesters defied police orders and went ahead with the vigil.

As the event went ahead in March 2021, an escalation of assaults by police officers emerged online, showing them aggressively pushing protesters to the ground – with the protesters chanting 'Shame on you' (*Evening Standard*, 2021). Some arrests were made, while some of the protesters were also filmed damaging police vans. The way in which the police handled women on that night was quite forceful – considering the sensitive nature of that event. In fact, the way the police handled the vigil received widespread criticism from the public, with the mayor of London, Sadiq Khan, referring to the response of the police as 'neither appropriate nor proportionate' (Khan, 2021). Similarly, MP Fay Jones indicated, in a speech to the House of Commons, that the police should have been more compassionate in their handling of the event, and that it was surprising to see a peaceful vigil collapse into violent protests, with placards reading 'ACAB' – 'All cops are bastards'. She argued that such important events 'could be hijacked by those who would seek to defund the police and destabilise our society, making it even harder for women to come forward and report assaults' (Jones, 2021).

It is important to note that this event not only damaged public trust of the police, but it also further weakened women's confidence in the police. For example, the End Violence Against Women (EVAW) coalition (2021) indicated in their report that '47% of women and 40% of men reported declining trust in the police following the case's publication surrounding the rape and murder of Sarah Everard'. As Patsy Stevenson (the woman in the viral footage who had been pinned down by the police) concluded in her interview with *Good Morning Britain* in 2021, 'the dialogue has now been opened and we need to come together as a society and make sure everyone is talking to each other about their experiences'. Simply, dialogue remains an effective tool in bringing about change and restoring public confidence going forward.

It is important to recognise that while police agencies have continuously tried to regain public trust, following several cases of misconduct involving some of its officers, each of these cases can be argued to have further intensified tensions between the police and the policed to the point that British activists are now calling to 'defund the police'. This leads me to my final case study – where the events of the Black Lives Matter (BLM) movement also recorded a series of violent attacks from both the protesters and police officers.

The Black Lives Matter movement

During the pandemic, the BLM protests in the UK emerged out of solidarity with those protesting the killing of George Floyd by a serving police officer in Minneapolis in the USA. Racial tensions between the police and the Black population have always been at the centre of public debates in the USA, and the issue of racial discrimination, racial profiling and police injustice against the Black population has continued to dominate recent scholarship (Ward, 2018; Lavalley and Johnson, 2020; Radebe, 2021). In May 2020, a graphic video began to go viral on social media showing the killing of George Floyd, an unarmed Black man in Minneapolis, by a police officer. George Floyd's last words were, 'I can't breathe mama!' – words that were visible on demonstrators' placards to echo the violence that Black people face at the hands of the police.

This killing quickly sparked public outrage across the world – with BLM protesters taking to the streets to express their grievances against the killing. In the UK, thousands of BLM protesters had swiftly done the same in British cities where they held demonstrations over the common theme of unequal treatment of Black people in the UK, and stood in solidarity with the family of George Floyd. Several other anti-racism protests also took place throughout 2020, with some reportedly peaceful, while others were marred with violence. Arguably, the relationship between the Black population and the police over the years can be described as 'frosty'. For example, David Lammy has previously drawn attention to the racial disparities and the unequal treatment of 'Blacks and Ethnic Minorities' in the criminal justice system in the UK (Lammy, 2017), while recent studies have maintained that policing during the pandemic was 'disproportionately targeting Black and Minority Ethnic communities in the UK' (Harris et al, 2022: 92). On 8 June 2020, former Home Secretary Priti Patel expressed her views in the House of Commons, noting that George Floyd's 'treatment at the hands of the United States police was appalling and speaks to the sense of injustice experienced by minority communities around the world'. She added that 'I fully appreciate the strength of feeling over his senseless killing, the inequality that black people can sadly still face, and the deep-seated desire for change. I know that it is that sense of injustice that has driven people to take to the UK streets to protest' (Patel, 2020).

According to BBC News (2020c), protests were peaceful in some locations, while others turned violent in other locations. For example, the demonstration at the US embassy in London was reportedly peaceful, and the same was reported in Glasgow. However, in Whitehall, BBC News reported that the violence that erupted was caused by a minority of protesters who attacked and were throwing bottles at police officers. In June 2020, demonstrators in Bristol pulled down and 'drowned' the statue of Edward Colston for his connection with the slave trade. In an interview with *The Guardian*, one of the police officers defended their action in not intervening during the toppling of the statue, explaining that 'they decided not to intervene and they came to a view that to take action would have involved significant use of force and confrontation with otherwise peaceful protesters, he said. It was a non-intervention that led to a de-escalation and constraining of criminal acts' (quoted in Sabbagh and Dodd, 2020). There were reports (BBC News, 2020d) that 'members of football hooligan networks' alongside some far-right activists had organised a counter-demonstration on the same day as the BLM movement. The groups claimed to be defending the British heritage and war memorials, and clashed with the police.

At Parliament Square, for example, BBC News (2020d) reported that these 'groups looked for opportunities to attack the police. Bottles and cans were thrown at their lines and horses – smoke bombs and fireworks set off. Journalists who came too close were threatened.' Outside Downing Street, images of violence and physical altercation between the police and protesters circulated in the media space in June 2020 (*The Sun*, 2020). Drawing from testimonies of protesters and witnesses, another report published by the Network for Police Monitoring (Netpol, 2020: 4) highlighted the 'excessive use of force being disproportionately targeted at Black and other racially minoritised protesters'. The report also indicated the police's failure of their duty to protect Black protesters from far-right attacks during the far-right's counter-demonstrations. Other images of police engaging in violent confrontations with protesters were also in circulation on Twitter, YouTube and mainstream media outlets during this period.

Understanding pandemic policing

Throughout the pandemic, the aim of government across the world had been to limit public gatherings in an attempt to curb the spread of COVID-19 infection. However, it could be argued that each of these cases has demonstrated how the events of the pandemic have further intensified pre-existing tensions between the police and the policed. On the other hand, they have shown how the enforcement of strict adherence to restriction laws may have further damaged police legitimacy.

It is important to recognise that heavy-handed policing destroys channels of communication, and if police agencies are aiming to lessen the likelihood of escalating violence during the policing of protests, there is a need to improve on their interactional approach with protesters. The third guideline of Reicher et al's (2007) model focuses on the centrality of communication with crowd members. It states that the police must be able to establish good relationships and foster positive interactions with protest organisers in order to ensure smooth demonstrations. In the case of the police and the organisers of the protests for Sarah Everard, it is clear that there was a breakdown in communication. The organisers of the vigil had initially approached the police to notify them of their intention to conduct a silent vigil but they were refused due to COVID-19 regulations in place at that time. Meanwhile, in the recent ruling by Lord Justice Warby and Mr Justice Holgate, the court upheld in March 2022 that the police had breached the rights of the organisers, and that the way they had engaged with the protesters at the vigil was not in accordance with the law. According to the judgment,

> None of the [Metropolitan Police Service, MPS] decisions was in accordance with the law; the evidence showed that the MPS failed to perform its legal duty to consider whether the claimants might have a reasonable excuse for holding the gathering, or to conduct the fact-specific proportionality assessment required in order to perform that duty. (Judiciary of England and Wales, 2022: 2)

If the police had taken a more sensitive approach, and allowed the vigil to proceed (with an acceptable mutual agreement by both parties), perhaps those violent events would have been better curtailed.

Further, in some of the footage that has surfaced online, police officers did not respond verbally to the some of the protesters at the vigil as they were being removed from the protest ground. This again suggests the need for police agencies to be more coordinated and effective with regards to dialogue during protest policing. As Reicher et al (2007) suggest, when people are being contained during violent confrontations and outbursts, it is important for police officers to quickly establish a means of addressing the crowd, and to explain to the organisers what they are doing and why they may want to adopt a different tactic in dealing with issues. This, they argue, 'may involve the development of new communications technologies such as high-powered mobile loudspeaker systems and giant LCD screens' (Reicher et al, 2007: 411).

Generally, traditional police operations have been identified as being about collating criminal intelligence that treats the crowd as one entity (Reicher et al, 2007). However, 'Knowledge-based public order policing' recommends that rather than treating the whole crowd alike, police forces may benefit from ensuring deep knowledge of the group's behaviours and identifying transgressors with a known history of violence who may wish to disrupt legitimate demonstrations prior to the event.

Crowd violence is usually contagious during mass actions, and we have seen how the violence of the minority sometimes overshadows collective action. I highlighted earlier how the former home secretary Priti Patel admitted in her speech to the House of Commons that the clash witnessed between the police and the BLM protesters was caused by a minority of protesters. The admittance of this minority suggests the need for police agencies to enhance their intelligence gathering by making the most of crowd aims. In his essay, Peter Joyce (2009: 31) distinguishes two particular types of groups in a protest, namely the 'contained' and 'transgressive' groups. He argues that the contained groups are the legitimate entities who are willing to abide by the law. They are willing to cooperate with the police and accept police suggestions. The transgressive groups, however, are the opposite. This group 'may possess anti-authoritarian views that make them unwilling to negotiate with the police and instead pursue confrontational actions' (Joyce, 2009: 31). The report by the All-Party Parliamentary Group on Democracy and the Constitution concluded that officers in Bristol 'failed to distinguish between those protesting peacefully and those engaged in acts of violence', which resulted in 'excessive force' being used (APPGDC, 2021: 63, 7).

I do not infer that the police should abort the enforcement of the law whenever negotiations are breached, and nor do I condone the aggression that some protesters have shown towards the police. The argument here is that by identifying the transgressive groups, the police may be predisposed to identifying certain risks – instead of pre-empting the violence that has not yet occurred.

It is also important that police agencies 'maintain a differentiated approach with the crowd' at all times (Reicher et al, 2007: 410). As already mentioned, one of the most crucial elements of policing is treating the public with respect and, in the face of violence, it is important that innocent and legitimate protesters are not treated like others who are participating on an illegitimate basis. Studies have indicated that when people are treated with procedural fairness (Myhill and Quinton, 2011), there is very little chance that they will behave irrationally – and, as I (Famosaya, 2020: 943) concluded, 'when citizens are respectfully treated, positive interactions are highly likely'.

The COVID-19 pandemic created an enormous challenge, not only for the members of the public, but also for policing in the UK. Undoubtedly, police officers were put in a very difficult position during the pandemic because they were tasked to carry out their duty at a time of serious emergency while implementing rules that they themselves were not accustomed to. Some of these guidelines were complex in nature, and police officers were having to adjust to these guidelines as they changed sporadically. It could be argued that the changing and ambiguous nature of these rules may have further contributed to some of the failings of the police. In enforcing strict adherence to the regulations, this also meant that police officers were put at a considerable risk as they could have unknowingly come in close contact with those who were infected with the virus. These were the police's duties. Therefore, it is important to recognise the efforts of all the diligent police officers who put their lives on the line to protect the public to the extent that some of them were physically attacked, ridiculed and abused while they were simply doing their job.

Maintaining public order at protests is one of the hardest tasks to manage in modern policing, and this chapter maintains that de-escalating confrontational situations may continue to prove difficult to achieve in the absence of partnership and dialogue between the police and protesters. This means that police agencies must endeavour to position themselves in a situation where the protesters do not perceive them as obstructing their goal, but rather, as an organisation assisting them to exercise their rights.

Activists are very important in any democracy, and their role cannot be overemphasised. I classify them as the immune system of any society that fights against attacks, and in a real sense, they are the groups that challenge the systems of oppression attacking the dignity of humanity. Police agencies will therefore need to support the system and demonstrate open hands in cooperating with legitimate protesters while facilitating partnership arrangements with protesters. The onus does not rest on the police alone, however. Protest groups, through their organisers, will also need to ensure cooperation with the police at all times by (for example) notifying the police of an upcoming assembly or processions or demonstrations and ensuring strict adherence to their risk assessment. Both parties must engage in discussions, conduct frank and genuine pre-match meetings, and clarify risks as well as police officers' mode of engagement on the day. Finding reconciliation and ensuring positive interactions via a procedurally fair approach and dialogue is the goal.

DYING DECLARATION

Anjana Nair

I forgive the unmasked
Who thronged the malls, theatres and beaches
Consuming the pleasures
As if there is no afterward

I forgive the travellers
Who toured tracing territories
trespassing the rules –
Written and unwritten

I forgive the crowds
Devouring the words spilling out of a *neta
Who somehow seems to care less –
For us and ours

I forgive the police
Who had already forgiven those
Breaking the law and dancing to the tunes
Of careless rhythm

I forgive the election commission
Who forgot to enforce protocols
With more fervour and passion
Rules, were there for a reason!

I forgive the governments
Who made us sitting ducks,

Failing to make arrangements – Oxygen and beds
On time, for me and the likes

I forgive the airs
That carried the virus,
Into my lungs – choking me,
And squeezing life out of me

And I forgive my lungs
For failing me

I forgive my mouth
For gasping. ...

I forgive everyone failing me

I forgive myself. ...

Note: *Neta = political leader

6

Legal education after COVID-19

Patricia Tuitt

This chapter explores the implications of the coronavirus pandemic on the education and training of prospective lawyers. It argues that the pandemic has drawn attention to the fact that much of legal education presumes a normal state of affairs existing within the state wherein the laws that are the subject of study are enacted and implemented. Consequently, prospective lawyers are not adequately equipped with the appropriate knowledge and skills to ensure that the rule of law is maintained in those exceptional occasions when a general state of emergency is declared.

Focusing on the English university law school, the chapter offers one way of addressing the current deficiency. It suggests that the law curriculum be redesigned so that prospective lawyers are exposed to a deep and sustained exploration of the encounter between the law, various organs of the British state and certain marginalised communities – such as migrants and resident non-nationals. As the chapter seeks to demonstrate, the experience of living in the context of laws that can be set aside or ignored in favour of political and strategic considerations – which many individuals reported during the 'lockdowns' that were imposed during the coronavirus pandemic – is indicative of the way in which marginalised communities are routinely managed.

A brief explanation of the law during the pandemic

The rule of law is most threatened when the boundaries between law and non-law become blurred or are deemed to be irrelevant to a proportion of the population – which is significant in size – who would otherwise not dispute the existence of a general duty to obey the law. During the coronavirus pandemic, various organs of the state took measures – or endorsed measures taken by others – that resulted in restrictions on the fundamental rights of individuals. In many cases these measures were not authorised by the law. Neither the law school nor other institutions involved in legal education and training adequately equip prospective lawyers with the means to respond effectively to the widespread disregard or breaches of the law by state officials, which, as with the pandemic, often occur when emergency situations affecting whole populations emerge.

This chapter argues that lessons gleaned from the COVID-19 pandemic about how the letter of the law can be abandoned in favour of the political and strategic interests of politicians and other state officials must be learned and incorporated into legal curricula. For this to happen, however, not only must the pandemic and the effect of its various lockdowns become an object of legal studies, the law curricula must also better incorporate the study of other historical and contemporary situations that have prompted state officials to engage in the kinds of lawless actions that government ministers, the police and university officials, among others, engaged in during this health emergency. This would entail a redesign of the law curricula to enable compulsory study of how various organs of the British state – notably, the police and immigration officials – have governed certain marginalised communities. As the chapter aims to demonstrate, migrants, resident non-nationals and criminalised young Black men, in particular, are *routinely* governed by the strategies that were *exceptionally* visited on the entire population of England during the coronavirus lockdowns.

The argument in the chapter is organised in two parts. The first draws on two reports produced by the Joint Committee on Human Rights (JCHR) on 8 April 2020 and 21 April 2021 that verify and record several instances of the conflation of law and guidance by various organs of the British state in implementing coronavirus restrictions across England. I juxtapose these instances with the way in which immigration officials dealt with resident non-nationals of Caribbean origin during what has come to be known as the 'Windrush scandal'. Underpinning this analysis are extensive references to Amelia Gentleman's *The Windrush Betrayal: Exposing the Hostile Environment* (2019).

The second part of the chapter reflects on the instances explored in the first part in the context of well-established theories on the relationship between law and violence. It argues that the conflation of law with guidance, which was a frequently observed phenomenon during the coronavirus lockdowns, is inherently undesirable because the distinction between 'legal violence' and 'natural violence' on which the very rule of law depends is eroded. The conflation of law with guidance evident in the management of the general population of England during the coronavirus emergency, and which marginalised communities (such as the Windrush descendants) routinely experience, raises the prospect that all of human life might be regulated by *unregulated* physical and non-physical violence.

Given that the chapter is concerned with the ways in which state officials interpreted and, where empowered to do so, purportedly applied laws governing restrictions on movement and social interaction during the pandemic, the examples used in the first part are confined to England – which is also where the author's knowledge of university law school curricula is gleaned. However, the arguments in the second part – concerning the impact on the rule of law of state officials setting aside law in favour of 'guidance' or political and strategic considerations – are intended to have a more general application.

Part 1: Law, guidance and governance

In an attempt to restrict the spread of the coronavirus, ordinary activities across England and other areas of the devolved nation, such as gathering in public, mixing in various households, attending educational institutions, non-essential shops, gyms, pubs and restaurants, were significantly curtailed. While only those restrictions – colloquially known as 'lockdown restrictions' – in the form of Regulations made under the Public Health (Control of Disease) Act 1984 were legally binding on individuals, the requirement of the law was only one factor among many that determined the extent of social interaction during the near two-year period, during which the virus and its many variants took hold. Other competing factors included government advice and guidance, peer and family pressures, the organisational preferences of employers and the organisational preferences of schools, universities and other educational institutions.

This chapter argues that the coronavirus situation, especially as it was observed to play out in England, is a classic illustration of how, in situations of perceived emergency, the space of the law can be seized or occupied by entities that seek to mimic the structure of law's force with a view to intensifying or heightening its effects. In other words, during times of emergency, the law is loosely interpreted and/or applied in furtherance of the political and/or strategic objectives of state officials who, in normal times, can usually be relied on to simply uphold the law. This is often justified on the basis that what is being upheld is the 'spirit' if not the precise 'letter' of the law. In the context of COVID-19 restrictions, words like 'rules' or 'instructions' came to symbolise the language in which the 'authority' or the 'force' of law was appropriated – seized or occupied – by state officials.

From the commencement of coronavirus restrictions, the Joint Committee on Human Rights (JCHR) has monitored the effects of lockdown restrictions on the human rights of individuals. In particular, its Chair's Briefing Paper of 8 April 2020 and its report on government responses to COVID-19 fixed penalty notices of 21 April 2021 provide ample evidence of government ministers and representatives of organs of state, such as the police and university officials, seeking, consciously or otherwise, to stand in the place of the law. For example, the JCHR expressed general concerns about '"announcements", "directions" or "instructions" from Government which have no legal force, but which are communicated in such a way as to appear binding' (JCHR, 2020: 3), and found that 'government guidance has at times been more restrictive than the legislation' (JCHR, 2021: 24). So restrictive were some of the government 'instructions' that 'sometimes … members of the public feel intimidated into not leaving their homes' (JCHR, 2020: 11).

It is important to note that in all of the instances recorded by the JCHR, the effect was that the measures that the state officials sought to impose were more 'forceful' than the law permitted. This is because few, if any, laws are couched in absolute terms. In the context of coronavirus lockdowns, the law would only prohibit social interactions if they took place either without *reasonable* excuse – thus allowing for a number of potential considerations particular to the individual to be taken into account – or without *lawful* excuse – that is, beyond the usually non-exhaustive list of potential exceptions that the law recognised. State officials, however, would frequently ignore these qualifications – interpreting, and, in the case of some officials such as the police, applying the law as if it imposed a 'strict' or 'absolute' obligation that permitted no derogation.

For example, when 'Northamptonshire's Chief Constable threatened to search people's shopping trolleys to ensure they were only buying "essential" items and to mount roadblocks to stop non-essential travel' (JCHR, 2021: 12), they sought to impose *by force* a condition relating to consumer activity that was not enshrined in the law – since such a general response was inherently at odds with a qualified legal rule. Another widely reported example occurred in January 2021 when two women were each given £200 fines by the police for supposedly breaching the 'spirit' of lockdown when they drove, with pre-prepared coffees, approximately seven miles from their home to visit a beauty spot. As the JCHR report recorded, 'at the time, there was no restriction on how far people in England could travel to take exercise, although guidance was to stay local' (JCHR, 2021: 23). In the course of time, the police admitted that the fines were not lawfully imposed, but that was not before the secretary for health and social care endorsed the police's assumption of the authority of law by stating that he 'absolutely backs' the decision of the police to issue a fine (JCHR, 2021: 25). As stated in the introduction to this chapter, state officials – especially politicians – frequently presented 'guidance' as bearing the force of 'law', leading to an undermining of the rule of law.

Government ministers have been as determined as the police to make statements and take actions that mimic the force that can only be legitimately exercised by the law. As noted in the JCHR report, 'the Home Secretary has ... publicly described large gatherings as "illegal" and "unlawful", when the law did not impose a blanket ban' (JCHR, 2021: 25). Again, the use by JCHR of the term 'blanket ban' draws attention to the essential difference between how the law that is *legitimately* in force operates, and the manner in which state officials sought to 'appropriate' the force of law. Legitimate legal rule is not *absolute* legal rule – exceptions being a necessary feature of legitimate rule. By contrast, those who sought to appropriate the law did so with the intention of imposing greater force on individuals than the law itself permitted.

The occasions when representatives of government or organs of the state have sought to occupy the space of law are too numerous to mention. However, some reference must be made to the actions of university officials who have not only encouraged the police to effectively patrol university halls of residence with a view to issuing potential fines (see JCHR, 2021: 31), but also, as Professor Fiona de Londras and Daniella Lock observed in their written evidence to the JCHR, have 'interpreted and applied general guidance as justifying requiring students to remain in their accommodation, resulting in arbitrary restrictions on and deprivation of liberty' (de Londras and Lock, 2021: para 2.1).

Law schools and other sites of legal education and training produce prospective lawyers who are well prepared to encounter the criminal or other legally disobedient behaviours of ordinary individuals. They are also adequately prepared for, and they largely welcome, the occasions where an organisation or individual may operate according to standards that are higher than those imposed by law – in the interests of consumer protection, for example. However, in the absence of sustained engagement with the question of how marginalised communities are governed by key organs of the state, there is very little in the legal curricula that would enable comprehension of the actions of representatives of governments and public bodies that assume the role of regulators; or, to put the point more forcefully, who *act as if they were the law* in order to impose a stricter rule on an individual than the law allows. As stated in the introduction to this chapter, the COVID-19 emergency has called attention to the need for legal education to better equip prospective lawyers with the knowledge and skills to effectively address those occasions when state officials seek to govern populations by abandoning the formal law in favour of 'rules' or 'guidance' that further their political and/or strategic interests.

A discrete module on law in times of emergency could incorporate the lessons of COVID-19 together with the study of situations of emergency occurring in other geographical locations. However, any such module must also acknowledge that although a general state of emergency affecting a whole population is still a relatively rare occurrence, certain communities within a politically stable state are managed precisely through strategies that assume that a state of emergency exists. To put the point another way, the coronavirus emergency is novel in that the conflation of law and guidance has been a feature of how the *general* population in England has been *temporarily* governed. However, *specific* communities in the same locale live in a *perpetual* state of emergency – to borrow a term from the philosopher Giorgio Agamben (2021) – and have seen their human rights compromised through the conflation of law and guidance – with far more devastating consequences to them than evident in any of the JCHR's reports.

There can be no more compelling instance of this than in what has come to be known as the 'Windrush scandal'. This concerned a number of men and women of Caribbean origin (commonly referred to as the 'Windrush descendants') who arrived in the UK as children during the 1950s and 1960s. Although without the formal status of British citizenship, the men and women were all legally entitled to remain indefinitely in the UK as a result of a provision of the Immigration Act 1971, which conferred that entitlement on anyone who had arrived in the UK before 1 January 1973. In other words, all were resident non-nationals. Almost without exception, the men and women had remained in the UK since arriving there – not even taking holidays abroad (Gentleman, 2019: 6, 8, 52, 60, 70). Mainly for that reason, they formed part of a group of approximately nine million UK residents who, while residing in the UK perfectly lawfully, do not possess a British passport (Gentleman, 2019: 62, 180).

In 2014, the Immigration Act, which was intended to create a 'hostile environment' for those considered to not be lawfully in the UK, was passed. While the Immigration Act 2014 did not alter the legal status of the Windrush descendants as such, it requires every person resident in the UK to prove, by providing supporting documentation, their entitlement to be in the UK before they can access basic resources, such as public or private rented accommodation. It is important to note that although a valid passport would usually be sufficient proof, nowhere in the Act is it stated that other documentation cannot stand in place of the passport. The principle that legal requirements are not absolute extends even to immigration rules that are known to be harsh and restrictive, comparatively speaking.

Unfortunately, for the Windrush descendants, Home Office officials took a much more restrictive approach to the range of valid documentation that could be taken into account than required by the Act. This is why I offer the Windrush case as an example of the abandonment of legal rules by state officials (Home Office personnel) in favour of their own 'guidance'. No general state of emergency relating to the security of the UK's borders existed. However, migrant communities or those like the Windrush descendants – who are wrongly classified as migrants without formal legal status – are governed through tactics that assume in respect of them the existence of a *perpetual* state of emergency. As Amelia Gentleman observed, the way in which Home Office officials interpreted their powers under the Act disproportionately impacted on the Windrush descendants who would see their 'security disintegrating simply because of the absence of a faded stamp in a passport' (Gentleman, 2019: 12). In essence, the effect of the Act was that 'the occasions on which it would be necessary to produce a passport were set to multiply' (Gentleman, 2019: 124).

Of crucial significance to the overall argument in this chapter, and for comparison with the management of the general population during the coronavirus lockdowns, is the fact that the Home Office demanded proof of lawful entitlement that went well beyond what even the harsh requirements of the Immigration Act 2014 demanded. Indeed, as Gentleman documents, the Home Office requirements were practically impossible for anyone to meet. Gentleman is the *Guardian* journalist who first brought the plight of the Windrush descendants to the attention of the public. In her book, she deftly summarises the Home Office's unreasonable and, as subsequently established, unlawful demands when she questions: 'how many of us are able to lay our hands on our first passport? How many of us can supplement this with three or four pieces of official documentary evidence showing where we were living every year for the past four or five decades (Gentleman, 2019: 181)? In default of a passport, most of the Windrush descendants were able to gather official documentary proof of at least 30 years of National Insurance (NI) payments (see Gentleman, 2019: 24, 36, 51, 73, 171). The Home Office rejected this entirely cogent proof of long-term residence as insufficient. In all cases, NI payment records were supplemented by other official documentation. In the case of one woman, this documentation included 'copies of archive records from Shropshire Council showing that she had been in care in 1971' (Gentleman, 2019: 36), and in the case of another they included 'seventy-five pages of evidence proving she had spent a lifetime in the UK – bank statements, dentist's records and medical files ... tax records, letters from her primary school, from friends and family – but, inexplicably, this was not enough to satisfy immigration staff' (Gentleman, 2019: 171). Having failed to discharge the impossible burden of proof, the Windrush descendants suffered a de facto loss of status. As Gentleman puts it, 'the government reclassified a large, wholly legal cohort of long-term residents as illegal migrants' (2019: 8). All in all, the actions of this crucial arm of the British state amounted to nothing less than 'an unjustified persecution of a whole generation of people' (Gentleman, 2019: 74).

Without wishing to trivialise the impact on individuals of the lawless actions of state officials during the coronavirus pandemic, these simply do not compare in degree to the losses suffered by the Windrush descendants. The experience of losing, first, long-held jobs, then being denied unemployment benefits, and then being forced to use food banks was a recurrent theme of Gentleman's book (see, for example, Gentleman, 2019: 30, 67, 72, 141). Some of the Windrush descendants were rendered homeless (Gentleman, 2019: 73), and forced into street begging (Gentleman, 2019: 178). Others were denied the fundamental right to private and family life, with the devastating consequences that they were robbed of the chance to attend the funerals of close family members (Gentleman, 2019: 67, 72). In one of the cases that attracted substantial media attention, a man, known by the pseudonym of 'Albert Thompson' (see Gentleman, 2018), was refused the cancer treatment that medical tests had deemed necessary (Gentleman, 2018, 2019: 75–6). Knowing of the Home Office's harsh treatment of undocumented migrants, another man decided that he would not apply for his state pension (Gentleman, 2019: 71).

The degree of both physical and non-physical violence deployed against these lawful residents was also remarkable and disturbing. One of the men interviewed for the book described opening his door 'to find seven officers, six men and a woman'. In an effort to force individuals to 'self-deport', the 'private outsourcing company, Capita ... bombarded individuals with an alarming combination of phone calls, letters, and, most controversially, text messages' (Gentleman, 2019: 163).

The occasions when officials attempt to appropriate the force of the law raises the prospect that all of human life might be regulated by *unregulated* physical and non-physical violence. As Part 2 of this chapter argues, law does not operate without violence, but it is the law itself that determines the nature and extent of violence needed to bring individuals – including state officials – under its rule. The law's violence is what I refer to here as *regulated* violence. The violence meted out by state officials during the COVID-19 lockdowns and to the Windrush descendants is referred to as *unregulated* violence – precisely because it occurred without the authority of law. The consequences of unregulated violence are grave. Indeed, the JCHR contemplated the 'relationship between the police and citizens and perhaps even between citizens' being 'fundamentally, if temporarily, altered' (JCHR, 2020: 12) by the frequent occasions when state officials sought to punish individuals without the authority of law. The spectre of unregulated violence is quite evidently raised by 'concerns that the police are now able, and even required, to enquire into every citizen's private life, for example through questioning, in order to ascertain whether they have a "reasonable excuse" for leaving the place where they live' (JCHR, 2020: 12), and further, by 'concerning reports of individual police forces establishing online forms seeming to encourage people to report on their neighbours for potential infringements ... [leading] to members of the public confronting other members of the public and asking them to account for their behaviour' (JCHR, 2020: 13).

The management, in England, by various state officials of the coronavirus health emergency offers an intimation of how easily a society can be governed by unregulated violence. However, if the attention of legal educators and policy makers is solely focused on these still exceptional situations, a very partial understanding of the significant threat to the rule of law that arises whenever state officials seek to appropriate law's force will emerge. Resident non-nationals form one example of the marginalised communities that are frequently subjected to extraordinary rule – Windrush being one of the most publicised examples of this worrying phenomenon. In Part 2 I situate the examples explored in this part within a broader theoretical and philosophical discussion on the relation between law and violence.

Part 2: Legal violence and natural violence

In Part 1, I made frequent allusions to the 'force of law'. This was not merely the result of an arbitrary or careless choice of words, but was intended to draw attention to a particular quality of the law. Law coerces. Law compels individuals to act or refrain from acting – and it does so in language that is uncompromising and always backed by the threat of violence – both physical and non-physical – in the event of non-compliance. To put the point another way, law is violent. In the words of Robert Cover in the essay 'Violence and the word' (1986), law authorises the 'imposition of violence upon others' (1986: 1601).

The foregoing comments on the nature of law are relatively uncontroversial. However, for the purposes of the argument in this chapter, it is necessary to go further than to merely acknowledge that violence is inherent to law. More fundamental is the proposition that violence is only ever justified when it emanates from the law. Violence not authorised by the law – that is, violence that is meted out by some entity outside the law – cannot be justified in principle.

One of the most authoritative statements of this position is to be found in Walter Benjamin's 1921 essay 'Critique of violence', in which he stated: 'all violence as a means is either lawmaking or law-preserving. If it lays claim to neither of these predicates, it forfeits all validity' (Benjamin, 1996 [1921]: 243). Violence, for Benjamin and for Jacques Derrida, too – who wrote an extended commentary of Benjamin's essay several years later (Derrida, 1992) – is to be given a broad meaning to encompass not simply the enactment of traumatic physical force but also other acts, and statements too, that have the potential to compel or coerce. In other words, their definition covers acts of both physical and non-physical violence. For example, Benjamin's essay makes clear that 'extortion' is a form of violence (1996 [1921]: 239). For Derrida, violence or 'force' – to use the term he expressly deploys – can be 'direct or indirect, physical or symbolic, exterior or interior, brutal or subtly discursive and hermeneutic, coercive or regulative' (1992: 11).

The treatment meted out to the Windrush descendants would unequivocally meet the definition of violence in the extended sense in which both Benjamin and Derrida use the concept. However, so, too, would several of the instances identified in the JCHR reports on the coronavirus lockdowns. For example, the impositions of fines for alleged violation of lockdown 'rules' clearly fall within this extended definition of violence. It constitutes a threat of economic harm in the event of non-compliance. Further, a home secretary who attaches the label 'illegal' or 'unlawful' to the actions of private individuals (see JCHR, 2021: 25) would be enacting a form of 'discursive' or 'hermeneutic' violence – in the sense that the mere allegation of illegality would be traumatic to anyone who considers themselves law-abiding. And when the Derbyshire Police used drones across the Peak District in order to detect and draw attention to people who were exercising outside their homes (see JCHR, 2020: 10), they were enacting what for Derrida would surely be an act of 'symbolic' violence. In this instance, no individual was specifically targeted, but the existence of the drones was clearly intended to make communities conscious that they were being placed under surveillance.

According to Benjamin's 'Critique of violence' these and the other forms of violence that are recorded by the JCHR and by Amelia Gentleman can only ever be justified as a means to bring about law – described by Benjamin as 'law-making violence' – or as a means to subordinate the citizen to law – which Benjamin alludes to as 'law-preserving violence' (1996 [1921]: 243). Being outside the law – as much of this activity was later found or admitted by the perpetrators to be – they, in Benjamin's words, forfeit all validity.

Specifically in relation to the coronavirus emergency – applying Benjamin – we would say that when using violence to subordinate individuals residing in England to their advice or guidance or organisational preferences, government ministers, the police and university officials used violence in pursuit of *their own ends*. This use of violence is that which most threatens the survival of the law. To put it another way, law breaks down when it loses its exclusive right to deploy violence. A legal order loses its exclusive right to deploy violence when an individual subject exercises violence in defiance of the dictates of the legal order, or – in the situation that is the focus of this chapter – when an individual, especially where that individual represents an organ of the state, seeks to appropriate and then augment the law's force. As Benjamin writes, 'law sees violence in the hands of individuals as a danger undermining the legal system' (1996 [1921]: 238). I strongly hold to the position espoused by Benjamin. There can be absolutely no justification for a deployment of force that is not authorised by law. To put the point again in Benjamin's terms, 'all the natural ends of individuals must collide with legal ends if pursued with a greater or lesser degree of violence' (1996 [1921]: 238).

Consistently with its overall terms of reference, the JCHR has examined the aforementioned instances, and many others, in light of their compliance with human rights standards. Its conclusion that the actions and statements of, among others, the police, government ministers and university officials have imperilled human rights, ranging from 'the right to a fair trial (Article 6 ECHR), the principle of no punishment without law (Article 7 ECHR), the right to family and private life (Article 8 ECHR) and freedom from discrimination in the enjoyment of other Convention rights (Article 14 ECHR)' (JCHR, 2021: 5), is extremely worrying. However, the primary concern of this chapter is not with how these actions undermine particular laws, *but how they challenge and undermine the very idea of law itself.* To emphasise the point, what the individual acts of violence that the JCHR document bears witness to put at stake is not only the survival of any particular legal right (such as that contained within Article 8 ECHR), but also, and crucially, the very survival of law itself – for 'a system of legal ends cannot be maintained if natural ends are anywhere still pursued violently' (Benjamin, 1996 [1921]: 239). No state – whether it declares itself a democracy or not – has yet been able to find a way to govern its populations without the use of violence. The state, however, maintains its legitimacy for as long as that violence is authorised by – that is, *regulated* by – the law. The example of the coronavirus lockdowns and the Windrush situation demonstrates that, in times of perceived emergency – whether affecting a *whole* population or *particular* communities within that population – state officials use violence for their own ends, rather than in the legitimate interests of law creation or law preservation. Currently, there is insufficient attention given in the legal curriculum to this phenomenon.

Conclusion

In *Where Are We Now? The Epidemic as Politics*, Giorgio Agamben urged commentators on the coronavirus emergency to 'consider the events we have witnessed within a broader historical perspective' (Agamben, 2021: 7). This is what I have sought to do in this chapter. From the perspective of the UK – England specifically – such a contextual enquiry would lead to a qualified acceptance of Agamben's claim that Western governments manage their populations on the basis of a perpetual state of emergency or 'perpetual crisis' (Agamben, 2021: 28). To the extent that a state of emergency is characterised by 'the end of a world ... built on rights, parliaments and the division of powers' (Agamben, 2021: 42), or, as Guillermo Andrés Duque Silva and Cristina del Prado Higuera put it, by a 'vacuum space of law. That is a zone of anomie in which all legal determinations are deactivating' (Silva and Higuera, 2021: 512), there is, I think, a still meaningful distinction to be made between a 'normal' state of affairs and a situation of 'exceptional 'emergency – at least insofar as majority populations are concerned.

However, over several decades, Agamben has written persuasively on the ways in which marginalised communities – especially refugee communities – exist under a regime structured almost entirely through the meting out of violence by state officials in pursuit of their own political and/or strategic interests, rather than in pursuit of the law. To be more specific, the unregulated exercise of violence – unregulated because it sits outside the law – that has been evident in the ways the coronavirus lockdowns were managed in England may be novel and exceptional as far as majority populations in the UK are concerned, but are the norm by which specific populations – migrants, resident non-nationals, criminalised young Black men – are managed. The routine treatment to which these groups are exposed foreshadows the ways in which majority populations may be managed when a general state of emergency is declared. It follows also that as the number of such supposedly 'suspect' communities increases, the 'state of exception … [that] is not characterised by its abnormality and contingency, and … is not explained in terms of "normality to come," but instead by its permanence' (Silva and Higuera, 2021: 506) – which Agamben already discerns – will be visible to all.

The law cannot be rescued by lawyers alone, but they have a leading role to play if physical and non-physical violence is not to be meted out by any official whenever they feel that the circumstances warrant it. And if lawyers are to effectively repel any exercise of violence that is not authorised by law, they must be more alert to the occasions when state officials may seek to occupy the space of the law. We know that this dangerous impulse occurs when a general state of emergency is declared and as a means of managing some marginalised communities. In this regard, then, law schools and other institutions of legal education and training must learn from the lessons of COVID-19, but even more pressing for them is the need to learn the lessons from Windrush and from the other all too frequently occurring instances when the human rights of the most marginalised are denied – often because of the deliberate or negligent conflation of law with guidance.

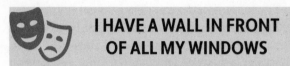

I HAVE A WALL IN FRONT OF ALL MY WINDOWS

Manca Bajec

*Note to reader: This extract is at the start of the play, just as the two characters begin to develop and their interaction becomes clearer. The **Main character** is becoming increasingly frustrated by the space she is living in. The **Wall** is her only interaction and engagement with the outside.*

Extract from a one-act monodrama.

Characters:
Main character
Wall

Scene:
Small one-bedroom flat in East London, March/April 2020. The living room/kitchen is half the size of the bedroom. The main character contemplates moving her bed into the kitchen in order to have more 'living room/working room' space. The thought of the smell of her latest culinary-experiment-gone-wrong and the effort of moving everything deters her from going ahead, even though she has gone so far as to measure the size of her bed and realise that it would fit.

Main character:

'I have a wall in front of all my windows. Sitting down at my desk in the kitchen, where I do most of my work and spend most of my days, I can see the sky but nothing else. I am not really sure what its purpose is but it's there. It's made life over the past year easier in many ways. I guess not seeing empty streets allowed me to forget, for longer periods of time, that anything outside my little flat is any different than normal. Images of what is happening outside appear in my head based on what I hear and for some time things were incredibly quiet.'

Wall:

'Before the pandemic, I would pass a woman called Elizabeth almost every day. She sat by my front door, next to the ATM, and would wait for people to give her change. I often spoke to her, she called me darling, she called everyone darling. She would ask me for a cigarette every once in a while, she must have seen me smoking outside (though I ought to/must mention I am not an "outside" smoker – growing up in a Balkan household, smoking wasn't considered an act of evil one needs to be punished for, to stand outside hiding away). She would sometimes share a detail or two about her life, but more often she would make a comment about the weather. She had what I thought was an American accent, but maybe I'm wrong.

I haven't seen Elizabeth since the start of the pandemic, I have no idea what happened to her, but I think about her often. The last time I saw her she mentioned she got an apartment from the council but was unable to pay for her heating, so I gave her some money. I don't know whether that was true or not, it didn't really matter, she was always friendly and was obviously not doing as well as I was so I figured if I can offer her a bit of money then I will. It is not my place to judge the people that gather around the Sainsbury's ATM. I often think about what led them there, but to be honest, in a large city like London, and in the current times we live in, most of us are not too far from that state.'

Main character:
'At the start of the first lockdown I was in quarantine for two weeks with a cold or flu. Like everyone else I was glued to the news watching as things progressed by the hour. I imagine we all had similar thoughts about the surreal situation we were suddenly experiencing. It felt like an apocalyptic end. I wondered what all those people from various religions and cults, who had been preparing for The End for some years now, must have felt. Were they experiencing some kind of relief... that their predictions were right? All those years when they were often ridiculed for stockpiling supplies, the rest of us were now the idiots waiting in queues outside supermarkets concerned about toilet paper and pasta. I wondered if they had moments of "I told you so". In my hometown there was a group that thought a flood was going to destroy humanity at the end of the century and dragged boats to the highest point in the city, the hill with the castle on it. I wonder if they still think about floods or if they just imagine this period as a metaphoric flood.'

Wall:

'So many things will define these years, among them the selection of new terms we have all become so accustomed to hearing and saying or the importance of human contact or how the lack of it affects us. But we know most of these things already. We know about the effects of physical contact and solitude but for many of us we just weren't used to experiencing them on this level. More than anything, I think these years will be defined not by the acts of humanity that we see but by the many acts of inhumanity. If anything, these times should not be defined by applause and back-patting but rather shame. Have we now proven that we are the cruellest being?

And how will we remember these times? As only the cruellest being can: we will sprinkle all the cruelty with stories of glory, leaving in the shadows the stories of those who were truly forgotten, tormented, shamed and proclaimed guilty without trial. Forgotten because they are old and irrelevant, tormented because they are fighting for their survival, shamed because they cannot feed their families or provide their children with lavish homes, and proclaimed as guilty because they didn't abide by the rules – which we now know even those who created them broke. Because this period has shown that it isn't good enough to have what most of us thought was a middle-class existence. In this period the middle class became working class, the working class became poor and the poor were the starving. We have seen how well organised nations and mass populations of people can be. And we have seen how seemingly democratic political structures can manipulate populations by restrictions set in place to protect them.

This will define these years, this moment when we have become aware of how quickly we can become manipulated and how – regardless of the size of the mass of bodies we can create – we have limited power. Our power is restricted to words, which are often muzzled and divided to exist in small and segregated communities. We have become accustomed or even programmed to be satisfied with the "lesser evil".

So, should we be concerned with how we will memorialise this time? Perhaps we should start thinking about how this period will be remembered or should we instead hope that we will have the possibility of forgetting. Or should we rather concern ourselves with what will come next. Will the new decade bring anything more than a continuation of what we are slowly becoming accustomed to? We try to resist the urge to go beyond – remaining in a new state of normality – creating a new state of normality.'

Main character:
'In this new state of solitude, shadows become strange companions. As do sounds or their absence. I felt my hearing was getting much better. I used to complain that I had terrible hearing in one ear because of an injury I had as a child. Ironically, I put a tiny rubber key note, which I pulled off a tiny piano, and shoved it deep into my ear. Of course, the more I tried to get it out, the more my fat little fingers pushed it in deeper into the ear canal. I told my parents, but they had a look and

couldn't see anything. Many, many years later I had a terrible earache accompanied by high fever and was rushed to the hospital. Upon everyone's surprise and my parents' embarrassment … a tiny rubber piano key was flushed out of my ear.

So, my obsessions continued drifting towards the wall. It's not really a full wall but kind of reaches up to my neck. So even when I went to the "terrace", that I wasn't supposed to go on to, I couldn't really see over the wall. It's a tease. It gives you a bit of the sky but denies you the ability to understand what else is out there. You are left to imagine what the noises that you are hearing are really related to. Most of the time that allows my imagination to go wild and I come up with terribly overcomplicated stories about the odd noises and various associations, but during the period of the pandemic it was mainly silence that I heard. It's odd to think about what silence sounds like, but my wall made this silence even more deafening. My wall became my muse, we spoke, we stared at each other, she saw me laughing and crying, and she was the only witness to my life for those months.'

7

Border harms in a pandemic

Amy Cortvriend

It was 26 June 2020, and it was my birthday. We were slowly starting to emerge from the first lockdown with many restrictions still in place. These are the things I remember from that day. A few of my friends did doorstep drop-offs, bringing thoughtful gifts. My sister was living with me after being forced to return home from India due to COVID-19, and she had bought me flowers. Roses and lilies. Probably chosen by my daughter named Lily. I chose the online workout of the day because that was my birthday privilege. Yet the thing I remember most vividly is the newsreader on the radio informing us of a stabbing in Glasgow with multiple victims. A man, the 'perpetrator', had been shot dead by the police. In my head I was pleading 'Please don't be a Black, Brown, Muslim or migrant person'. I could not stand the thought of more racist and Islamophobic headlines, more equating foreigners with terrorism. It was worse than I could ever have imagined. Badreddin Abdallah Adam Bosh was a Sudanese asylum seeker who had been accommodated in the Park Inn Hotel in Glasgow throughout lockdown. It later transpired that he had suffered with mental ill health and had reached out for help 72 times. Having worked with and researched asylum seekers for a number of years, and knowing the stigma attached to being an asylum seeker in society, politics and the media, I knew the media would immediately reach for terrorism, despite the police asserting it was not. This was not the first incident of its kind during the pandemic. Another asylum seeker, Adnan Olbeh, had been found dead in his guest house after his mental health had deteriorated following his experiences in the asylum system and poor housing conditions during the pandemic. Although his cause of death is not known, Smina Akhtar (2020) argues that he was a victim of the hostile environment.

Hotels have been used increasingly in recent years to accommodate asylum seekers, but this was particularly problematic during the COVID-19 pandemic, bringing to light some of the Home Office practices at this time. Many of these problems were present prior to the pandemic but were intensified, particularly during lockdown. The incident at the Park Inn Hotel in Glasgow was one in a series of tragic events and abhorrent conditions imposed on asylum seekers throughout the pandemic, a marked event on what Claudia Aradau and Martina Tazzioli (2021) call a 'confinement continuum' – a racialised and classist continuum in which some have the freedom of mobility, and others, such as asylum seekers, face extreme confinement, at times in carceral spaces such as immigration removal centres (IRCs). While Aradau and Tazzioli (2021) refer to the confinement continuum on a broad and global scale, this chapter focuses on the experience of asylum seekers more specifically during the pandemic. From the use of initial accommodation in 'ordinary' times to hotels and barracks during the pandemic, this chapter evidences extreme confinement and its consequences for people seeking safety during the pandemic.

The UK asylum system

The UK has two primary streams of entry for refugees. The first consists of refugees who arrive with 'leave to remain', usually with refugee status. To be recognised as a refugee in the UK, an individual must have fled their country of origin because they feared persecution, in accordance with the 1951 United Nations (UN) Convention Relating to the Status of Refugees, which states:

> As a result of events occurring before 1 January 1951 and owing to well-founded fear of being persecuted for reasons of race, religion, nationality, membership of a particular social group or political opinion, is

outside the country of his nationality and is unable or, owing to such fear, is unwilling to avail himself of the protection of that country; or who, not having a nationality and being outside the country of his former habitual residence as a result of such events, is unable or, owing to such fear, is unwilling to return to it. (UN Convention and Protocol Relating to the Status of Refugees, 1951)[1]

Those who arrive with 'leave to remain' do so through a UK government quota system in conjunction with the UN High Commissioner for Refugees (UNHCR), which identifies and processes refugees and assesses the appropriateness of resettlement. Of those eligible for resettlement, the UK prioritises vulnerable people such as survivors of violence, women, girls, children and adolescents at risk. As these refugees arrive with 'leave to remain', they have access to benefits, employment and housing.

Asylum seekers face very different conditions, challenges and legal status. Asylum applicants in the UK must evidence their experience of persecution or risk of it, and the inability to seek protection within the country from which they fled. This includes evidencing that they were unable to relocate internally within their country of origin, and that they have not passed through a safe third country. They face a series of interviews, have their credibility questioned in a culture of disbelief (Jubany, 2017), and throughout the asylum process are forced into poverty, dispersal accommodation that can be unsanitary and unsuitable (House of Commons Home Affairs Committee, 2017), are prohibited from employment and are at risk of detention and deportation throughout the entire time. The asylum process is intended to be concluded within six months (UK Visas and Immigration, 2022b), and although the pandemic meant cases were not being processed as quickly (Finlay et al, 2021), even before COVID-19 hit there were lengthy delays. In my current research, the average time the women I interviewed had been waiting for their asylum claim to be processed so far was 4.8 years. In my experience, the 'simple' cases, such as people who had fled conflicts in countries such as Syria, had been granted a positive decision within a few months, and the more complex cases, which included appeals and submission of further evidence, lasted up to 10 years and were still ongoing at the time I conducted interviews.

Immigration law in the UK has become increasingly punitive, purposely creating a 'hostile environment' for asylum seekers. The term was immortalised when Theresa May outlined her goal as home secretary in an interview: 'The aim is to create, here in Britain, a really hostile environment for illegal immigrants' (Theresa May, 2012, quoted in Kirkup and Winnett, 2012). Yet this hostile environment began long before Theresa May was home secretary. In the UK this has been demonstrated in the sheer volume of legislation criminalising migrants. Between 1999 and 2016, 89 new immigration offences were introduced compared to 70 new immigration offences between 1905 and 1998 (Aliverti, 2012). A majority of the recent offences originated from just six Acts of Parliament passed during the New Labour government as a response to public concern over the abuse of the asylum system. The response was the hyper-criminalisation of immigration (Aliverti, 2012) and the increased convergence of immigration and criminal law, known in border criminology circles as 'crimmigration' (Stumpf, 2006). At a time when the media was prolifically publishing images of migrants entering the UK underneath Eurostar trains and suffocating in lorries (Cohen, 2013), the Immigration and Asylum Act 1999 was passed, which affected the physical and social lives of asylum seekers by implementing dispersal orders for accommodation that removed asylum seekers' ability to choose accommodation. This piece of legislation was instrumental in leading us to those events on 26 June 2022.

Housing asylum seekers

Housing asylum seekers between IRCs, initial accommodation and dispersal comes after a claimant has lodged an asylum application. People seeking safety are required to make a claim as soon as they arrive in the UK (preferably at the port of entry), or as soon as they think it is unsafe to return to their country of origin. At this point they undergo a screening interview to determine the basis of their claim, and to consider whether the case can be considered in the UK.[2] After the screening interview, asylum seekers are often placed in temporary initial accommodation before moving to longer term accommodation while awaiting a decision on their claim. While in this initial accommodation, asylum applicants will usually be provided with meals and basic toiletries, and therefore will not receive cash support. This is known as 'Section 98 support'. Once longer term (but still temporary) accommodation has been sought, asylum applicants are then dispersed and moved on to Section 95 support, which includes accommodation and, at the time of writing (2022) £40.85 per week, per person.

During the first few weeks after arrival, asylum applicants are often moved multiple times in a short period of time, transported from one place to another in a minibus or coach with no explanation of where they were going, arriving in initial temporary accommodation that is often shared with others. Asylum seekers can face forced evictions and be moved around the asylum accommodation estate at any time. In my work with asylum seekers, I have spoken to people who were terrified when being transported from one place to the next. They often do not know where they are going, if they are being detained or deported. In one charity I worked with I was told that minibuses would meet at the back of a service station off the motorway and a bus full of people would move from the minibuses into taxis. The charity worker joked that it must look 'dodgy', but it was no joke to the newly arrived asylum seekers who spoke little, if any, English, and who did not understand what was happening to them.

Prior to the pandemic I spoke to Agnes[3] who was placed in a hotel for around six weeks with her three children. During this time, she was so scared that for weeks she would only leave her room to eat, until a cleaner who spoke the same language as her explained where she was and gave her directions to shops and other places in the local area:

> 'I'm staying one night in hotel, past midnight the Home Office dropped me at hotel with my three kids. After this night they send me Barry House, a hostel Barry House. I stayed one month in London, Barry House. After I had again interview in Home Office,

and they send me in hotel. I like this place to live in because I stay one and half months with my kids. I have everything I need. It was very safe here. I didn't go out. Just I stayed inside because I'm scared. I did nothing, just I stayed inside. And one lady come in and knock door. "Please you want to go out, you want to kill your children just inside, go out".'

Agnes was accommodated in three different places in as many months. Although she says she felt safe, this was only within the confines of her room that she shared with her three children. She was scared to leave the hotel, and only left her room to eat in the hotel's restaurant. She was completely isolated for those few weeks until one of the cleaners encouraged her to leave the room. The cleaner drew her a map of the area, pointing out the local shops and how to get a bus, but Agnes never did leave the hotel, except on the few occasions when the Home Office required her to attend an appointment. Even before the pandemic, this was an initial push towards social exclusion and isolation (Hynes and Sales, 2009). Agnes was fearful due to her previous experiences. She had fled a lifetime of gendered violence and was evidently traumatised. She was fearful of her past abusers finding her in the UK. Agnes was not alone in this self-imposed isolation. A young Pakistani women, Mariam, also reported isolating herself, but rather than being fearful of her past, she was fearful of her present:

'We just never got out of our rooms. Like we was too scared to go and get food or the men would be like "come here, do this, sit here". We was too scared. So like my brother – we had one brother – he would like just go and get two plates and we would all just share … if we would go toilet we would go at night when everyone sleeping 'cos there'd be drunk men just walking around so we'll just stay in there, do nothing. Erm, my brother would just come in there, go and get food.'

Mariam and her family were staying in what she describes as a church but was in fact a hostel – short-term shared accommodation for new arrivals. Mariam was with her mother, sisters and young brother. She was fearful of the single men in the accommodation who would often drink and would look at her and her sisters. There were shared bathrooms, toilets and eating areas, and food was not allowed to be taken to the rooms, so Mariam's brother would smuggle what he could back to their room. Having come from an area in Pakistan where there was an expectation that women should not be in the presence of men without a male guardian, the perceived threat of the male residents was amplified for Mariam, who believed she was at risk of sexual violence. The perception of risk was not only due to the cultural expectations she had grown up with but also resulted from suggestive comments and looks from some of the men. In this instance, the accommodation was culturally inappropriate for her.

Housing during the pandemic

These two examples show the inappropriateness of hotels and similar accommodation even before the pandemic, so it was inevitable that circumstances would deteriorate, particularly during lockdown. From the onset of the pandemic, the use of hotels by Home Office contractors increased in part because the Home Office and its contractors were unable to seek enough suitable accommodation, and second, because failed asylum seekers and those whose claims had been granted were not able to be evicted during the peak of the pandemic (Home Office, 2020). This meant that there were a greater number of people in temporary hotel accommodation. However, there were a number of asylum seekers who were moved out of self-contained flats and houses into hotels at the onset of the pandemic.

Just before the first lockdown, after former Prime Minister Boris Johnson had asked residents of the UK to avoid all essential travel, Home Office housing contractors were moving people between accommodations. An asylum seeker contacted John Grayson (2020) to ask for help: 'We were in a refugee house in Newcastle for two weeks, then five days ago they brought us here. I don't know why they did that.' The family were moved over a hundred miles from a self-contained house in Newcastle to Urban

House in Wakefield, shared accommodation for up to 300 people. Mears, one of the Home Office contractors responsible for asylum accommodation in the north of England, Scotland and Northern Ireland, later moved over 300 asylum seekers in Glasgow from self-contained flats to hotels, some with less than one hour's notice (Brooks, 2020). Most of the people moved were men, and there was also reportedly a pregnant woman, a family with a toddler and possible victims of trafficking (Brooks, 2020).

In a time when people were being asked to respect social distancing, these moves prevented the people affected from keeping any distance from others. In evidence submitted to a House of Commons Select Committee (2020), Mears' chief operating officer, John Taylor, justified the use of hotels to protect the health and wellbeing of asylum seekers and his staff by helping them avoid unnecessary journeys, and to 'ensure better access to healthcare'. Although there were some safeguards in place, such as arranged meal collection times in hotels, it was impossible to avoid people in public spaces such as lifts, stairwells and shared dining areas. Thus, the aims of reducing risk contradicted the outcome: residents were in contact with more people than if they had remained in their self-contained accommodation.

There were a number of problems with the use of hotels during the peaks of the pandemic. There were practical issues, such as having no access to kitchen facilities (Finlay et al, 2021), or even a fridge in many hotels (House of Commons Select Committee, 2020). Considering the warm weather, particularly in the first lockdown, this meant that asylum seekers accommodated in hotels had no immediate access to chilled food and drinks, and in addition, they had no money to purchase additional refreshments due to the ceased cash payment element of Section 95 support to asylum seekers living in hotels at that time.

The Home Office had withdrawn this support as it argued that there was no need for it since asylum seekers had been provided with food, drink and basic toiletries (Philp, 2020). This created harm by limiting autonomy (Pemberton, 2015), preventing people seeking safety from making choices about when, where and what they ate. This also impacted Muslims during Ramadan who were not able to get food at appropriate times, according to a BBC *Disclosure* report (2021). This added to autonomy harms, preventing people from religious practices, despite the assurances of Chris Philp (2020) (then parliamentary under-secretary of state [minister for immigration compliance and justice]) that food would be provided late evening and early morning for those observing Ramadan.

Housing lots of people in one venue also heightened both perceived and actual risks of contracting the virus, and therefore increased isolation (Finlay et al, 2021). In some cases this isolation was enforced by hotels managed by Home Office-contracted Clearsprings Ready Homes, which implemented a 23-hour curfew (Gold Jennings Solicitors, 2021). Gold Jennings Solicitors launched judicial review proceedings when an asylum applicant claimed he had been told that if he was absent from the accommodation for more than one hour, he would be reported to the Home Office and his claim could be in jeopardy (Taylor, 2021). This was despite there being no legal restrictions within coronavirus lockdown rules to limit time spent out of their homes to exercise and do essential shopping. The case was brought by an asylum seeker who had fled persecution, which included state detention, so an enforced curfew was particularly difficult for him. In effect, what these restrictions created was immigration detention within the community. Despite a decreased use in carceral spaces, this was nevertheless confinement, and criminologists know that confinement causes harm (Canning, 2017).

It is clear, then, that there were a number of problems within the hotels in which people seeking safety were accommodated. This was compounded by the closure of face-to-face support from non-governmental organisations (NGOs) that ordinarily support asylum seekers. NGOs provide a range of support, such as practical support, advice and information, but also emotional support that helped them to manage the stress of navigating – or suffering – the asylum system (Cortvriend, 2020).

While many migrant support services moved online, some asylum seekers did not have access to the internet or internet-ready devices (House of Commons Select Committee, 2020). This not only prevented people from accessing support from NGOs, but it also prevented communication with family and friends. Even when asylum seekers had access to a smartphone, some hotels charged to allow access to Wi-Fi in their rooms, meaning they would have to go to a shared area, risking virus transmission to access the internet. The lack of cash support further compounded communication issues as asylum seekers living in hotels would not be able to purchase phone credit to contact lawyers and family members, as well as having restricted access to healthcare services such as GPs and mental healthcare (House of Commons Select Committee, 2020). Restricted access to healthcare further exacerbated existing inequalities during the pandemic (Fu et al, 2022).

Impact on asylum seekers

The combination of lockdown restrictions, extreme limits to autonomy for those staying in hotels and other shared accommodation, and the inability to socially distance had a negative impact on the mental health and wellbeing of asylum seekers. One asylum seeker wrote:

> The day becomes the month becomes the year becomes the decade. ... Our mental faculties started to break down.
>
> Because the system, maybe unintentionally, was designed to break people as vulnerable as us. Our sense of self and identity started to fragment. Even though we stayed strong, we declined.
>
> We went from fit and capable to talking about suicide ideation. When your life is the only thing that you have choice over in the end, you'd probably contemplate it, too. Locking a traumatized person up in a hostel for an indefinite time. ... It just cuts through everybody's emotional and psychological state. It just diminishes. ...
>
> I survived McLays. ... (Anonymous, 2020)

'The day becomes the month becomes the year becomes the decade ...'

Waiting is a significant stressor in the lives of asylum seekers (Sinnerbrink et al, 1997; Reesp, 2003; Cortvriend, 2020), but this was compounded for those who were living in hotels with no money for an indeterminate length of time during a pandemic in which we were all feeling uncertain. Waiting is stressful, in part, because it is an exertion of power (Bourdieu, 2000). This power is exercised by the state in determination of asylum claims but also due to neoliberalism in the asylum system, by corporations contracted by the Home Office that have power to move and hold the asylum-seeking populations in these hotels and hostels. The indeterminate length of stay in these conditions compounds the impacts of this exertion of power, as it does in immigration detention (Bosworth and Vannier, 2016).

'Because the system, maybe unintentionally, was designed to break people as vulnerable as us'

Sadly, this asylum seeker was wrong. Many of the harms created by immigration policy and practice are intentional and integral to building and maintaining a hostile environment for asylum seekers. Two of the aims of the hostile environment are to control migrants (Bowling and Westenra, 2020) and to minimise migration into the UK by acting both as a deterrent as well as coercing migrants to leave, as outlined by Theresa May when proposing 'the hostile environment' (quoted in Kirkup and Winnett, 2012).

'Our sense of self and identity started to fragment'

This phrase stood out to me and reminded me of the works of Erving Goffman (1961, 1963) in relation to identity. One of the concepts Goffman proposes that I argue is relevant to asylum seekers is the idea of the 'total institution'. Goffman's *Asylums* (1961) shows how social institutions have the power to subjugate and control the identity of its residents. While Goffman (1961) considers carceral institutions such as asylums and prisons, this can also apply to the use of hotels to accommodate asylum seekers in lockdown. Even prior to the pandemic, asylum seekers reported feeling like they were in a symbolic prison (Cortvriend, 2020). The total institution is a site of control over its inmates, including daily routines (Goffman, 1961). This was evidenced in the use of hotels where residents were served meals at particular times of day, with some hotels enforcing a curfew (Taylor, 2021), which prevented movement outside these hotels. This was in addition to the coronavirus lockdown rules imposed on the wider population of the UK.

Goffman also introduces the concept of a 'civil death' in relation to residents of mental health institutions (1961: 25), where legal rights are removed, and it is a similar case for asylum applicants who have limited rights in comparison to the majority population. The limiting of rights contributes to the social exclusion of asylum seekers (Hynes, 2011). Civil death begins with admission procedures, which Goffman (1961: 25–6) suggests include 'taking a life history, photographing, weighing, fingerprinting, assigning numbers, searching, listing personal possessions for storage ... instructing as to rules and assigning to quarters'. Most of these (with the exception of weighing and lesser controls over possessions) are undertaken when applying for asylum. Biometrics are taken at the time of the screening interview, rules are provided and reinforced with the use of immigration bail and quarters are assigned via dispersal policies. These practices, Goffman (1961: 26) argues, reduce the subjects to the most basic categorisation of human being. However, I suggest that this process goes beyond that, reducing asylum applicants to less of a human being than British citizens, again fragmenting identity.

Total institutions contaminate the physical identity of their inmates by marring the physical environment and objects associated with the self (Goffman, 1961: 33). This is evident in the asylum system where claimants are moved between asylum accommodations, which was particularly relevant in Glasgow, with the removal of hundreds of asylum seekers from self-contained accommodation to hotels (House of Commons Select Committee, 2020). The effect this has on identity is amplified when there are human agents of contamination (in this case, the Home Office and other agencies, corporations and people who are effectively deputised by them) with whom inmates are forced to have social interactions (Goffman, 1961: 35). Goffman (1961: 35–6) describes this as physical contamination that contributes to the mortification of the self, or, as this anonymous asylum seeker describes, a fragmentation of identity and self.

'We went from fit and capable to talking about suicide ideation. When your life is the only thing that you have choice over in the end, you'd probably contemplate it, too'

Asylum seekers pre-pandemic already had limited rights such as exclusion from the labour market and immigration bail conditions. The housing of asylum seekers is just part of the web of policies that seek to control the everyday lives of people seeking safety (Canning, 2017: 86). Dispersal policies control where asylum seekers live and enable surveillance, particularly in hotels and hostels that have staff permanently onsite. This anonymous asylum seeker writes about their life being the only thing they have autonomy of. Prior to the pandemic I have found similar in my own research. One woman told me she cleans compulsively because inside her asylum accommodation was the only thing she had control of; everything else was in the hands of the Home Office. Monish Bhatia (2021) has also found that asylum seekers use their bodies to actively resist the harms caused by the asylum system. The participants in his research had been subject to electronic monitoring, and one participant went on hunger strike to protest the conditions in which he was living (Bhatia, 2021). It is clear that during the pandemic the use of hotels and other shared accommodation has had a widespread impact on mental health. In Glasgow, Adnan Olbeh was found dead in his room in McLays Guest House after telling Mears staff he had suicidal thoughts and repeated attempts to seek help (Akhtar, 2020). Adnan was not alone in the deterioration of his mental health. Concerns relating to self-harm and suicide among asylum seekers more than tripled in just three months (Laing and Tierney, 2020). In addition to contributing to mental ill health, contingency accommodation in the asylum system later contributed to physical ill health, including a series of outbreaks of COVID-19.

Throughout the pandemic the numbers of asylum seekers rose, as new arrivals came, often via boat across the Channel, claims were being processed much more slowly, and there were fewer deportations, and of the people who were detained, most were foreign national offenders as opposed to failed asylum seekers (Home Office, 2021; UK Visas and Immigration, 2022a). In the second quarter of 2020 there were a total of 109,456 asylum claims in progress, which includes claims awaiting a decision, appeals and those subject to removal action (UK Visas and Immigration, 2022a). A year later, this figure had increased to 125,316 (UK Visas and Immigration, 2022a). The increased demand meant the Home Office required additional accommodation, and in response they housed asylum seekers in disused former army barracks including Napier Barracks and Penally Camp.

This contingency accommodation came under intense scrutiny for a number of reasons. Public Health England was critical of the use of the barracks during COVID-19, advising that they were unsuitable due to the use of shared dormitories, which contradicted the guidance at the time (Neal, 2021). The Home Office ignored this advice and continued to house hundreds of asylum seekers there. In addition to the harms to mental health (Doctors of the World et al, 2021), the use of the barracks also posed a risk to physical health. This included poor sleep due to sharing dormitories, weight loss due to poor food quality and the risk of COVID-19 outbreaks, a risk that was realised in January 2021 (Doctors of the World et al, 2021). During this major outbreak, over 100 residents were forced to remain in their dormitories for up to four weeks, only allowed to leave to use the bathroom and shower, and if they attempted to leave they were threatened with arrest (Neal, 2021). In addition to risking the physical health of residents, this also evidenced this group's confinement and social control.

Conclusion

Prior to the pandemic, asylum accommodation and dispersal policy has been found to create social exclusion, remove autonomy and break down trust (Pearl and Zetter, 2001; Hynes, 2011). Frequent moves, particularly in the first few weeks and months in the UK, mean asylum seekers find it difficult to build relationships within the community, and the lack of agency in where they can live removes autonomy. Victoria Canning (2017) argues that asylum policy and practice contributes to structural violence as the harms it causes are foreseeable, avoidable and impact on the basic needs of asylum seekers. The pandemic exacerbated these harms. Indeed, many of the harms created by immigration policy and practice are intentional and integral to building and maintaining a hostile environment for asylum seekers.

With an understanding of asylum accommodation during the pandemic we might begin to understand what happened to Badreddin. Having endured a treacherous journey to a hostile Europe, moving from one European country to another, attempting to seek one more welcoming than the last, Badreddin lost hope (Tsilivakou, 2021). When in Glasgow, he withdrew even from his family, contacting them less frequently (Tsilivakou, 2021). Living in a hotel during the pandemic exacerbated this and there were reports that fears of contracting COVID-19 exacerbated his mental health before his death (BBC, 2021). Fearful of catching the virus he withdrew, isolating himself from others, appearing paranoid and agitated (BBC, 2021). His room had no view, so even looking out of the window he faced a wall (Tsilivakou, 2021). When Badreddin attacked the asylum seekers, hotel staff and police officer, he had suffered a severe breakdown in his mental health (Carrell, 2022). He had made over 70 calls to the Home Office, Mears and Migrant Help[4] (Carrell, 2022). Badreddin faced a hostile environment not just in the UK but in Europe as a whole, and he was coerced to leave, having requested a voluntary return to Sudan (Tsilivakou, 2021). He was not an evil perpetrator of a violent attack but a victim of the hostile environment and its neoliberal policies.

Our borders are not only killing people outside them through push-backs and by forcing migrants to take dangerous journeys, but the hostile environment is responsible for deaths within our borders too. Asylum accommodation throughout the pandemic has created, for people seeking safety, borders within borders, an intensified experience of bordering. The structural violence inherent within the asylum system (Canning, 2017) was magnified during the early stages of the pandemic, intersecting with coronavirus lockdown rules to compound the already difficult life conditions in which asylum seekers in the UK live.

These deaths could have been avoided. There could have been solutions. Evictions from self-contained accommodation into hotels that felt unsafe and like prisons to asylum seekers could have been prevented. Pip Fisher (2020), a GP who works regularly with asylum seekers, asks, if schools could reopen with social distancing, why could services not reopen for vulnerable people who rely on them? Asylum seekers are reliant on NGOs for practical support, information and English language skills, all of which contribute to positive emotional wellbeing in a population that already has increased levels of trauma (Cortvriend, 2020). If some of these things had been put into practice, the deaths of Adnan Olbeh and Badreddin Abdallah Adam Bosh might have been avoided.

Notes

1   The UN Refugee Convention can be found at: www.ohchr.org/en/instruments-mechanisms/instruments/convention-relating-status-refugees
2   If the Home Office determines that an asylum seeker has travelled to the UK through a safe country, it may decide that the case should be considered in that country.
3   Names have been anonymised.
4   Migrant Help is a charity that has been appointed by the Home Office to provide information about asylum, and is a point of contact for housing maintenance issues, assistance where there is a risk to health and wellbeing, asylum payment issues and complaints.

PART III

Caring for the dead

RECKONING WITH GRIEF

Mark Brown

Mark Brown ✅
@MarkOneinFour · **Follow**

I really don't think the UK is doing a very good reckoning with the grief, sadness and loss of the pandemic because overall it feels we still listen too much to the voices of those not affected that much by the pandemic at the cost of those really harmed by it **#partygate**

8:52 AM · Apr 20, 2022   ⓘ

Mark Brown ✅
@MarkOneinFour · **Follow**

We seem to be unable to situate such a massive (and ongoing) event within our public sense of what the world is about, and so desperately look to reassuring voices that tell us little has changed. I don't know I have the language to really discuss it from my own experience

8:55 AM · Apr 20, 2022   ⓘ

Mark Brown ✅
@MarkOneinFour · **Follow**

I sometimes feel a terrible rending of my own thoughts, where I wonder whether someone like me is allowed to be angry and let down and filled with grief. Helping with vaccinations over the last year and a bit was a kind of harnessing of that rage at loss.

8:59 AM · Apr 20, 2022   ⓘ

Mark Brown ✅
@MarkOneinFour · **Follow**

I don't know what to do with the reconstruction of the world needed, both of my own tiny world and the wider world and I can't find a frame to get my head around it. In part that's because I feel like we haven't admitted a reconstruction is needed, because it's 'back to normal'

9:01 AM · Apr 20, 2022   ⓘ

Mark Brown ✅
@MarkOneinFour · **Follow**

We've been, and are going through, a massive death and disablement event as a result of covid-19. Johnson's apologies had those affected as a kind of insubstantial other to vaguely reference, a sort of empty seat at the table to be nodded at, but never really considered as real

9:09 AM · Apr 20, 2022   ⓘ

Mark Brown ✓
@MarkOneinFour · **Follow**

It feels like our public dialogue about the impacts of the
pandemic is too often a dialogue that excludes the reality
of those intimately affected and forms a series of
reassurances from those standing unscathed to those
afraid of being affected.

9:12 AM · Apr 20, 2022   ⓘ

Mark Brown ✓
@MarkOneinFour · **Follow**

It's so weird that we have an entire set of cultural
expectations that we should be able to talk about life
changing events, but we don't really have the apparatus
to discuss a life change two years. Or apparatus to discuss
large collective change as part of an ongoing situation

9:17 AM · Apr 20, 2022   ⓘ

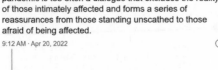

Mark Brown ✓
@MarkOneinFour · **Follow**

You and me have been through the same two years of
pandemic, but you and me might have had very different
experiences. I don't get to be glad I didn't lose anyone,
because I did. So a reckoning with what happened feels
important, both privately and collectively

9:21 AM · Apr 20, 2022   ⓘ

Mark Brown ✓
@MarkOneinFour · **Follow**

The bumbling, blustering path through **#partygate** has
been on a personal level incredibly difficult. It's impossible
not to match the date of actual and alleged breaches with
my own personal calendar of loss and grief. I won't get to
argue my way out of the impact of the pandemic

9:27 AM · Apr 20, 2022   ⓘ

Mark Brown ✓
@MarkOneinFour · **Follow**

I feel boxed in a corner where it's difficult to authentically
experience and process my own loss and grief. I think
there's a few reasons. One is that the precipitating events
are not over. Another is somehow my experience feels
malleable, like it could be rewritten from outside

9:39 AM · Apr 20, 2022   ⓘ

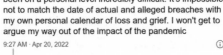

Mark Brown ✓
@MarkOneinFour · Follow

Pandemic grief is weird because your bereavement is part of a story in which everyone else has been taking part. We often experience mass death events as something singular and removed from the mundane. Something that happens outside of the mundane and to others we can identify

1:47 PM · Apr 21, 2022   ⓘ

Mark Brown ✓
@MarkOneinFour · Follow

In such terrible events we can see very easily how those bereaved are living something different to us, and can focus very easily on the run up to the event and its aftermath allow for a collective response of compassion and an effort to provide help from our place of safety

1:49 PM · Apr 21, 2022   ⓘ

Mark Brown ✓
@MarkOneinFour · Follow

The pandemic is different to this because everyone has been 'in' the pandemic along with everyone who has died during it and as a result of it. This makes the deaths of those to covid seem less exceptional and makes them seem less of a rupture with the 'normal' state of things

1:54 PM · Apr 21, 2022   ⓘ

Mark Brown ✓
@MarkOneinFour · Follow

As someone trying to bumble through pandemic grief, I feel this lack of a popular sense of an antagonist keenly. We usually compartmentalise death due to illness and make the illness the enemy, but in a pandemic the illness and the general context are all blurred for people

6:20 PM · Apr 21, 2022   ⓘ

Mark Brown ✓
@MarkOneinFour · Follow

'We're going to beat covid' gets mixed together with 'we're going to get back to normal' gets mixed with all manner of feeling and experiences around the pandemic. The upshot of this is the distinct loss of people's lives gets diluted into a set of general impressions of the time

6:21 PM · Apr 21, 2022   ⓘ

181

Mark Brown ✔
@MarkOneinFour · Follow

It's so weird. There's been lots of great grassroots work in communities during the pandemic but we've not seen anything like a national fundraising campaign to help to support the bereaved or injured by covid-19. It's like the reality of those harmed is ungraspable

6:23 PM · Apr 21, 2022   ⓘ

Mark Brown ✔
@MarkOneinFour · Follow

It's so odd to me that over two years 172,000 odd people can not be here anymore because of one particular cause and yet we can't seem to muster a national sense of anything regarding that reality. Millions of people are harmed, hurting, lost, bewildered and just nowt

6:25 PM · Apr 21, 2022   ⓘ

Mark Brown ✔
@MarkOneinFour · Follow

For me personally, it's hard because the situation is not over. Losing Alison doesn't feel real (which I know is not uncommon in grief). My grief has been staggered, is arriving in installments and is tied to the news cycle of the pandemic in Westminster and beyond

6:27 PM · Apr 21, 2022   ⓘ

Mark Brown ✔
@MarkOneinFour · Follow

My loss is linked to the loss of thousands and thousands of other people by tiny, almost invisible threads of commonality but it feels like those threads are not allowed to be reinforced because the net they might form would begin pull a sense of something having happened tighter

6:32 PM · Apr 21, 2022   ⓘ

Mark Brown ✔
@MarkOneinFour · Follow

At the moment there are those who have lost loved ones, and there are those that haven't and the connection between the two is weak. Where's the forum for telling the story of those no longer here and those who survive them?

6:35 PM · Apr 21, 2022   ⓘ

Mark Brown ✓
@MarkOneinFour · Follow

Can we stomach bearing witness the reality of something that at one point might have scared us that it might happen to us, once the reality of it happening to us recedes? Can those relatively untouched by the pandemic share some of their blessing with those not so lucky?

6:37 PM · Apr 21, 2022   ⓘ

Mark Brown ✓
@MarkOneinFour · Follow

I realise **#partygate** is a lightning rod for those feelings of loss, but I don't feel that's been fully integrated into a sense of what has been lost by those who lost people or have faced great damage. We're arguing about rules breaking with death as a spicy modifying flourish

6:41 PM · Apr 21, 2022   ⓘ

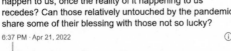

Mark Brown ✓
@MarkOneinFour · Follow

I can't unremember my sister being dead. I can't bounce back to her still being here. My experience of the pandemic has diverged in one significant way which I share with thousands of others. But I don't feel like all of us thousands are recognised as thousands

6:53 PM · Apr 21, 2022   ⓘ

Mark Brown ✓
@MarkOneinFour · Follow

What I'd like, I think, is some kind of space to explore these feelings with others. I've had counselling for my grief in a personal sense, but the result of the pandemic isn't just my own personal butthurt. This grief is not just atomised into individual upsetting stories

6:57 PM · Apr 21, 2022   ⓘ

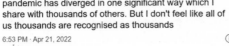

Mark Brown ✓
@MarkOneinFour · Follow

As I've said before, the reality of loss within a pandemic is that the chapters of the story of loss don't have clear beginnings and ends. I feel like we are at risk of collectively equivocating so deeply that we eventually end up concluding that no one was really lost at all

7:00 PM · Apr 21, 2022   ⓘ

8

Lessons from a mortuary

Lara-Rose Iredale

For as long as I can remember, I've always wanted to work with the dead. I cannot explain what drew me to this line of work, and speaking to colleagues across this profession I can honestly say that very few of us can answer the question 'why?' A vocation, a calling – no one enters this line of work lightly. We are all individuals – there is no stereotypical mortuary professional (although with my all black everything attitude to clothing, multiple tattoos and piercings, I would say that I definitely look like what you would imagine a stereotypical mortuary dweller to look like). One thing that does tie us together, though, is our passion and dedication to the job.

As an anatomical pathology technologist (APT), to give my full job title, I am responsible for the continued care of the deceased. I work in an NHS hospital, but APTs also work in council/local authority-run public mortuaries. My job is to look after the adults and children who die in our hospital and local borough. We also provide post-mortem services for coroners from all over London, the southeast and as far afield as Hereford and Nottingham. For APTs in general, our day-to-day job involves admitting and releasing deceased patients, assisting with post-mortem examinations, and facilitating families visiting their loved ones, alongside the administration and maintenance of the mortuary environment. Truly, no two days are the same in this line of work, just as no two mortuaries are alike in how they operate; some do not conduct post-mortems at all, for example, and each will have their own standard procedures and paperwork.

My job is gruelling and rewarding in equal measure, and for those of us who enter this career, it is usually a path we remain on for life.

The following account comes from a place of reflection in 2021, nearly two years since the beginning of the pandemic. I remember Dr John Troyer from the University of Bath's Centre of Death and Society observing how whenever there is a 'controversial' news story regarding death and dead bodies, on Monday the media will be full of righteous anger and indignation but by Friday opinion pieces will be more introspective and well rounded. Had my account been written during the first half of 2020, the rage and desperation would have been palpable. The passage of time has enabled me to write a more balanced account of the facts, decisions made and my feelings around them. I hope I can present my pandemic experience with clarity and fairness. As ever, I do not speak for all APTs when writing this. I could write several essays and talk for days about the challenges I faced, both personally and professionally – the prolonged intensity of the work, the separation from loved ones, the uncertainly of every aspect of work and home life – for us, COVID-19 was inescapable.

When trying to organise my thoughts and memories of the past two years into a coherent narrative, almost memoir, it became clear that this is not what I needed to do. I am not the sole authority on mortuary work, and nor am I trained in emergency preparedness. However, I do believe I have something worthwhile to say on the lessons I have learned personally, and the lessons that we should take away from the pandemic as they relate to care of the deceased. What follows can therefore be described as a warning. I know, in the case of COVID-19, it's a bit late for that now. Maybe instead this short piece can serve as a warning about what happens when warnings are ignored.

Business as usual to chaos happens faster than you think

January 2020 seems like a lifetime ago, but when news first started breaking about this new coronavirus with pandemic capabilities, I can honestly say that I wasn't worried from a work perspective. We are well versed in handling excess deaths – we do it every winter – but as the virus spread and death tolls were increasing across the world, we started to get concerned about our ability to cope with the projected death rates. From mid-March, it was clear that this was on a scale like we had never experienced before. We received out first COVID-19 patient in the mortuary on 14 March, and less than three weeks later had reached capacity. Our day-to-day job became that of management of the deceased.

The increased death rate did not happen in a vacuum. It is important to contextualise everything that happened in those first few weeks with what was going on nationally compared to what usually happens when someone dies in our hospital.

Let's say there is an expected death in hospital, which is a death in which a medical certificate of cause of death (MCCD) can be issued without the need for the involvement of the coroner or a post-mortem examination. What happens?

The patient is brought down to the mortuary within four hours of death and placed in a fridge by two porters. They arrive maybe with some small items of personal property (jewellery, cards, religious tokens and so on). The patient is then 'checked in' by a member of mortuary staff – three points of ID on two hospital wristbands, their property is accounted for, they are weighed and measured (in case of a post-mortem examination) and we look for evidence of any implanted devices, such as a pacemaker. We change their sheet and clean them up if needed. We then transfer this information onto our bespoke mortuary database – each mortuary has their own way of tracking and recording patients. This will be very important later.

Meanwhile, the patient's hospital notes and any other property is taken to the bereavement centre by a nurse or ward clerk where the bereavement staff input the patient's details onto the database (we use the same one – it's a shared system). They document the property and start to phone the wards to see if there is a doctor available to write the MCCD. The doctor has to come to the bereavement centre to do this. The family of the deceased get in touch (if the family were present on the ward at the time of death, they will often go straight to the bereavement centre), and they will be called when the MCCD is ready to be collected; we have a time frame of 48 hours for doctors to complete this paperwork.

The family also collect the property of the deceased from the bereavement centre, or make other arrangements (it is brought down to the mortuary to be collected with the deceased by the funeral director, or it can be disposed of by the hospital, should the family not want it). The family then make an appointment to register the death at the local town hall – this is a face-to-face appointment – where they are provided with the necessary paperwork to proceed with a funeral. Finally, a funeral director comes to collect the deceased. If the family want to see their loved ones in the mortuary, an appointment is made with the mortuary and the ward staff where the patient died, as a nurse must accompany the family when they visit.

This is a very basic run-through of what happens, but read again and take note of how many people are involved in this process and, notably, how much of this happens face to face. This is pre-COVID-19, happening daily, and, of course, there are far more complicated deaths than this standard example, with families experiencing difficult emotions, some who do not speak English as a first language, who have specific religions or cultural needs and so on.

Now imagine that process happening when the country is on lockdown, when people are not supposed to leave their homes, the hospital is shut down to all visitors, doctors and nurses are overwhelmed on the wards and the mortuary is receiving more and more patients, not only from the wards, but also from the community. Timing is everything.

During winter, when the excess deaths see an increase in pressures on the mortuary and on our capacity, the cogs are still moving. There is an increased volume of work, but people can still attend the hospital and collect paperwork and property and register deaths. With COVID-19 and the lockdown, things ground to a halt. Very specifically, *legally* there was no way of registering a death remotely. Between next of kin themselves testing positive for COVID-19, or at least having to isolate because of their contact with someone with COVID-19, then the hospital shutting down to visitors, we were all stuck, waiting. The only thing moving was the dead, and they were coming to us.

'Not my problem' becomes your problem in unexpected ways

How to deal with the property of the deceased soon became a major issue. This was something that I had never really given a second thought about, as it wasn't anything I ever saw – it was the bereavement office that dealt with it. As it turns out, people bring *a lot* of their own property to hospital with them – clothes, books, electronics, personal hygiene products and so much more. This property all needs to be returned to the family. With the death of a patient, these items are no longer just comfort items that make a lengthy hospital stay more pleasant; they are now the last link between the living and the dead. We can't judge based on the financial value of the items what is valuable to relatives in these circumstances, especially when the hospital closed to visitors and families were not allowed to physically be close to those dying. A hairbrush, a signature fragrance, birthday cards, an heirloom piece of jewellery, receipts from the last meal shared together – everything is to be made available to return to the families.

Concerns about how long COVID-19 remained on surfaces (at this early stage in the pandemic, there were a lot of unknowns and uncertainties) and there was an extra layer of complexity to contend with – how do we deal with property *safely*? A new process was created by those higher up the chain than us, involving specific ways of decontaminating and separating, documenting and tracking the property before it even reached us. I wish I could say it worked well. On paper it was easy, but practically ... less so. I can honestly say that the most frequently recurring, contentious and infuriating aspect of the pandemic was the 'property problem', which really boiled down to communication problems between those who designed the new system, those whose job it was to use the new system, and those whose job it was to implement and clearly communicate these changes to all involved. The mortuary was not responsible for any of these aspects, as this was all about what happened to the property before it reached us. It just so happens that we were the ones who were at the end of the chain and spotted errors in the process, and by then, it was too late. The burden fell on us to fix the issues. Property was building up, and documenting and sorting through it was an entire job on its own, and we simply didn't have the staff or capacity to deal with it alone.

Thankfully, redeployments were happening all over the NHS trust. With outpatient clinics, research departments and so on not running, staff were available to work elsewhere. We were able to have a two-person team dedicated to dealing solely with property. Honestly, it was such a relief to have people who could focus their whole attention on this, coming up with systems and a database to document everything. It was not an easy job, both practically and emotionally. These people were now responsible for contacting the families of the deceased and having conversations about what they wanted to do with the belongings their loved ones had left behind, packing it up and mailing it out. They were trying to trace missing property, property that relatives weren't sure existed, property that we realised hadn't been sent with the patient when they had been transferred to us from another hospital. There was no training as such, just doing what needed to be done, and I cannot express enough how important this job was and how well they did it.

Interestingly, I read an article about a hospital in the USA that was also facing the same problems regarding property – this was certainly an issue I imagine all hospitals faced. The solution the US hospital put in place was extraordinarily similar to what we did.

Trust your mortuary staff – aka: subject matter experts – use them!

National lockdown was announced on 23 March, quickly followed by the Coronavirus Act 2020 receiving Royal Assent on 25 March. This was what we had been waiting for as this Act was effective at streamlining and enabling swift death certification and registration. This solved the problem of how to get the paperwork moving, but we were worried that this would not necessarily translate to the movement of deceased patients. Between the mortuary and bereavement staff, we predicted that families would be reluctant to book a funeral, given that restrictions in place meant that there could be no attendees. Seeing as the lockdown measures were going to be in place for three weeks, people would refrain from making arrangements until they could have the service they wanted. And if there is one thing the dead can do, it's wait. In the grand scheme of the mortuary world, three weeks is a bit long for a deceased person to stay in our care, but it is by no means unusual. A couple of things were becoming very evident, very early on. First, higher management had no idea how the mortuary worked on a day-to-day basis. Routine things such as the movement of the deceased, as described above, the hold-ups that can occur even with the introduction of online death registration (you cannot force people to make funeral arrangements), the lack of space at funeral directors' premises – all of these we had to explain, it felt, on a near daily basis. Second, this lockdown was going to last a lot longer than three weeks.

We made our concerns clear from the start about our capacity – we needed more, and quickly. I remember vividly an almost comical exchange between my boss and local health and emergency planning leads about the amount of COVID-19 positive patients in the mortuary. When we said that we were getting full and we needed extra space urgently, we were met with disbelief. How could we be running out of space? There weren't that many deaths, surely? We sat open-mouthed, looking into the fridge room at our rapidly declining spaces – how could they not believe us? The answer was paperwork. Every death due to COVID-19 had to be reported to NHS England, and this was done by filling in a paper form that then made its way up the chain. Of course, with the overwhelming demand on ward staff, there were delays in the forms leaving the wards. On paper, there were few COVID-19 deaths. Our fridges told a different story. When patients die in hospital carrying certain infections (along the lines of hepatitis, HIV, tuberculosis and now COVID-19), they are placed in a specific, separate fridge bank, as more personal protection equipment (PPE) precautions are needed when handling the deceased. The separate fridge banks serve as an easy visual cue more than anything else. Contrary to what may be a common misconception, there is very little danger posed from the deceased in terms of infection transmission. With COVID-19 deaths on the increase, the deceased were now placed wherever there was space. We made a note on the fridge doors if the deceased had COVID-19, another easy visual cue for us and the portering staff who are responsible for transferring the deceased from the wards to us. A quick glance at our fridges showed the majority of our residents had had COVID-19.

From here began an eventual daily situation report (sitrep) meeting (virtual, of course) regarding mortuary issues, namely, capacity. It turns out there is quite a bit to consider when procuring extra mortuary space, and one of these is, well ... space. Where do you put it? Issues like security, ease of access and how public it would be all had to be weighed up. During previous excess death scenarios, we were fortunate enough not to have to use outside excess storage as we could utilise the space at our (much smaller) satellite mortuary, so we'd never dealt with that before as a mortuary or as a trust. Of course, there were cost implications too, and yet again, *timing*. Every mortuary in the country was looking at obtaining more space, and with few companies actually being able to provide such bespoke equipment, and with lead times increasing every day, a decision wasn't made, and things were looking bleak. London and national mortuary capacity databases were set up that were fed into daily to enable the NHS and the government to monitor the situation. It was around this time that there were rumblings of large temporary mortuary facilities being put in place, quite separate from the Nightingale Hospitals that were being built.

I received a phone call from someone in a council department who had been tasked with helping with the logistics of one such temporary mortuary facility that would be situated in Breakspear Crematorium. This was due to be operational only one week later. Those where the mortuary was being built wanted advice on how to keep track of the deceased moving in and out of the facility. The specific question will be burned into my memory forever: 'What system does the NHS use for keeping track of the deceased?' As if such a system exists and it would be a simple case of access to this supposed universal NHS system. I broke it to them – there wasn't one. A brief silence followed by a despondent 'oh'. A conversation followed where I explained how every mortuary uses a different system to track the deceased in their care, and that some may still use paper registers. That not everyone dies in a hospital; certainly our patients may arrive with us after dying at home. The paperwork that is generated after you die in relation to burial and cremation is another matter altogether. This was clearly not the conversation the person on the end of the phone was hoping to have. My boss had the pleasure of following up these conversations, each email and phone call brought more bad news for the designers, and disbelief from APTs that this was ever going to work.

At the same time, our own temporary storage facilities were close to being built, but the Breakspear facility would be operational first. The teething problems of how to organise the transfer of the deceased seemed to have been ironed out and a system was in place. This was not without fault and was very labour-intensive for APTs and brought with it a lot of frustration and upset, but we really had no alternative but to use the facility as we had nowhere else. I know other mortuaries were in a seriously dire situation, and I don't want to think what would have happened had the facilities not been ready.

The use of emergency mortuaries is the most difficult aspect to reflect on. APTs have high standards and expectations when it comes to management of the deceased; it is what we do on a daily basis, and to have this taken out of our control was very difficult to accept. APTs and funeral directors alike had an opinion on how this could have been done better. We'd pick apart every detail and perceived fault as a bonding activity. Because the deceased were still our responsibility, we felt comfortable passing judgement on those who dared enter our realm uninvited and uninitiated. It was an easy target and somewhere very tangible to direct our frustrations, but later on I would come to realise just what limited expertise the people in charge of setting these up had at their disposal.

When the first peak of COVID-19 seemed to be settling and we were moving into summer, things that were very strange and unfamiliar soon became routine. Our own onsite excess storage was up and running with no need to use the temporary mortuaries any further. Reporting systems for mortuary capacities were streamlined and reduced in frequency as mortuaries became less pressured for space. Knowledge about COVID-19 in general had advanced in part because of the information that post-mortem examinations had yielded. This information aided medicine in real time as it was understood more the effects that COVID-19 and the current treatments were having, and the benefits to the living cannot be overstated. We were able to help other departments that were eagerly waiting to reopen their clinics as we were able to test various fluids and areas to see if COVID-19 was present and transmissible – things like orthopaedic surgery and ophthalmology – and guide risk assessments and PPE. This was down to the generosity of the families who consented for post-mortem examinations on their loved ones, and I cannot thank them enough.

Do the best you can with the tools you are given

When it was time for the national temporary mortuary facilities to be stood down, we were invited to attend a review and reflection of the process. This included council workers who had been involved in setting it up, funeral directors and, of course, APTs. The APTs were very vocal about what we thought had been done badly. This was one time when our voices could well and truly be heard, and no one was spared; there was criticism of every aspect – the setting up of the facilities, the eventual roll-out, the heavy burden of paperwork and organisation that was put onto mortuary staff and the general user-unfriendliness of the whole system. We weren't harsh or cruel, but we made it clear that the best time to ask for our input into matters concerning mortuaries was *before* and not after the event. The biggest complaint from APTs was that a system that was supposed to help us ended up being more of a burden.

On reflection, I one hundred per cent stand by what I said in that meeting and where I think things went wrong. I am not an emergency planner, and I cannot claim expertise in the area of mass fatalities, disaster planning and so on. And honestly, neither were the people in that meeting. The people who were in charge of implementing emergency mortuary facilities and monitoring were people who worked in the local authority whose regular day job did not involve the deceased in any capacity. They were called in to a meeting and were told that their role was to get the sites up and running, pronto. I still maintain that subject matter experts should have been drafted in earlier, that a quick phone call could have established contacts in the industry who could have helped, but, ultimately, there should have been a plan that could have been provided for them to follow. And that falls directly onto the UK government. Exercise Cygnus, the 2016 pandemic simulation, should have dealt with this (Public Health England, 2020b). One of the recommendations was for excess death management to be reviewed. It may surprise you that no one who actually works in a mortuary, who has knowledge of how mortuaries function and the relationships we have with other statutory bodies, is involved in such planning. It is clear when you get asked, in all seriousness, one week before the opening of emergency mortuaries 'How does the NHS track the deceased?' that something has gone very wrong. Local authorities and the NHS are involved as stakeholders, but when senior staff in the NHS have repeatedly demonstrated they don't know how their mortuaries work, how on earth are they supposed to have meaningful input into planning that directly affects us?

Ultimately, the temporary mortuaries were designed to be just that – temporary. They were relief for overwhelmed hospital and public mortuaries that bought time for local excess storage facilities to be built onsite. As it was rightfully pointed out by someone on the call, in a rather sharp tone (having just been berated by angry APTs), the Breakspear facility was the first excess mortuary storage facility to be opened – before any hospital or local authority had secured any extra space – and without them we would have been up a very particular creek without a paddle. Once trusts had their own storage sorted, there would be a move to a mutual aid model, where mortuaries could utilise space in other established mortuaries in the future, without the need for the larger emergency mortuaries. The purpose of the meeting was to receive feedback and learn for the future, and I am sure that what we said was heard that day.

Look after your staff

During the pandemic, there were regular regional meetings involving managers from mortuaries, registrars, cemeteries and crematoriums along with our local coroner. These had been more like update and sitrep-type meetings to keep each other informed of any issues we were facing that might impact services and were wound down in 2021. I was able to attend the final meeting on behalf of my boss, which was an opportunity to share our experiences and what we thought went well, what needed work and what might happen during a future pandemic. Towards the end, the coroner brought up that in any future excess death situations, he would prefer less disruption to post-mortem services, specifically that there should be fewer delays in getting post-mortem examinations carried out in his mortuaries. An honourable aim, but one I fear is not necessarily achievable due to mortuary staff being a finite human resource.

Throughout the pandemic, there was such a focus on mortuaries' capacity for storing the deceased, but no one questioned the mortuary staff's ability to keep up with the workload. No one was asked if any staff were off sick at any point, if they had to shield or if the mortuary was adequately staffed pre-pandemic to begin with. Our mortuary was reliant on locums pre-pandemic, and thankfully we were able to retain them for the duration, but we were unable to gain further locum staff as everyone was already snapped up. We were not the only mortuary to be in this situation. There simply aren't enough of us. We also experienced the knock-on effects of having a mortuary in another jurisdiction having all their staff off sick with or isolating because of COVID-19 – yet another example of 'not our problem' becoming our problem unexpectedly. In our mortuary, we undertook work from multiple coronial jurisdictions due to our paediatric specialty, not just the work for our local coroner, and that work did not stop during the pandemic. There were backlogs of work because, *of course*, they were inevitable.

Pre-pandemic, the ebb and flow of workload and capacity in the mortuary could never truly be predicted day to day. There would be a plan of action for the next 24 hours, and we knew what work had been referred to us by the coroners and hospital we served that had to be scheduled over the coming days, but all it would take is one phone call for the plans to be thrown into disarray. A forensic post-mortem that had to be arranged quickly, staff calling in sick, an issue at our satellite mortuary that required attendance immediately – this is all 'normal' chaos in a mortuary setting. Late finishes and overtime come as standard. I can only describe a standard day at the mortuary at the beginning of the pandemic as being like a regular day where *everything* goes wrong. Every day was now 'one of those days'. I can't remember a day when we finished work on time. Ten to twelve hour days were becoming standard, plus weekend on-call work. We didn't have the luxury of *choosing* to work an extra hour or so to catch up on any paperwork or preparing for the following day's workload. It was unrelenting and hard to keep up with the ever-changing rules and ways of working. I was overwhelmed and exhausted. We all were. There was also the fear that everyone was feeling about COVID-19 itself. How much risk was there to us commuting to work? I was living in a flat share with two other people, one of whom was clinically vulnerable. My other flatmate contracted COVID-19 in March and developed long Covid that they were still struggling with throughout 2020 and into 2021. I was very conscious of not just keeping myself safe, but others too.

Lockdown created a source of conflicting emotions for me. I had a stable job and had the 'luxury' of being able to leave the house and go to work every day. Yes, work was hell, but I still had it. I have a lot of friends who are self-employed and in creative fields, and my heart broke for them. I was fortunate that my team were such good friends, so we had each other for support. After a tough day at work, it was common for us to blow off some steam in the local pub, but this wasn't something available to us once the pubs closed. Not that we would have had the energy to do anything but go home and sleep. If I was able to go home. My weeks doing on-call were spent staying over at a hotel opposite work. The hotel provided rooms for trust staff, and it was a much-needed respite when having to attend daily at weekends while on-call to provide up-to-date capacity numbers and manage the little space we had. I remember the first 'clap for carers'. I had just rolled back to the hotel and climbed straight into a bath. I missed it completely. I was sent a video from my flatmates clapping and banging pans outside the windows, and I may have cried. The following week, we actually finished work at 8 pm and made it outside the hospital just as the clap was starting. I'm pretty sure we all had tears in our eyes. Overwhelmed, guilty, undeserving, thankful, tired. With nothing to break up the weeks stretching ahead – no time off (what was there to do?!), nowhere to go and nothing to do but work, my days were a constant loop of same-but-different.

Our mortuary also had a COVID-19 scare. A 24-hour window was all that saved us all from having to isolate and the mortuary effectively grinding to a halt (as the rules at the time stood on testing and isolation periods). A resilience plan was non-existent for the circumstances of the entire mortuary staff being unable to attend work for an extended period of time. One had to be devised very quickly, and it was clear that we would not be able to run the service 'business as usual' – post-mortems would either have to be diverted or put on hold. I know that other mortuaries had been able to plan around this scenario by splitting up their staff and having them work different days or shift patterns so that there would be some cover if one team had to isolate. But this was not feasible for us due to our reliance on locum staff who were not able to use the trust systems we rely on every day for every aspect of the job.

In the meeting, this revelation turned out not to be limited to mortuary staff. Registrars and crematoria staff are also in the position where no one else can do their job without prior training and up-to-date knowledge. It would seem that the majority of roles in post-death care are specialised, in part because there is so much legislation and the huge legal ramifications should something be done incorrectly. It takes a minimum of two years of on-the-job training to qualify as an APT; it is not something you can spot-train people to do. Yes, once trained, the practical skills are transferable to any mortuary, but the operation of each mortuary is very much non-standardised (remember, there isn't one way to track the deceased in the NHS!). In theory, having a cohort of people on standby should they be needed in the future to provide emergency cover (which was a suggestion made) sounds great. In practice, however, it would not work for an established, fully operational, post–mortem active mortuary.

The mortuaries built into the Nightingale Hospitals benefited from having input from the Association of Anatomical Pathology Technologists (AAPT), which is the non-statutory body for our profession. The AAPT got involved as the pathologists who were consulted about the various laboratory needs of the Nightingales were aware of the AAPT's existence and recognised the valuable input from actual mortuary staff that was needed in the setting up and *training* of the people needed to run the mortuaries. Similarly, the temporary mortuaries that were built only needed to function as storage for the deceased, and did not provide post-mortem examination facilities, hence why very specific training could be given in the receipt and release of the deceased only.

You are not as alone as you think you are

The first few months of the pandemic have really put the efforts of mortuary staff and funeral directors – people whose jobs are usually hidden – into the spotlight. We are used to being left to our own devices and are a self-sufficient department in many ways. I have often complained of the mortuary being 'forgotten about'; we are seen as mysterious, operating under a cloak of misery in the basement of the hospital. I found myself suddenly thrust into the world of higher hospital management, feeding into Gold Command and having daily dial-ins with very important people. I have seen my colleagues in other mortuaries appear on the news, their work, their struggles and their humanity documented for all to see. We are being recognised for the important role we play in healthcare. At the beginning I felt very much out of my depth, especially as everything was so fast-paced, and parameters moved almost daily; it was very difficult to keep track. Later I recognised that those in the mortuary were very much being *included* in decision making, and that we were, in fact, the experts in our area of work, and our input was invaluable in driving the needs of the service.

The one thing that really stood out for me during the pandemic was the solidarity and support we received from others working in death care. Almost immediately we had offers of help with capacity issues from funeral directors (little did we all know back then just how hard hit *everyone* was going to be). I had friends in the industry privately message me asking for advice around PPE, and I was able to share the latest guidance with them as this was a constantly evolving landscape.

Being a member of the AAPT was especially useful as we were able to access and share resources in almost real time. Any time new PPE guidance or advice on best practice was published by the Royal College of Pathologists, the Human Tissue Authority, the government, it was published on the AAPT website and on our Facebook group. We could all interact with each other and share advice on practical issues and offer each other some emotional support in the process.

Personally, the pandemic put in sharp focus what was important in my life. At the end of 2019 I began a long-distance relationship. The national lockdowns in 2020 and 2021, and the intervening tier system of restrictions meant that we spent more than six months apart. I made the decision to leave London and move north, which obviously meant leaving my beloved St Thomas'. Coincidentally, a vacancy came up in a mortuary relatively locally and I now work in a solely paediatric hospital. As such, my current workload is less affected by COVID-19, which, going into Christmas 2021, is a world of difference to this time in 2020.

A warning

Shortly after I began in the paediatric hospital in the summer of 2021, a trust-wide email went out – 'Tomorrow's Major Incident Exercise – what you need to know'. I quote from the email:

> It aims to test the 'Day 2' procedures and explore issues which could emerge post a major incident. … The testing of these plans is a legal requirement but more so, it provides a safe environment to use procedures that may be unfamiliar or new for our colleagues. It also provides an opportunity to identify lessons that can go on to improve the Trust response.

I ask my boss about this – a live exercise?! Are we involved?!

No.

This was part two of the exercise, the first being before I started at the trust. My boss had approached the organisers at that time to enquire about being involved, only to be shot down.

No. The mortuary does not need to be involved.

In the shadow of Hillsborough (22 victims aged under 18) and the all too recent 2017 Manchester Arena bombing (7 victims aged under 18) it was decided to run a major incident exercise in a paediatric hospital with an A&E department in which there are ZERO deaths.

No one dies. Especially not children.

No need for a plan.

No lessons to learn.

MY IMPENDING ADVENTURE, A STORY FOR ANOTHER DAY

Irene Naikaali Ssentongo

Walking down a lonely path with no one to hold nor kiss goodbye. The oxygen mask gives me the calm assurance that all will be well soon.

Taking a leap of faith into the unknown, I look ahead towards my guiding star. The assurance I get is that the path I have chosen is the one I am destined to take. Where are we headed? I ask, I hear no voice in return. I turn my head to fill in the void.

I must cooperate and spread out my wings, well knowing that this game of life is working for me not against me.

I then cross over to the other side with confidence. I have endured the race and now it's time to cheer on the helplessly medical teams that watched silently as I negotiated my path.

Weep no more my beloveds, my impending adventure on the other side is a story for another day.

9

Funerals, cemeteries and crematoria: different community experiences

Avril Maddrell, Danielle House and Farjana Islam

Early in the spring of 2020, the COVID-19 pandemic was widely represented as a great social equaliser that placed everyone 'in the same boat'. However, it swiftly became clear that this was not the case. Most struggled to adapt to the new normalities in terms of adhering to the lockdown restrictions and social distancing rules while working, raising families and taking care of older and COVID-19-affected family members, and fulfilling responsibilities to neighbours and relatives near and far; but the quality of these experiences depended on resources and responsibilities. Households' experiences of lockdown varied with accommodation, access to outdoor space, loss of earnings and employment, and the burden of isolation or family responsibilities. Moreover, the disease itself adversely affected certain communities, largely key workers, the elderly, those with health vulnerabilities and those already suffering from pre-existing socioeconomic inequalities. Restrictions on hospital and care home visits and attendance at funerals caused additional grief for the bereaved, and had a particular impact on the challenges of fulfilling end-of-life and funeral religious requirements for certain faith groups.

We reflect on our personal experiences of the pandemic including illness and bereavement, and bridge between this, ongoing research with the funerary sector, and new research with Bangladeshi Muslim communities, drawing on interviews in Dundee, Edinburgh and London. We explore inequality, death and bereavement during the pandemic, including the unequal risk of death from the disease, the restrictions that COVID-19 placed on funerary rituals and varying impacts on bereavement during the pandemic. The pandemic has highlighted overlapping socioeconomic inequalities and health risks, and new questions relating to what constitutes a 'good' or 'bad' death, but also what is necessary for a 'good' funeral ritual, reflecting the particular spiritual, emotional and religious norms of given communities set against uniform public health regulations during the pandemic.

This chapter reflects on the impact of COVID-19 on cemeteries, crematoria and funerals during the first 18 months of the pandemic in the UK, when the country experienced high rates of hospitalisation and deaths, coupled with periods of school and nursery closures; furlough or unemployment for many and overwork for others; and strict rules on people's movement and interactions in an effort to slow the spread of the virus. This period, prior to the majority of the population being fully vaccinated, was characterised by uncertainty, fear, risk of severe illness and death, as well as 'stay at home' mandates during periods of 'lockdown' and prolonged social distancing rules.

At this time, the threat of contracting COVID-19 and uniform public health restrictions put in place to reduce the spread of the virus was viewed as a 'great equaliser' in society, placing everyone 'in the same boat' – a phrase that circulated in politicians' statements, the media and everyday conversations (Milne, 2020). However, it soon became apparent that we weren't *all* 'in the same boat'. In the UK, experiences of the first wave of the pandemic were very different for individuals, families and communities. Those identified as 'key workers' – including doctors, nurses, hospital workers, food processors and retailers, and bus, taxi and delivery drivers – continued with face-to-face delivery of necessary services at considerable health risk. Others lost their jobs or experienced reduced earnings while on furlough; those who could continue their work from home during lockdowns had varied experiences depending on their household space, digital connectivity and caring responsibilities (for example, for those working from home *and* caring for children, people with disabilities and/or older people's needs in multigenerational households). Those who had access to private outdoor space were privileged compared to those who had no outdoor space; and while some had the burden of heavy family responsibilities, others suffered from social isolation, felt insecure or were physically unsafe in their own homes or accommodation.

It was reflecting on these inequalities that prompted UK writer and broadcaster Damian Barr to tweet on 20 April 2020: 'We are not all in the same boat. We are all in the same storm. Some are on super-yachts. Some have just the one oar.' This social media post, and Barr's subsequent poem on the same theme (Barr, 2020), captured in a nutshell the role of inequalities in differential experience between individuals, households, communities and even countries during the early pandemic. The impact and legacies of bereavement during and as a result of COVID-19 have been felt by many but, as we will demonstrate in this chapter, were especially impactful on lone mourners; on those unable to support their loved ones emotionally and spiritually at the end of life; those who believe their loved ones may be disadvantaged in the afterlife because of missing religious rituals; and professionals, such as clergy, funeral and cemetery and crematoria workers, who were unable to provide best practice services.

The idea of the 'same storm but different boats' was also true of us, the authors of this chapter, all living in the UK during the pandemic but our experiences mediated by different privileges, challenges and losses. One author's partner contracted COVID-19 through public-facing key work, and was required to isolate for two weeks caring for her sick partner and young child in a small flat, relying on emotional support via transnational phone and video calls with kith and kin living in her home country. Another experienced pregnancy, childbirth and the challenges of juggling childcare and paid work during nursery and school closures, as well as the absence of otherwise everyday parental and community companionship and support. All had parents made vulnerable by age and/or health conditions, but one had a parent who died in a care home, separated from family at the time of death during a period of strict lockdown restrictions. This experience of parental loss was not due to COVID-19 but shaped by the pandemic: communication with and support for the dying in those last days limited to short phone or video calls. When the funeral was finally possible, ongoing travel restrictions meant that some immediate family members were unable to be present and could only view the funeral online.

These experiences of different sorts of separation, isolation, stress and loss were shared by many. Even for those geographically close to loved ones, visiting the dying was at first prohibited and later restricted to short visits by next of kin, with both the dying and their loved ones shrouded behind face masks and other PPE (personal protective equipment). Many died in hospitals or care homes without family present and, significant for many, without end-of-life spiritual support. Restrictions on attendance at funerals varied across the nations of the UK, but most were limited in terms of numbers and/or as a consequence of restricted travel or international quarantine requirements. Many had to join funerals online, and even next of kin allowed to be present in person experienced very basic funeral rites, not able to shake hands, offer the comfort of hugs or share memories over refreshments. One interviewee, a Christian minister in Dundee, commented on the lasting impact of limitations to participation in funeral rites as experienced by so many of the bereaved at this time. She observed, 'I think this will come up in the future. I think it will come back to people in terms of mental health and so on, because the bereavement process has been interrupted.'

However, some social and faith communities were more impacted than others. During the first pandemic wave in the UK, it soon became clear that age and pre-existing health conditions were also strongly correlated with vulnerability to severe illness and death, and more men died than women. Most of all, the disease itself disproportionately affected certain communities due to pre-existing socioeconomic inequalities, creating intolerable overlapping burdens for the poorest families, including many migrants and minorities (Ho and Maddrell, 2020; Islam and Netto, 2020; Platt and Warwick, 2020). In August 2020 a government agency report on the uneven impact of COVID-19 confirmed that 'the impact of COVID-19 has replicated existing health inequalities and, in some cases, has increased them' (Public Health England, 2020a: 4). This impact was compounded when combined with other factors such as race-ethnicity and deprivation: a disproportionate number of those from minority ethnic communities were dying of the disease. This prompted National Health Service (NHS)

Providers to stress to their members that the impact of COVID-19 was greater for those who lived in more deprived areas, who were twice as likely to die from COVID-19 than those in wealthier areas. NHS Providers also found that 'Black men were four times as likely, and Asian men were three times as likely to die from coronavirus than their white counterparts ... [and] deaths were almost three times higher in Black, Mixed and Other females, and 2.4 times higher in Asian females compared with White women' (NHS Providers, 2020). While many mourned often unexpected deaths, there were particular challenges for those who hold specific religious rituals as vital to the wellbeing of the deceased, and for mourners who have an obligation to fulfil those rites.

In this chapter, we share the experiences of people from across the funerary sector in Dundee, particularly those involved in Muslim burials, and bereaved members of British-Bangladeshi communities in Edinburgh and London. The experiences from the funerary sector in Dundee were shared with us through interviews as part of the 2019–22 CeMi research project on inclusive cemeteries and crematoria across six countries in northwest Europe (https://cemi-hera.org), which extended its remit to include the impact of the pandemic in the first wave. The research with British-Bangladeshi Muslim mourners in Edinburgh and London was undertaken by Farjana Islam, which extended her previous doctoral research with British-Bangladeshi families.

In the early stages of the pandemic, medics explained the harmful impact of 'viral load' resulting from repeated exposure to the COVID-19 virus. Here, we use the idea of 'emotional viral load' (Maddrell, 2020), that is, repeated exposure to stress, grief and loss, which has a cumulative effect. The idea of emotional viral load is coupled with evidence of multilayered inequalities to reflect on the nature of loss for those in very different 'boats' in the storm of the early pandemic. The chapter is divided into two sections: we first look at the experiences of funeral service providers, and then turn to those of the British-Bangladeshi community.

The emotional toll on funeral service providers

In spring 2020, it became clear how important 'key' or 'essential' workers are to our societies, yet key workers in cemeteries, crematoria and the wider funerary sector seemed to be less visible than staff in health, care and service industries. Funeral directors and cemetery-crematoria staff were at the forefront of dealing with the death toll of the virus; they were also at heightened risk of infection themselves through delivery of direct services for the living and the dead. Having to work within strict public health restrictions, many reported they were unable to deliver what they considered to be a 'good' or 'proper' service for the deceased and their families. At times this caused them personal and professional anguish, as evidenced in this section, which explores the experiences of people in the funerary services in Dundee, Scotland, including staff from the City Council's burial service, such as cemetery supervisors and workers, as well as funeral directors, Christian ministers and Muslim imams who delivered burial services during the pandemic, and staff and volunteers from the private Dundee Muslim Cemetery Trust.

In common with other local authorities, in Dundee, the municipal burial service rapidly trained new staff in order to ensure continued service if regular cemetery staff were ill or there was a very high death rate. Numerous council staff from other departments – leisure attendants, gardeners, street cleansing staff – volunteered to be seconded to work in the cemeteries and to take on this challenging job. Funeral sector staff reported extremely high workloads for funeral directors and the crematorium during 2020, with the crematorium running funeral services during evenings and on Saturdays for a period. In the cemeteries, staff prepared graves in readiness, in case of overwhelming need. Pre-digging and temporary backfilling allowed graves to be made ready quickly when needed. Cemetery staff were very aware of how the preparation of a row of empty graves would have appeared foreboding to cemetery visitors. It had an emotional impact on staff, too, with one experienced cemetery supervisor describing it as feeling 'morbid' to see a large number of pre-prepared graves in the context of the pandemic.

One funeral director explained they were overseeing a lot of unattended or 'direct' funerals at this time, because families were not allowed to travel to attend. Direct funerals take place without mourners present, are the cheapest form of funeral, and have been gradually increasing in number in the UK in the years preceding the pandemic. However, a funeral director explained that they took place during the first wave of the pandemic due to the lockdown restrictions: 'they [the family] were perhaps abroad or they were isolating themselves or were a vulnerable group that couldn't move, and we were arranging funerals whereby we had to carry out an unattended service, collect the ashes, and then they would have their gathering later on'. In the face of the pandemic restrictions, cemeteries, crematoria and funerary service staff tried hard to deliver dignified funerals, but many of these professionals found it emotionally challenging when the services they were able to provide fell short of what was culturally defined as a 'good' funeral. As with health workers dealing with death during the pandemic, many funeral sector professionals were overstretched, physically and emotionally exhausted; that is to say, they suffered from an emotional viral load.

Funeral rituals were greatly restricted at this time, and the short graveside rituals attended by a small number of mourners created a different atmosphere at funerals. One cemetery supervisor explained how these funerals felt more 'intense'; with so few mourners present, they found the emotions of the mourners to be heightened. They also described the affect social distancing regulations had on their interactions with mourners:

> 'I think with the funerals, you don't realise how much you comfort people until you can't. And I didn't realise before that you'd maybe just go and put your hand on someone's arm or something and say "Take care, I hope you're okay". I think sometimes emotionally it's got me more than it would … we had one [deceased] woman who was 99 just turning 100 and the only one there was her daughter. And the priest was there and he got upset because he wanted to cuddle the daughter and she got upset and I just thought "oh God", I just wanted to cuddle her.'

In general, faith communities, which require prompt burial or cremation (such as Muslims, Jews and Hindus), have had to negotiate with local authorities over many years to reduce the normal time frames of administrative processes such as the registration of death. The importance of timely funerals cannot be overstated, as an imam explained: 'it's one of the last rites that you give to the deceased, and it feels a very very important rite'. Dameer,[1] a representative of Dundee Muslim Cemetery Trust, shared how this impacts on the mourning family: 'One is always in tension until their loved one is buried. So the longer it is, I think it adds more pressure to the family.' During the pandemic, funerals were particularly challenging for minority faith communities. For many faiths, deathbed rituals, the treatment of the deceased and funerary rites are important for the eternal wellbeing of the deceased. It is only when the dead 'rest in peace' that their mourners can also be at peace; meaning that for many, the wellbeing of the living is closely tied to the welfare of the dead (Maddrell et al, 2021).

In Islam, funerary rites demonstrate respect for the dead as well as showcase shared values and beliefs at the community level (Ansari, 2007). Muslim funeral rituals, including those adhered to by British–Bangladeshi Muslims, include washing the body (*ghusl*), shrouding the body in white clothes, prompt burial and funeral prayers (*janazah*) in the presence of a congregation. In some parts of the UK during the first lockdown, some Islamic end-of-life and funeral rituals were not performed because of the contagious nature of the virus. Clergy and families were not able to visit, and there were periods of time when it was not possible to perform *ghusl*, with some substituting this ritual for *tayammum* (that is, dry washing of the deceased body using a purified stone) due to insufficient PPE and a shortage of trained staff or volunteers (Maravia, 2020).

In Dundee, the City Council and the Muslim community have been collaborating for years to meet the religious requirement for prompt burial, but these arrangements were challenged by COVID-19 pressures. The Muslim communities in Dundee have established a private Muslim cemetery in order to ensure best Islamic practice for burials. Dameer explained that the council opened up several graves ('lairs') in the Muslim cemetery, as in other local cemeteries, in readiness for potential need: 'Dundee City Council have, as a partnership with ourselves, they've been very good, they've been proactive in making sure that they had plenty lairs [graves] open because they understand the Muslim community have to get the burial done within 24 hours.' He went on to say that the community also felt supported by the city's registrars when trying to get same-day death certificates in the early pandemic; when all appointments were booked up due to working restrictions and the high death rate, the registrars worked through their lunch breaks in order to release death certificates promptly for Muslim families: 'they were going out of their way to certainly help whichever way they can to make sure things are performed on time, which we are extremely grateful for'.

Despite these positive experiences of collaboration to overcome challenges presented by the pandemic, public health restrictions on funerals still had a strong impact on required rituals during 2020–21. Dameer explained again: 'it's impacted the Muslim community itself quite a bit. Because, it's affected all communities obviously, but our rituals and our way of doing things have changed *completely*.' As with other places of worship, the city's mosques were closed during early lockdown restrictions, so the usual community funeral prayers at the mosque were not possible. The number of mourners at the Muslim cemetery was limited to very close family, whereas the norm would be for a large community turn-out, and practices such as communal backfilling of graves was reduced to the few mourners in attendance throwing a handful of soil into the grave, and the rest filled by machinery.

The Muslim cemetery is supported by numerous volunteers who serve the community on occasions such as funerals. Aarif, a volunteer who backfills graves at Muslim funerals, estimated he had attended over 90 per cent of funerals in the Dundee Muslim community over the last decade. He explained how he understood the need for the regulations but felt excluded from his community participation and support role nonetheless:

> 'I went to a funeral and I got a phone call saying I
> shouldn't have been there. But I was paying my respects
> because I knew this gentleman from a young age and
> he had been a part of my life in the mosque. So I just
> went for a mark of respect but then I got told by the
> Council they're not happy and I accept that and there's
> been a couple more deaths there where I've known

them very well, and I've not participated just to respect what rules have been set out.'

Aarif added that mourning families were also impacted by these regulations, but took comfort from the burial:

'I know the families will be understanding, but the thing is it'll be 10 people from a family at the funeral and they have to pick who was the closest and they go. And they maybe get to throw in a couple of handfuls of mud and the digger's doing the rest, where before they would probably backfill the grave with the volunteers. So in that way it'll maybe affect them to bury their loved one. But they'll know they've been buried properly as well, and safely. And they can go back and tell their loved ones that it went well.'

Pandemic restrictions also impacted on families and community volunteers who perform the ritual washing of the body, or *ghusl*. In the uncertainties of the first lockdown, some bereaved families in London we spoke to were so anxious that they wanted to hide knowledge of COVID-19 as cause of death for fear of stigmatisation and of the deceased being denied *ghusl* and proper shrouding according to Islamic tradition. In Dundee, the Muslim community across several mosques decided just one mosque would provide the space to perform this important ritual for all the local Muslim deceased at the time. Under normal circumstances, *ghusl* would be performed by several imams and volunteers at a mosque, along with family members, with women washing female bodies and men washing male bodies. Due to health risks and social distancing regulations, *ghusl* practices were greatly adapted, limited to four people wearing full PPE, which presented physical, emotional and spiritual challenges. An imam from this mosque explained the practical challenge of moving bodies during *ghusl* with so few people:

'[W]e decided to try not to move the body and just where we wash the body we dry that place and put the white sheets of cloth that we cover the body with, we

just put it on that table so we try as much as possible
to reduce the amount of moving the body around.'

Furthermore, health risks, especially when dealing with those
who had died as a result of COVID-19, meant that the age
and health of *ghusl* volunteers, who were typically elders in the
community, had to be considered. Aarif explained the necessity
of recruiting new younger *ghusl* volunteers, a process replicated
across the country:

'In some cases if family members are [aged over] 50
and they have underlying health issues, they were
not allowed to perform the ritual with their loved
ones. We had to have some volunteers or even other
family members come in to do it. So as a result it
has upset some families, but they understand the
circumstances as to why it's happened. We're having
to make sure the under-45s are trained up to do these
things and I think that's really the issue at the moment
that we have.'

The imam added that performing *ghusl* for the first time could be
daunting, especially for close mourners, and this was made more
challenging in the context of the pandemic:

'[S]o we have one or two family members that join, so
for them it's an unusual experience for them anyway,
doing it. And then having to do it under PPE. So in
a way you feel a bit more like a daunting experience
than the usual process of the washing.'

Performing *ghusl* during the pandemic not only meant a potential
risk to physical health; it also presented additional emotional
challenges for new young volunteers. The imam was sensitive to
potential overload and explained, '[we] try to rotate the volunteers
as much as we can so that everyone don't feel too overwhelmed'.
We now turn to the emotional toll on members of the British-
Bangladeshi community bereaved as a result of COVID-19 in the
first phase of the pandemic in 2020.

The emotional toll on British-Bangladeshi families and communities

Analysis from the UK Office for National Statistics (ONS) showed that during the first wave of the pandemic (24 January 2020 to 11 September 2020), people from all minority ethnic groups had higher rates of death involving coronavirus compared with the white-British population (ONS, 2021c). More specifically, this data showed that British-Bangladeshi males and females were three times and nearly two times at greater risk of death respectively when compared with the white-British group during that time frame. British-Bangladeshis are one of the most socioeconomically disadvantaged communities in the UK (Barnard and Turner, 2011), and Public Health England's (2020a) analysis of the pandemic highlighted that longstanding ethnic inequalities associated with housing, occupational risk and low socioeconomic status increased the vulnerability of British-Bangladeshi people to COVID-19.

Overcrowding and intergenerational households are common in British-Bangladeshi communities, where men are often the sole earner and work in sectors that were 'shut down' during lockdown (for example, restaurant work, taxi driving), resulting in high levels of financial insecurity (Platt and Warwick, 2020). These combined conditions led to higher mortality rates due to COVID-19 within this community (Islam and Netto, 2020).

We now turn to accounts from the mourners of six men of Bangladeshi heritage who died during the UK's period of strict lockdown, March–June 2020, focusing on their experience of bereavement in relation to their religious and customary end-of-life and burial rituals.

For Muslims, including British-Bangladeshi Muslims, the ability to perform spiritual end-of-life and burial rituals are part of what constitutes a 'good' or 'bad' death. These rituals typically include listening to holy Quranic verses and reciting the *kalema* to reduce the pain of death (Maravia, 2020; Yarrington, 2010), the ritual washing and wrapping of the corpse, prompt burial and communal funerary prayers. When someone dies alone, family members and kin can develop feelings of guilt and discomfort 'for not being there' to support the dying person (Baldassar, 2014;

Bravo, 2017), and the people we spoke to reflected on the pain of unexpectedly losing loved ones who died separated from family and without spiritual end-of-life support.

Because of the highly contagious nature of the virus, across the UK family and clergy were barred from visiting those dying in hospitals and care homes during the first phase of the pandemic. Mariam, a woman in her late thirties, shared how her husband had been infected by COVID-19 while in intensive care, recovering from a routine treatment, in spring 2020, and died without family present and spiritual support. Her grief at her husband's untimely death was further exacerbated by the fact that he died while being separated from herself and children and without listening to the Quranic verses in his dying moments. Her emotional load was immense as she dealt with her husband's premature and unexpected death, while supporting their four children in this crisis. She added:

> 'Once [a few days before his death] my husband called me from the hospital and asked for his mobile and other necessary things. When I started my journey to the hospital to give him those things, my children started to cry. They hugged me tightly while my elder child cried out loud saying they did not want me to visit hospital as they did not want to lose me to coronavirus. On that day, I rushed to the hospital leaving my children at home with a hope to see my husband, but the hospital did not allow me to visit his ward, I left the mobile for him with a hope that he would call me, but he never called me again.'

During these stringent restrictions, hospital and care home staff facilitated final family conversations via phone or video conference call when they were able to do so, but not everyone was fortunate enough to have this opportunity to say goodbye. End-of-life spiritual support was made possible due to amended regulations towards the end of the first wave of the pandemic, which allowed clergy to have access to the dying, and some families were able to say their goodbyes and to perform and observe end-of-life rituals using digital platforms. But feelings of sadness and guilt that traditional familial embodied interactions and rituals were not possible persisted for many nonetheless.

As mentioned earlier, it has long been a challenge in the UK to meet the Muslim need for a rapid burial due to slower administrative norms and the impact of longstanding budget cuts on the responsible local government services (Gardner, 2002; Beebeejaun et al, 2021; Maddrell et al, 2021). In contrast to the supportive experience of registrars in Dundee, mourners we spoke to in London and Edinburgh experienced delayed release of death certificates due to pandemic pressures, which was a barrier to prompt burial. This was compounded during the early stages of the pandemic when local government offices in London and Edinburgh reduced their hours of service. Mariam's bereavement experience was aggravated by the delays of her husband's burial because of the slow process of death registration following her husband's death in hospital. Mariam could not visit the Registry Office because of the lockdown, and had to use an online service to obtain the death and burial certificates. She had support from her community to do so, but had to wait two to three days for each email reply, and had to attend a virtual interview with the Registry Office to obtain the certificate for burial. Because of these delays, the Islamic ideal of quick burial was not possible.

The British-Bangladeshi community suffered significant loss of income during the first lockdown, and this put financial strain on low-income families having to organise and pay for funerals during the pandemic. Dhyia, a gentleman in his late forties who lives in Edinburgh, reported that his late friend who died during the pandemic had sent most of his earnings to Bangladesh to support his family there, and so did not have any savings that could be used for his funeral expenses. While it is possible to apply for a government funeral allowance, this delays burial as the funding requires authorisation from the local authority. Dhyia further described the barriers and community response:

> 'The coffin costs £700, funeral is expensive. Government reimburses £1,000 to contribute to the funeral cost for the people who receive benefit. But the people who don't receive benefit, they have to arrange their funeral cost. My friend who died during

the lockdown was not a benefit recipient as he was a chef in a restaurant. He did not have any family here and so his Bangladeshi friends in Edinburgh paid the [funeral] expense.'

During the first lockdown, all places of worship were closed and attendance at funerals restricted, although those restrictions varied by nation within the UK. In Scotland, numbers of attendees and other restrictions at funerals were determined by funeral directors, cemeteries, local authorities and clergy interpreting the guidelines. Men we spoke to in Edinburgh and London expressed feelings of guilt and pain when the *janazah* (communal funeral prayers) for the deceased were attended by just a few people. In Edinburgh, Dhyia reported that during 2020–21 the Scottish Muslim Funeral Services (the only Muslim funeral director in Edinburgh) arranged the funeral prayers in the cemetery and allowed up to 16 people to attend, adhering to social distancing rules (see Figure 9.1).

Some mourners, who could not attend the funerals in person due to lockdown restrictions, attended the funerals virtually,

Figure 9.1: *Janazah* prayer and burial in Edinburgh for a COVID-19 death

Source: Photograph taken by Dhyia (pseudonym), April 2020, with permission granted for its reproduction here

although such provision was also dependent on funeral director approval. Dhyia also personally facilitated the virtual attendance of immediate family members of a deceased Bangladeshi man through a video conferencing call to Bangladesh. He recounted the added distress to the deceased's wife and daughters who could not even see his face properly for the last time because his face was necessarily covered by a surgical mask.

Constrained by lockdown restrictions, use of online communication tools by British-Bangladeshi community members went some way to providing bereavement support to the affected families, both locally and transnationally. However, despite socially distanced and digital community support, British-Bangladeshi families reported a sense of guilt for not being able to offer usual face-to-face bereavement support, which impacted on their sense of community, but also acknowledged the catch-22 situation restrictions presented. Alam, in his early forties in London, recalled that his neighbour, who had died from COVID-19, had been a social person who used to host gatherings for friends and family. When he died, Alam and others could only support his bereaved family from a distance, leaving food on the doorstep but without visiting to offer condolences face to face. Alam was accepting of the necessity of restrictions, but felt their impact.

Conclusion

The COVID-19 pandemic resulted in health risks, illness, death and bereavement, as well as wide-ranging restrictions on travel and social interactions, which, in turn, impacted on support for the dying and bereaved, and limitations on funerals, cemeteries and crematoria. While these impacts were widely felt, representations of the whole population 'in same boat' was rendered hollow by the disproportionate impact the virus had (and continues to have) on certain ethnic, gender, health and age groups. As evidenced by funerary sector workers and volunteers and by the bereaved British-Bangladeshi families who shared their experiences with us, many suffered from multiple and repeated stresses and losses, causing them to experience and carry a heavy emotional viral load, which may have implications for their longer term wellbeing.

Professionals described the emotional toll of their work during this time, and their frustration and sadness, as well as acceptance, at having to deliver services that lacked dignity for the dead and comfort for the bereaved that they strive for in their work. British–Bangladeshi mourners described deep and multifaceted grief as a result of unexpected death, public health restrictions on visiting the dying and attending funerals during the pandemic. For families, loved ones' deaths without normal emotional and spiritual rituals were experienced as a 'bad death', leaving feelings of guilt in the minds of their kin and community. Locally, professionals, community volunteers and networks collaborated, often creatively and successfully, to mitigate these impacts on the bereaved. Nonetheless, the experiences of both bereaved families and funeral sector staff discussed in this chapter highlight the need for public health restrictions to be sensitive to varied faith needs, and the long-term emotional and spiritual harm done when the bereaved cannot be with their loved ones and perform religious and informal last rites. It also underscores uneven access to municipal bereavement services, the emotional drain of slow administrative processes such as the registration of a death, and the particular spiritual toll this has on those of minority faith requiring prompt burial or cremation for their loved ones.

Note

1 This and other names are pseudonyms.

PART IV

Commemorating lives lost

PHOTO STORY

Led By Donkeys

London, England – APRIL 20: The Archbishop of Canterbury Justin Welby, Rabbi Daniel Epstein and Imam Kareem Farai visit the National Covid Memorial Wall on April 20, 2021, in London, England. Bereaved families created a vast COVID-19 Memorial Wall, on the Embankment opposite the Houses of Parliament in Westminster, London. Painting 150,000 individual red hearts for each of the lives lost to the virus in the UK, the group hopes to put personal stories at the heart of the government's approach to learn lessons from the pandemic. The project was started without permission and the bereaved families group are now campaigning to make it a permanent site of remembrance.

Photographs by Chris J. Ratcliffe for Covid-19 Bereaved Families for Justice/Getty Images

10

Walking the wall: COVID-19 and the politics of memory

Mark Honigsbaum

On 29 March 2021, Matt Fowler, a Jaguar Land Rover engineer from Nuneaton, travelled to Westminster to draw a red heart on a pale stone wall directly opposite the Houses of Parliament. Inside the heart, Matt wrote his father's initials 'IF', before drawing another heart, followed by another.

Matt was not the only person crouched beside the wall on the Albert Embankment that morning. If you'd been standing on Westminster Bridge looking towards Lambeth Pier, you would have seen five groups of individuals, each comprising six people, spaced two metres apart, as per the government's then lockdown regulations, drawing red hearts on the Portland stone wall. Wearing hi-vis jackets emblazoned with the words 'National Covid Memorial Wall' in order to deflect the authorities' suspicion, they appeared to be on official business. In fact, they were members of the grass-roots activist group, Covid-19 Bereaved Families for Justice, and were engaged in an audacious act of guerrilla memorialisation.

Within days, Matt and his associates had drawn 150,000 hearts – one for every British victim who, by March 2021, had died with COVID-19 on their death certificate – and by the end of April the Albert Embankment had become a site of pilgrimage for bereaved families from across the UK and a symbol of the public's growing discontent with the government's handling of the coronavirus pandemic.

According to Matt, shaming the government had not been his intention when he dedicated the first heart to his father, Ian, also a Land Rover engineer, who had been hospitalised in April 2020 during the first national lockdown. 'The idea wasn't to cast aspersions or try to get recompense', Matt told me when I interviewed him for my podcast a few weeks after the unauthorised action. 'It was to try to save as many lives going forward as possible, not just in this pandemic but in any sort of future pandemic as well' (quoted in Honigsbaum, 2021a).

If that was the intention, however, it was not how others saw it. Viewed from the opposite bank of the Thames, the hearts resemble what one writer described as a 'dirty, bloody smudge' (Knight, 2021) and another as 'a reproachful smear of blood' (Wynne Jones, 2022). The power of the memorial comes from its juxtaposition with Parliament. As Fran Hall, of Friends of the Wall, a group of volunteers who visit the wall every week to retouch the hearts, told me: 'The political nature of the wall lies in its position, not in individual statements written on it.' Indeed, Friends of the Wall removes graffiti and inscriptions it considers inappropriately political. 'The ethos is that each heart represents one person and that person's family and friends' grief', Hall explained.[1]

Nevertheless, the memorial, which at time of writing had not been recognised by the government, is as much a symbol of Covid-19 Bereaved Families for Justice's demands for an independent, judge-led public inquiry into the pandemic as a place of mourning. To add to the pressure on the government, whenever new stories emerge about alleged breaches of the lockdown restrictions involving former Prime Minister Boris Johnson and Downing Street officials, you will find reporters lining up to film pieces-to-camera on the Albert Embankment. Little wonder that by the wall's anniversary in March 2022, Johnson had not accepted Covid-19 Bereaved Families for Justice's formal invitation to visit the memorial.

I first heard about the National Covid Memorial Wall when a colleague forwarded me a link to Covid-19 Bereaved Families for Justice's Facebook page in April 2021. At the top of the page was a video of the Archbishop of Canterbury Justin Welby walking the wall accompanied by Rabbi Daniel Epstein, of the

Western Marble Arch Synagogue, and Kazeem Fatai, Imam of the Old Kent Road Mosque. Wearing a clerical shirt and a blue face mask, Welby appeared visibly moved. Addressing the camera, Welby said:

> 'I was unprepared for the visual force of this wall. Because it's high it feels like a wave of grief and sorrow breaking over us. To talk about feeling inspired … it's much more than that. It's awe at the commitment and love that this wall represents, as well as the sorrow.'

Welby concluded his remarks by urging people to 'listen to what the hearts are saying to you, reach out with your heart to those who are represented … walk the wall' (Covid-19 Bereaved Families for Justice, 2021a).

In the days and weeks that followed, Welby's video racked up 13,000 views, prompting others to follow in his footsteps. Nazir Afzal, former chief crown prosecutor for north west England, whose brother, Umar, had died of COVID-19 two weeks after the first national lockdown, was one of the first to respond to Welby's call and, soon after, London's Mayor Sadiq Khan and Keir Starmer, leader of the Labour Party, visited the wall (BBC News, 2020a). Florence Eshalomi, MP for Lambeth, also paid her respects, as did the leader of Lambeth Council, which, together with St Thomas' Hospital, is responsible for the wall's upkeep and has the final say over whether the hearts should stay or be removed.

By now, journalists from all over the world were also descending on the Albert Embankment to interview visiting dignitaries and members of the bereaved. 'A million or more people grieving … that's a wartime number', Welby told a journalist from *The Guardian*. 'One of the things people want to know when something goes wrong is that something has been learned from it and mistakes won't be repeated' (quoted in Booth, 2021).

Watching Welby's video and the interviews with the bereaved afterwards, I felt as if I was witnessing a new kind of secular ritual, one with the power to reshape the politics of memory around infectious disease and establish a new template for the memorialisation of pandemics. Welby's reference to war could not help but recall the martial metaphors employed by Johnson in his attempt paint the Conservatives as a 'wartime government' engaged in a deadly battle with a microscopic 'invader' (Irving, 2020). By inviting comparisons with the Second World War and the Blitz spirit, Johnson sought to underline the need for collective sacrifice and compliance with the rules in order to protect the NHS from collapse. But in the weeks and months that followed, as the government was wracked by a series of disclosures about Johnson's alleged flouting of the coronavirus restrictions and the Metropolitan Police (the Met) launched a formal investigation into the 'Partygate' affair, this rhetoric began to ring hollow, and the hearts became a potent symbol of the bereaved's displeasure at the apparent failure of politicians and government officials to observe the rules they had made.[2]

The bereaved's outrage reached a crescendo on 29 March 2022 when, on the anniversary of the first heart going up, some 200 members of Covid-19 Bereaved Families for Justice marched from the Albert Embankment to Downing Street to present Johnson with a 106,000-strong petition calling for the National Covid Memorial Wall to be made permanent. With ironic timing, the petition's delivery coincided with the Met issuing fines to 20 people found to be in breach of lockdown regulations for attending 'social gatherings' at Downing Street. Although the Met declined to disclose the names of the miscreants, the significance of the moment was not lost on Covid-19 Bereaved Families for Justice. 'It's crystal clear now that whilst the British Public [sic] rose to the challenge of making enormous sacrifices to protect their loved ones and their communities, those at 10 Downing Street failed', read a post on the group's official Twitter feed moments after the Met announcement. 'Frankly, bereaved families have seen enough. The PM should have resigned months ago over this' (Covid-19 Bereaved Families for Justice, 2021b).

A post on the Twitter handle of the National Covid Memorial Wall was similarly scathing: 'Those who lost loved ones, often being denied the opportunity to hold the hand of a dying relative for one last time or even to attend the funeral, have not forgotten or forgiven' (National Covid Memorial Wall, 2021).

The shifting politics of memorialisation

According to the art critic Arthur Danto, 'We erect monuments so that we shall always remember and build memorials so that we shall never forget' (1985: 152). Danto was writing about the Vietnam Veterans Memorial, which names all 58,000 US service personnel who died or went missing in the conflict. By contrast, the Cenotaph in Whitehall, Britain's memorial to the 'fallen' of the First World War and other military conflicts, makes no reference to individuals who perished in the fighting. Instead, it is dedicated to all the anonymous 'glorious dead'. Although memorials to wars and other controversial episodes in history have long been sites for fierce ideological struggles, such struggles have intensified in recent decades.[3] For instance, it took a decade to select and construct Reflecting Absence, the memorial to the 9/11 terrorist attacks on the World Trade Center in Manhattan in the USA. More recently, the Black Lives Matter (BLM) protests have revealed the way that past commemorative choices, such as statues celebrating the lives of colonial figures whose wealth derived from the slave trade, have contributed to a limited understanding of history and the persistence of racism and social inequalities in the present. An example is the toppling of the statue of Edward Colston, the transatlantic slave trader, by anti-racism protestors in Bristol in June 2020.

These past struggles remind us that grief, loss and remembrance are both personal and political processes. As Alexandra Barahona de Brito, Carmen González-Enríquez and Paloma Aguilar (2001: 33) have argued, memory is central to narratives of the past and the construction of imagined futures. 'Memory is a struggle over power', they write. 'What and how societies choose to remember and forget largely determines their future options.' The struggles often revolve around the meaning of the event being memorialised. In turn, these meanings determine whose memories are accorded prominence and in what form.

This politics of memorialisation is most evident in state-sponsored truth commissions and public inquiries into civilian disasters, such as the 1989 Hillsborough Stadium disaster and the fire that consumed Grenfell Tower in 2017, but it also encompasses unofficial social initiatives and efforts to rework the past in wider cultural arenas (Easthope, 2022b). This is hardly surprising given the way that memory is central to the formation of identities and vice versa. According to John Gillis, memories help us make sense of the world and are constantly being revisited and reworked in accordance with our ideas about ourselves and our place in society. In this sense, 'memory work', like other kinds of mental and emotional labour, is 'embedded in complex class, gender and power relations that determine what is remembered (or forgotten), by whom, and for what end' (Gillis, 1994: 3). As Judith Butler observes, such memory work is particularly important in situations involving mass death and where public expressions of loss and mourning have been curtailed, as was the case during the recurrent coronavirus lockdowns. On such occasions, according to Butler, private ceremonies or online acts of remembrance are insufficient as they 'cannot assuage the cry that wants the world to bear witness to the loss' (Butler and Yancy, 2020).

Like wars, pandemics occur with regularity throughout history. But while wars are able to draw on a stock repertoire of symbols and rituals, the same is not true of pandemics. For example, despite killing more than 50 million people globally, there were no contemporary memorials to victims of the 1918–19 'Spanish influenza' pandemic anywhere in Europe or North America (Honigsbaum, 2009; Beiner, 2022b). Nor, with one or two notable exceptions, have those who perished in the flu pandemic been commemorated since.[4] Memorials to the 14th-century Black Death and the outbreaks of plague and cholera that swept Europe in the 17th, 18th and 19th centuries are similarly rare.

An exception is HIV/AIDs, which, because of its stigmatisation in the 1980s as the 'gay plague', rapidly became the site for political consciousness-raising around lesbian and gay rights. Through patient-activist groups such as ACT UP (AIDS Coalition to Unleash Power) and Stonewall, memories of AIDS victims were instrumentalised in an effort to shame politicians and demand access to potentially life-saving medication (Epstein, 2016; France, 2016). Perhaps the best example is the US National AIDS Memorial Quilt (National AIDS Memorial, 2022). The first section of the quilt, comprising the names of 1,920 US AIDS victims, was displayed on the Mall in Washington, DC in 1987 during a march on the US capital in support of LGBT rights. Today it comprises 50,000 panels and weighs 54 tons, making it the largest piece of community folk art in the world and the weightiest memorial to any pandemic in history. However, like its smaller British version, the quilt is now in need of repair and is no longer on public display.

Why pandemics are not better commemorated in the public sphere is unclear but appears to be connected to the fact that they are natural events largely outside human agency and control. Despite politicians' frequent recourse to military metaphors and attempts to compare pandemics to wars, it is not easy to visualise a microscopic virus as the 'enemy'. And nor do pandemics lend themselves to compelling moral narratives, with clear heroes and villains. And when, as in the case of the 1918–19 influenza pandemic, the virus competes for the public's attention with a *real* war, the challenge is all the greater. This is one reason why few people, including historians, were struck by the significance of the 'Spanish influenza' at the time. Overshadowed by the First World War, individual experiences and memories of the pandemic failed to penetrate the public sphere, leading to what Guy Beiner has termed 'social forgetting' (Beiner, 2018: 17–30).

Another consideration is that, in contrast to military conflicts, where victims are able to draw on a familiar suite of rituals and heroic templates, pandemics suffer from what Astrid Erll (2009: 111) calls a lack of 'pre-mediation', whereby 'existent media which circulate in a given society provide schemata for new experience and its representation'. Without such mediation, collective memory struggles to find a consistent shape or form, hampering commemoration and the ability to incorporate 'lessons' for the prevention of future pandemic crises into the present. 'Pandemics just have not been sufficiently mediated ... so that they can then turn into a premediating force in the present', notes Erll (2020: 865). Beiner concurs, arguing that in the absence of mediation and a compelling political reason for remembering, the 'Spanish influenza' became 'a *lieu d'oubli* ... indiscernibly lodged between memory and oblivion' (Beiner, 2022a: 27).

By contrast, every second of the coronavirus pandemic has been documented in real time on digital media and distributed via social networks. As Erll (2020: 867) puts it: 'It is the first worldwide digitally witnessed pandemic.' Indeed, long before Matt Fowler and other activists applied red marker pens to the wall on the Albert Embankment, digital images of hearts and other expressions of love and loss were proliferating on Facebook and other online commemoration sites (see, for example, Yellow Hearts to Remember- Covid 19, 2022). Amplified by likes and retweets, these digital *memento mori* enabled those who had recently lost loved ones to COVID-19 to share their experiences of trauma and grief and connect with other members of the COVID-19-bereaved – a process that Andrew Hoskins (2011) has termed 'connective memory'. At the same time, social media, coupled with the unprecedented coverage of the pandemic by broadcast and conventional print media, facilitated social remembrance of the pandemic and the persistence of the bereaved's experiences on a scale that would have been unimaginable in 1918 or, indeed, in the 1980s and 1990s. The result is a new politics of memory, one in which activists, with the support of religious and moral leaders, have been able to instrumentalise the bereaved's grief in order to shame those they consider responsible for their losses and unequal treatment.

Walking and rewalking the wall

To appreciate the wall's impact you have to visit it. On the day I first walked the wall in late April 2021, the weather was cold and damp and, except for the occasional jogger, the embankment was deserted. Although I had seen countless pictures of the wall online, nothing had prepared me for its emotional power. Some of the hearts I saw that day contained a simple word or phrase, such as 'Truth' or 'Life – Love – Loss'. Others, the names of deceased individuals and their relationship to the bereaved: 'mum', 'wife', 'daughter', 'grandmother'. The most ubiquitous phrase was 'Not forgotten' followed by the name of the deceased and their birth and death dates (see Figure 10.1). In some cases, grieving relatives had traced vein-like blue lines from the deceased's heart to others bearing the names of close family members, mapping an intimate network of affection and loss. Among the personal inscriptions, there were also universal messages of bereavement. 'RIP to all of the victims of the virus', read one (see Figure 10.2). 'For all

Figure 10.1: 'Not forgotten'

Photo: Mark Honigsbaum

Figure 10.2: 'RIP to all of the victims of the virus'

Photo: Mark Honigsbaum

my NHS colleagues who lost their lives in the line of duty', read another. There was even a section of the wall dedicated to the Philippines – presumably the work of Filipino health workers – that read: 'Heal Our Land'.

In one spot, sandwiched between the inscriptions to British coronavirus victims, was one that read 'Li Wenliang, Wuhan whistleblower' (see Figure 10.3). This was a reference to the Chinese doctor who had been the first to raise the alarm about the coronavirus only to be sanctioned by the Chinese authorities and to die of COVID-19 at a hospital in Wuhan a few weeks later. Clearly, whoever had left the inscription considered Wenliang a martyr. Nearby someone had also dedicated a heart to Prince Phillip, even though he had died of natural causes on 9 April 2021 and, unlike Wenliang, could not in any way be considered a casualty of the coronavirus.

But perhaps the most surprising inscription I came across that day was to victims of bovine spongiform encephalopathy and variant Creutzfeldt-Jakob disease (BSE/vCJD), better known as 'mad cow disease'. It was not on a heart but on a brass plaque displayed on a section of wall abutting St Thomas' Hospital. The

Figure 10.3: 'Li Wenliang, Wuhan whistleblower'

Photo: Mark Honigsbaum

inscription read: 'In loving memory of the victims of Human BSE (vCJD). Always in our thoughts'. I later discovered the plaque had been erected in the early 2000s by the Human BSE Foundation, an organisation set up by the families of the 177 British victims of vCJD, the brain disease caused by the consumption of beef infected with BSE. In 2016 there had been calls for Lambeth to move the plaque to a more suitable location on the grounds that it 'had been unsympathetically placed' and disrupted the wall's listed façade (London SE1, 2016). But the plaque had remained in its original position, to all intents and purposes forgotten by the public until the hearts brought it new visibility. It struck me as an apt symbol of the way that, without constant reaffirmation in the public sphere, memorials to victims of infectious disease outbreaks are continually at risk of slipping into oblivion.

The initial genesis for the wall came from the grim coronavirus death counts that filled the evening news bulletins during the first year of the pandemic. Updated each day on the UK's COVID-19 dashboard, the statistics normalised the mortality, facilitating avoidance of the mass experience of loss. As Jo Goodman, whose father Stuart was among the first British casualties of the virus, told me when I spoke to her in May 2021: 'It felt like our loved ones were being reduced to numbers on a graph. The idea was to bring home the individualism and the scale [of the tragedy] at the same time.'

Like many of the COVID-19-bereaved, Jo was convinced that her father's death could have been prevented. A retired photographer, Stuart Goodman had been summoned to hospital on 18 March, five days before the first national lockdown, to be informed he had cancer. Fearing he might be at greater risk of contracting COVID-19 in a hospital setting, Jo had begged him to miss the appointment, but Stuart assured her he wouldn't have been invited unless the NHS thought it safe. A week later he developed symptoms of COVID-19, and by 2 April he was dead. He was 72. Afterwards, Jo struggled to shake the suspicion that the government had been too slow in locking down and that her father's life had been considered 'expendable', adding: 'It felt as if losing tens of thousands of lives of people like my father was somehow a price that we as a country should be willing to pay to protect the economy.'

Matt Fowler had been plagued by similar thoughts about his father. Ian, Matt's father, had been admitted to hospital on the first day of the lockdown and died on 13 April. He was just 56. According to Fowler, Ian had been 'the life and soul of every party, including the ones he wasn't invited to; he went from that to simply disappearing.' When Matt came across an article about Jo's father they bonded and decided to set up Covid-19 Bereaved Families for Justice. Initially, they saw it as a bereavement support group, but as more and more of the COVID-19-bereaved contacted them and shared similar stories, they sought a meeting with Boris Johnson in the hope of persuading him to visit the wall and convene a rapid public inquiry. The idea was that if lessons could be learned ahead of the expected second wave of COVID-19 in the autumn of 2020, it might prevent further needless deaths. But Johnson never responded to the invitation, and as Conservative backbenchers and lockdown sceptics in the Tory press urged him to resist calls for a second lockdown, Jo concluded that her father's death, and those of others like him, was being 'brushed under the carpet'.

On 5 November, with coronavirus case numbers spiralling out of control, Johnson was forced to bow to scientific advice and order a second lockdown. But by now Jo and Matt had concluded that they needed to do something more dramatic. Teaming up with Led By Donkeys, a collective of Greenpeace campaigners who had previously beamed anti-Brexit messages on the white cliffs of Dover, in December they projected a short film featuring bereaved relatives onto the Palace of Westminster (Lynskey, 2021). Later, Led By Donkeys helped Covid-19 Bereaved Families for Justice execute the guerrilla action on the Albert Embankment, although their involvement was deliberately kept secret for several months. As Fran Hall explains in Chapter 11, it was 'essential to minimise their role and let bereaved families take ownership ... for the wall to be approved of by the public, it was important not to allow it to be considered a political protest'.[5]

There was nothing inevitable about the hearts – initial suggestions included handprints, candles and shoes. They were primarily meant to symbolise 'an outpouring of love', explained Matt. But to the extent that they recalled the red poppies that had long been a symbol of Armistice Day, they also represented mass loss and the importance of national reflection.

Unlike the annual ceremony at the Cenotaph on Remembrance Sunday, however, the power of the memorial would come not from individuals projecting their emotions onto a blank marble slab in Whitehall but through the individual inscriptions on the wall and what the hearts collectively represented. Nor would the memorial await the inspiration of an architect or the approval of a bureaucrat in Whitehall. As Nathan Oswin, the group's media coordinator, told me: 'This was a memorial chosen by those who had lost loved ones. It wasn't waiting for a civil servant in a very fine suit with a very fine 2B pencil on a very fine bit of paper to sketch a very fine monument. This was people taking action directly.'

The key to the action was surprise. If they could get through the first hour, Matt figured, the memorial would be a fait accompli and it would be hard for the authorities to reverse it. To give their action the appearance of authenticity, Matt and his co-conspirators dressed the wall with two wooden signs bearing the legend, 'National Covid Memorial Wall' and laid bouquets beneath them. From a distance, the signs looked as if they were made of brass and the legend had been embossed in gold leaf.

Had Johnson accepted Covid-19 Bereaved Families for Justice's invitation to visit the wall and inspect their handiwork, it's possible the memorial would not have become as politicised as it has. Instead, Johnson chose to visit the wall under the cover of darkness on 27 April 2021, without informing grieving families beforehand. Johnson's surreptitious visit created the impression he was 'insincere' and was trying to 'dodge' a meeting with bereaved families (Wearmouth, 2021). But the event that more than any other energised Covid-19 Bereaved Families for Justice's campaign and made the politics of the wall apparent was the disclosure by the *Daily Mail* two days earlier that, in October 2020, when advisers had been urging Johnson to bring in stricter restrictions to relieve pressure on the NHS, he'd allegedly said that he'd rather 'let the bodies pile high in their thousands' than institute another lockdown (Walters, 2021). Although denied by Johnson, those comments provoked widespread outrage, particularly from those mourning the recent deaths of loved ones, and soon the hashtag

#BodiesPiledHigh was trending on Twitter alongside pictures of the wall. Significantly, Covid-19 Bereaved Families for Justice also retweeted the *Daily Mail*'s front-page story on its official Twitter handle accompanied by the post: 'Our loved ones should not be treated as collateral damage. No one should ever be treated as a "body". No wonder bereaved families worry about our loved ones being forgotten. Only a judge-led statutory public inquiry will reveal what went wrong' (Covid-19 Bereaved Families for Justice, 2021c).

Since then, hardly a week has gone by without some damaging new disclosure about the conduct of the former prime minister and Downing Street officials. In all, some 16 gatherings were investigated by the Met and civil servant Sue Gray. The timeline of the alleged infractions of the UK's lockdown rules stretches from 15 May 2020, after a photograph emerged of the prime minister and his staff with bottles of wine and a cheeseboard at a 'socially distanced drinks' in the Downing Street garden that day, to December 2020. One of the most egregious breaches occurred on Johnson's birthday on 19 June when his fiancée organised a surprise party for him in the Cabinet Room attended by 30 people. Although Johnson would subsequently claim that the birthday celebrations and cake-cutting had lasted just 10 minutes, the Met issued him with a £50 fixed penalty notice, making him the first prime minister in history to have broken the law while in office. At the time of writing, Johnson was also facing the prospect of further fines, including for an incident on 15 December 2020, when he purportedly hosted a Christmas quiz for No 10 staff.

Nearly every one of the gatherings coincided with the death of someone from COVID-19, making the alleged infractions a constant reminder of the bereaved's losses, and helping to ensure that the story remained in the public eye. Indeed, when in January 2022 ITV News obtained an email from Johnson's Principal Private Secretary Martin Reynolds, inviting Downing Street officials to the 15 May drinks in the garden of No 10 and to 'bring your own booze', it immediately broadcast interviews with members of the bereaved whose loved ones had died the very same day (ITV News, 2022). Other journalists followed suit, concluding their reports in front of the National Covid

Memorial Wall as the camera panned along the hearts to drive home the disconnect between the behaviour of Downing Street officials and the public's observance of the lockdown restrictions. And so it has continued, with every fine issued to Johnson and members of his staff providing the bereaved with a reminder of their losses and the media with an opportunity to draw attention to the double-standards of Britain's governing classes. The result is that rather than the coronavirus pandemic being forgotten, the wall has become a focal point for social remembrance of the pandemic and a place where the bereaved and others moved by their losses and their own experiences of lockdowns gather to reflect and express their collective outrage.

In an effort to understand how the wall had weaponised the bereaved's grief, I visited it again on 6 May 2021. Once again the Albert Embankment was deserted. However, at the midpoint of my perambulation I encountered a woman dressed in black drawing a fresh heart on the wall. Jayne Taylor-Broadbent had travelled from Hull earlier that morning, boarding a London-bound train at 7:20 am. She had been following the wall's progress on Covid-19 Bereaved Families for Justice's Facebook page for some time, but had waited until the anniversary of her partner Julie's death to leave a dedication.

Jayne and Julie had been inseparable since meeting on a train platform in 2011. 'It was love at first sight', she told me. In 2014, following the passage of the Marriage (Same Sex Couples) Act 2013, they became the first lesbian couple in Hull to be married in a church ceremony. But their married life was cut cruelly short when Julie, a former social care worker, was rushed to Hull Royal Infirmary on 4 May 2020 with a burst ulcer. At first, Julie responded to treatment, but on the second day in hospital she developed breathing difficulties and was moved to intensive care. Although Julie repeatedly tested negative for COVID-19, she was too poorly to be put on a ventilator. Instead, the hospital administered free-flowing oxygen. 'She couldn't speak but she could hear me. I sat with her and told her how much I loved her and that I'd always love her. I had to ask her if she was ready to have her mask removed. She was ready.' Within two minutes Julie was dead. She had spent just four days in hospital. Her death came four days short of her 50th birthday.

'I'd read a lot about the wall online', Jayne continued, regaining her composure. 'As soon as people started posting about it, I just knew I had to be here. It's where Julie belongs now and where people will see her, across from there. ...' She paused, pointing at Parliament, before turning back to face the wall. The spot she'd selected for Julie's heart was about a quarter of the way along. 'Thirty thousand people died at time Julie died, so I've tried to find the place on the wall, to map it out slightly.' Then, indicating all the people who had died before and since, she added: 'All these people are like me – they're grieving and they don't have answers.'

Jayne's visit coincided with the furore over Johnson's 'let the bodies pile high' remark, but she would not be drawn on whether she believed the reports, stating: 'If that statement was made, that was disgusting, unnecessary and cruel, not only to the people who have lost their lives but to their family and friends.'

Like Matt Fowler, she insisted that the original motivation for the wall had not been political: 'It wasn't to have a dig at the government. It was to stop all these people down there joining Julie.' However, she acknowledged that as long as questions about the government's management of the pandemic remained unanswered, there could be no closure for the bereaved:

> 'If they'd locked down two weeks earlier, I'm not saying people wouldn't have died – it was a pandemic, like we'd never seen before. But the things we were promised – the track and trace, that would've cut down these deaths – it never materialised. I've got so many questions to ask our Prime Minister. We need a public inquiry.'

After our meeting, I linked to Jayne on Twitter. She rarely posted comments in her own name but regularly reposted comments critical of the government. When in January 2022 Sue Gray's heavily redacted report into the Downing Street gatherings revealed several new events that had not previously been documented, she retweeted Keir Starmer's comment that people who followed COVID-19 rules 'will feel like they've been taken for mugs' (Taylor-Broadbent, 2022a). On 24 February, when Johnson declared 'freedom' from the coronavirus and ended free COVID-19 testing, Jayne reposted a tweet from Covid-19 Bereaved Families for Justice describing Johnson as a 'walking public health hazard' (Covid-19 Bereaved Families for Justice, 2022a; Taylor-Broadbent, 2022b). Come March, with Johnson doubling-down on his denials of rule-breaking and the calls for his resignation intensifying, Jayne could no longer contain her anger. 'How many inquirys [sic] illegal & criminal investigations and assessments does this government need to answer before the penny drops!!!' she tweeted, alongside the hashtags #ToryCorruption and #ToriesOut (Taylor-Broadbent, 2022c). This was followed by a series of posts supporting Covid-19 Bereaved Families for Justice's petition calling for the National Covid Memorial Wall to be made permanent. Soon after, the government announced the long-awaited draft terms of reference for the public inquiry, only for it to be revealed a few days later that the hearings would now not take place before spring 2023. The news prompted further angry retweets from Jayne, including one of a Covid-19 Bereaved Families for Justice post stating that although it welcomed the publication of the draft terms, the announcement had come too late for many of the bereaved: 'We will never know how many lives could have been saved had the Government had a rapid review phase in Summer 2020, as we called for at the time.'

My third and final visit to the wall came on its first-year anniversary. Unlike my previous two visits, the weather was sunny and there was a carnival atmosphere on the Albert Embankment. For weeks, Friends of the Wall had been restoring the hearts with fresh red masonry paint and reinstating the inscriptions. They had also removed the larger hearts and the elaborate, sprawling tributes to the NHS that used to fill the spaces in between. In addition, the Friends had reserved a section of the wall for babies, children and young people under 19. Official-looking signs on the wall made it clear that in future people should confine themselves to one heart, and that the hearts should be 'no larger than an adult hand'. However, policing the wall had become a Sisyphean task, and Fran Hall complained that every time the Friends visited the Albert Embankment they encountered inscriptions they considered 'inappropriate'. Fran also lamented the fact that although they had deliberately left the space around the BSE memorial plaque blank out of respect for those commemorated there, it was now surrounded by hearts. Unfortunately, Friends are a small group, and volunteers only visited the wall once a week for four to five hours: 'We would need to be there all day every day and would probably still find inscriptions that aren't in keeping.'

Nevertheless, to mark the wall's anniversary, Fran and her colleagues had found time to add several thousand new hearts to the Portland stone to reflect the fact that since the original action 34,000 more people had died with COVID-19 on their death certificates. They had also begun applying lacquer to protect the hearts from further decay. 'There are people who would like to see the hearts fade', Fran explained. 'We're not going to let that happen.'

Conclusion

Since the inception of the coronavirus pandemic, the government has sought to present it as a crisis comparable to war, one in which deaths are inevitable. 'We will get through this together', Johnson insisted, invoking the Blitz spirit as, day by day, the death toll mounted (Johnson, 2020a). This rhetoric was reinforced by the Downing Street press conferences where, flanked by his scientific advisers, Johnson would describe the measures being taken to curb infections and the progress of the vaccine roll-out. The result was that Britons, for the most part, were happy to give the prime minister the benefit of the doubt and go along with the lockdown restrictions. But this strategy began to unravel when Johnson relaxed the measures in March 2021, allowing bereaved people from different households to meet face to face for the first time in several months. Hearing about the National Covid Memorial Wall, many of them were drawn to the Albert Embankment to leave an inscription on one of the hearts. Those hearts gave a human face to the statistics and provided a focus for the grief of people like Jayne Taylor-Broadbent. The wall also provided the bereaved with a place where they could mourn and honour their loved ones, making it a site of pilgrimage. However, the true power of the hearts came from their placement on a stretch of Portland stone directly opposite Parliament and the implicit rebuke to the politicians opposite.

By refusing to visit the Albert Embankment in daylight, Johnson gave the impression he had something to hide, a suspicion that only grew with the Partygate revelations and his reluctance to name a date for a public inquiry. The result is that the wall was rarely out of the news, and every time the Met issued a new fine, its prominence grew.

However, perhaps the most remarkable aspect of the wall is that it is a work in progress. Unlike the Vietnam Veterans Memorial, new names are continually being added to it. And although many hearts and inscriptions have been erased or painted over, their traces persist just beneath the surface, making the wall a palimpsest and metaphor for ongoing social processes of remembering and forgetting. At the time of writing, no one can say if and when the National Covid Memorial Wall will become a permanent fixture on the Albert Embankment, but it has already demonstrated that there is no inherent reason why pandemics should not be better remembered.

Notes

[1] Private correspondence, 25 April 2022. I wish to thank all the members of Covid-19 Bereaved Families for Justice for their patience in answering my questions about the National Covid Memorial Wall and the politics of memory. I am especially grateful to Matt Fowler, Jo Goodman, Nathan Oswin and Jayne Bradford-Taylor.

[2] 'Partygate' is the media's name for the scandal over the Downing Street gatherings that are said to have breached the UK government's lockdown regulations.

[3] Rituals, such as the two-minute silence and the ceremony at the Cenotaph, which developed gradually from 1919, are good examples of this. Although these rituals and ceremonies now have a solemn, respectful tone, this was not always the case, and in the past veterans have used Remembrance Day to vent grievances about their postwar treatment (Gregory, 1994: 51–92).

[4] An example is the stained glass window in the Medical Library of the Royal London Hospital in St Augustine with St Phillip's Church in Whitechapel (Honigsbaum, 2017).

[5] Fran Hall makes a similar point in an interview with the memory studies scholar David Tollerton, explaining that when the bereaved visited the wall to honour their loved ones, 'they're not looking at the Houses of Parliament, they're looking at the hearts on the wall' (quoted in Tollerton, 2022: 29).

PANDEMIC EASTER

Herbert Woodward Martin

The cathedral is empty; the tomb is bare from the body
That occupied it from that tragic Friday no one
   envisioned
Emptiness as its own pain, brain wondering about loss
Who is responsible for this disturbance
Breathlessly searches for a lost coin.
Disturbance is aloft.
Who is responsible for vacating this tomb?
How will these mothers rest their eyes in
   contemplation?
What cautions will they take?
What Scribe takes responsibility for writing their story?
Will they remember to place their names and birth
   dates
And any other information relevant to these days?
What shall the late followers take from these days?
What shall we remember about of these convictions?
With what breaths shall we take to survive?

11

A wall of pain and love

Fran Hall

From the terraces of the Palace of Westminster, the view across the Thames to the South Bank has been a familiar one for years. Opposite the Houses of Parliament, the creamy white Portland stone wall between Albert Embankment and St Thomas' Hospital gleamed in the afternoon sun. At night, the wall is illuminated by the ornate Victorian lampposts spaced along its length, and the lights draped in the branches of the trees above. Part of the Albert Embankment Conservation Area, the busy walkway between Lambeth and Westminster Bridges has long been a popular destination for tourists and film crews alike. For decades it has looked the same, thronging with people walking below the wall, going about their business.

Then, in 2020, the virus began to spread in the UK, and the tourists and filmmakers vanished. The parliamentarian drinks parties on the terraces ceased. Local people stayed at home. Traffic disappeared, and the heart of London fell quiet, other than the sirens of ambulances ferrying stricken citizens to hospitals. For a year, as the country went in and out of lockdowns and tier systems, the number of people using the footpath along the Embankment ebbed and flowed, always fewer and more distant from each other than in years gone by. There was a strange, ongoing stillness.

And then, on Monday 29 March 2021, the day that the government-imposed 'stay at home' order was lifted after the third national lockdown, something began to change on Albert Embankment.

As Londoners cautiously emerged into the quiet city again after another three months at home, on the walkway between the two bridges, figures appeared and took up positions along the wall. From a distance, it would have been impossible to see what they were doing, but the few passers-by walking along the York stone footpath that morning saw around 20 people wearing grey tabards and black face coverings, spaced apart and focusing intently on a section of wall. They had red paint pens in their hands, and they were carefully drawing small, vivid hearts on the white stone of the wall.

Sandwich boards had been placed along the length of the Embankment displaying the same message as two large, black signs that had been fixed at eye level on the wall, one at either end. The signs read 'National Covid Memorial Wall', the same message on the tabards worn by the painters and the helpers who staffed a table with boxes of paint pens, branded face masks and piles of spare tabards.

To all intents and purposes, this appeared to be an official venture. Security cameras scan the entire length of the wall, and it is in one of the most heavily policed parts of London. The degree of organisation and professionalism of the activity looked completely authentic. But what was happening was unauthorised. No permission had been sought or given. The people painting on the wall were breaking the law.

Passers-by stopped and watched and took photographs, as the smatterings of red hearts began to spread. Camera crews appeared, and journalists asked for interviews with the people painting. Local opposition MPs responded to invitations that arrived in their inbox and walked across Westminster Bridge to see what was happening. Sir Keir Starmer, leader of the opposition, arrived in the afternoon and spoke to volunteers and endorsed the creation of the wall. More people arrived and joined in with the painting. They worked quietly, two metres apart from each other, along several sections of the half kilometre long wall. At the end of the day, specially commissioned security guards arrived to watch over the wall overnight. The next day, volunteers came back and carried on. And they kept coming, over the Easter weekend and into the following week.

Over the next 10 days, around 1,500 people took part in the biggest – and most audacious – grass-roots, commemorative action ever seen. By 8 April, the entire length of the wall had been covered in more than 150,000 hand-painted red hearts, one for every person in the UK who had died with COVID-19 as a contributing factor confirmed on their death certificate. The previously white stone wall had been transformed; from the Westminster terraces across the river, it now appeared as a blood-red rebuke, a reminder of the catastrophic death toll that the country had suffered.

The volunteers who had helped create the 'National Covid Memorial Wall' had given interviews to media from across the globe; the wall had been featured on all British TV channels and in multiple articles, in print and online. Photos and video footage of the 'wall of hearts' was all over social media. The wall had become established and accepted immediately, cherished even. It spoke to a nation that had been traumatised by the pandemic, a powerful, visual response to a deep, unarticulated need for something – anything – to mark the horror of what we all knew had happened, the sheer awfulness of so many devastating deaths.

The official opening ceremony on 8 April 2021 had been planned to coincide with the numbers of UK deaths from COVID-19 reaching the grim milestone of 150,000. As the Office for National Statistics released the latest exact numbers of deaths, the final few hearts were added. At that moment, there were exactly as many hearts on the wall as the official figure of people dead from the virus. The hearts had been counted by image recognition software as they were added, and the tally was as accurate as could be. The hearts filled all 25 sections of wall, stretching further than the eye can see. The scale of it was – and is – shocking.

On some of the hearts, dedications had begun to appear. Names, dates, heart-breaking messages from sons, daughters, wives and husbands, brothers and sisters and grandchildren of the people who had died. Some people had tucked photos behind the signs or propped them up against the wall, the faces of those beloved dead. Along the wall, bunches of flowers and single roses had been left, laid on the pavement or on the ledge running along each section. Here and there, candles flickered in glass lanterns.

The wall had become a place of pilgrimage for many, many people who had been grieving in isolation. It was a hugely public proclamation of a nation's sorrow, a startling visual representation of the scale of the loss we had endured. It had been created by bereaved people, for bereaved people, and it had become a vessel to hold the rage and grief and tears of millions. It was an anchor for the anger, the injustice, the impotence of a people who feel their government have failed them.

This extraordinary, unique installation, this iconic national legacy had begun with the death of one man, photographer Stuart Goodman, who had contracted COVID-19 most likely when he attended a hospital appointment, against the advice of his daughter.

Stuart Goodman died from COVID-19 on 2 April 2020, his death one of 1,007 recorded on that date, the first day where more than 1,000 people were reported to have lost their lives to the virus in a 24-hour period. Just 10 people were permitted to attend his funeral. His family were left reeling, shocked, bewildered – and angry at losing him, at a death that should not have happened.

Stuart's daughter Jo spoke to a journalist about her rage at the failure of the government to prevent the virus spreading in the UK, the failure that led to her father's death. When the article was published, she was contacted by another bereaved person, Matt Fowler, whose father Ian had died from the virus shortly after Stuart, on 13 April 2020. Ian was 56 years old and had just taken early retirement before he contracted COVID-19. He was admitted to hospital the day the first lockdown was announced and died three weeks later. Like Jo, Matt felt that the government's disastrous decision making had led directly to his father's death. Like Jo, Matt was angry and grieving, and desperate to try and stop others going through the same shattering experience.

Together, Jo and Matt set up a Facebook group, initially as support for others in the same position, but it quickly evolved into a campaign for an immediate public inquiry into the government's handling of the pandemic, calling for a rapid review phase to try and prevent similar mistakes from being made before the inevitable second wave.

Hundreds of bereaved people joined the group, and gradually Covid-19 Bereaved Families for Justice became one of the largest online communities for people grieving for a loved one who had died from the virus. Their calls for an inquiry continued to go unanswered, and their requests for the prime minister to meet with bereaved families were ignored, even though the virus continued to circulate as the summer continued. The government persisted with their strategy of lifting protective measures, allowing hospitality venues to reopen and introducing the 'Eat Out to Help Out' scheme to encourage a nervous public back into pubs and restaurants.

By September 2020, aware that there would inevitably be a second wave of infections and deaths, Jo and Matt realised that they needed to raise the group's profile to try and push the government to respond. The pair put out a call for experienced campaigners to support their campaign. The response came from four friends, Ben Stewart, Will Rose, Oliver ('Olly') Knowles and James Sadri, all seasoned Greenpeace campaigners. In 2018, the quartet had formed Led By Donkeys, a guerrilla activist group known for their anti-Brexit campaigning.

Together, Led By Donkeys and Covid-19 Bereaved Families for Justice created a short film of bereaved people telling their stories of grief, and in November the film was projected onto the Houses of Parliament. The impact was immediate, with the video of the projection circulating on social media, and the two groups began thinking about working together on some sort of memorial that would convey the scale of the death toll. When the number of people dead reached 100,000, in January 2021, and the prime minister said that a permanent memorial would be established 'only when we come out of this crisis', the two groups decided that they would not wait. They talked about various ideas, but the concept of a 'wall of hearts' was the one they agreed on – a simple, achievable and powerful visual statement. They just needed to find the right location for it.

Olly Knowles was the person given the task of finding a suitable wall to use. It didn't take him long – the elegant, 19th-century wall on the western boundary of St Thomas' Hospital was in the perfect location, and it was long enough for the immense number of hearts that needed to be painted.

Led By Donkeys organised the logistics – they funded the costs of 10,000 POSCA art pens[1] and did the calculations about size and numbers. They found the US scientist who could supply the software to count the hearts, and they supplied the tabards, masks and signs. They had learned from previous actions that if you look official, you could get away with all kinds of things.

Once all the plans were in place, the only missing element was the labour. The country was still under orders to stay at home, and the death toll was rising. The groups decided to put the call out for volunteers just before the restrictions were due to lift, with a view to starting painting on the first day the public were allowed out again in groups of up to six people.

During the week before 29 March 2021, a mysterious post appeared in the Covid-19 Bereaved Families for Justice Facebook group, asking if any members would be interested in being involved in a commemorative artistic installation in London. Those who showed interest were invited to a video meeting and sworn to secrecy. It was essential that word didn't leak out before work began.

No mention was made of Led By Donkeys' involvement. They felt it essential to minimise their role and let bereaved families take ownership of the wall. While the prominent location obviously made it an innately political statement, for the wall to be approved of by the public it was important not to allow it to be considered a political protest, but rather, an outpouring of grief and loss. The part that had been played by Led By Donkeys was not revealed for several months until an article appeared in *The Observer* in July 2021 – the bereaved families painting hearts on the wall had no idea of the real identity of the 'helpers' among them.

As part of the video meeting, an artist's impression of how the wall could look was shown, and then swiftly followed by the legal briefing, warning everyone that technically those involved would be committing criminal damage and could be liable to arrest and prosecution. The discussion fell rather quiet at that point, but nobody opted out. Around 30 people in total signed up for the three-hour sessions available, some on the Monday morning, which was identified as the time when the risk of arrest was highest, others for later the following week.

And this is how the wall came into being – the genius and organisational skills of Led By Donkeys combined with the determination of bereaved families. Among the 20 or so people who gathered on the Embankment at 8 am on Monday 29 March 2021 was Matt Fowler, and it was he who painted the first heart on the wall. He inscribed the letters 'IF', in his father Ian's honour.

Over the 10 days of creating the memorial wall, hundreds of bereaved people travelled from all over the country to help, supported by an army of well-wishers who also gave up their time over the Easter holidays. Through rain, hail, snow and unseasonably hot sun, the volunteers doggedly kept going. A community began to grow, people who had been living in isolation with their grief found others who completely understood what bereavement by COVID-19 feels like.

Volunteers went back day after day, drawn by a feeling of being involved with something profoundly important. In some of the interviews given to the media at the time, the volunteers referenced how creating the wall helped channel overwhelming feelings of grief and loss, that doing something purposeful was making a difference. It was as if there was a thawing of the icy loneliness so many had been living with after brutal separations and shattered lives. Tentative friendships blossomed as people worked alongside each other, and a shared determination to complete the wall in honour of those who had died united people who had been strangers a few days previously. A kind of magic was occurring.

Online, people who were unable to get to London supported from afar, some donating to the crowdfunder, others sharing posts and photos. Requests to have the names of loved ones added to the wall began to flow in, and a system was developed so that people received a photo of the heart written for their person, and a note of its location. A few of the volunteers agreed to go back to the wall now and then and add dedications on behalf of others who couldn't get there, and the others said farewell to each other and went back to their lives.

The wall was there to stay. The publicity it had gained for the campaign was extraordinary, and the impact it had had on bereaved people grieving in isolation around the UK was profound. At last, they had a place where they felt connected, where their loved ones' names were proclaimed, where they were no longer alone. 'I've felt like we were the nation's dirty little secret,' said one volunteer, 'nobody wants to think or talk about us, the people who have been bereaved. But now they can't ignore us. We're out in the light.'

Time passed. The wall continued to draw visitors through the spring and summer of 2021, but British weather and POSCA paint proved not to be a good combination. The vibrant red that had made the wall unmissable from Westminster began to fade, and the heart-rending dedications slowly blurred and became harder to read. The impact and power of the wall began to diminish. As the colour of the hearts grew fainter, the pain that had been inscribed in individual dedications gradually started disappearing, absorbed into the stone of the wall.

No doubt many Cabinet ministers secretly welcomed this waning of the intense, accusatory message that the wall silently conveyed. A fading away of the insistent, troubling reminder of the UK's disastrous pandemic handling strategies would have been very convenient for a prime minister who chose not to accept the invitation to visit the wall and meet bereaved families, but instead went under cover of darkness, most likely to be able to say that he had been to the wall if questioned.

Unfortunately for anyone looking forward to the view from the parliamentary terraces returning to its former, unchallenging paleness, the bereaved families had other ideas. In August, a new, small group of committed volunteers was formed with a mission to care for the wall and restore the colour to it. All women, the group met and discussed their thoughts. The wall was no longer the beautiful artistic installation that had been conceived in the beginning. Four months of unsupervised access to it had resulted in graffiti, scrawls by COVID-19 deniers, anti-vaxx slogans, newly painted enormous hearts that dominated whole sections of the wall and dedications that had been written in multiple hearts, defeating the original object of one heart for every life lost. And the whole wall was fading. It would be a Herculean task to restore it.

The first thing to do was to establish the 'Friends of the Wall' group as the accepted custodians of the wall, so the proposals put forward (removing the enormous and multiple hearts and rewriting the dedications in smaller, freshly painted ones, painting over original blank hearts with long-lasting masonry paint, rewriting just legible inscriptions) were put to a vote in the Covid-19 Bereaved Families for Justice group. There was overwhelming support; the few 'don't you dare touch my heart' responses had to be sensitively handled, but the consensus was endorsement of the plans, and gratitude that the wall would be cared for.

So, the group set to work. One of the 'Friends' wrote letters to various companies looking for support or help, and managed to get donations of masonry paint and black sharpie pens; others volunteered to take paint pots and brushes home each week and wash them; one had a husband whose company supplied paintbrushes for the team; one managed to get branded T-shirts, coats – and eventually warm waterproof winter coats – made for everyone; some brought Thermos flasks of coffee and home-made cake; one knitted scarves, another knitted hats and a third crocheted red hearts onto gloves.

By the end of 2021 they were kitted out in 'uniforms' that identified them on their weekly painting sessions, and their commitment to caring for the wall had become an important part of each of their lives. One of them travelled to London from Stoke-on-Trent every Friday, spending hundreds of pounds on train tickets each week. 'I could spend the money on therapy sessions instead', she said, 'But this is better therapy than anything anyone could give me. It's worth every penny.'

For this woman, and for all this second group of volunteers, the weekly time together at the wall was more than just a session of renovating and restoring the wall to its former beauty; it was a time of connection, and reconnection, a time to be with others who shared the churning feelings of rage and blame, who understood the emptiness of facing life alone, of missing someone beyond words. No explanations are needed at the wall. Everyone there understands. And everyone involved shares the same, absolute determination to never let the wall fade away.

'We will never let them forget. They will never be allowed to look away from what they have done', said one of the Friends of the Wall:

This is our wall. Our wall of pain and love. We should never have been placed in this position, of being devastated widows, bereft daughters, lonely sisters. We will keep coming here every week for the rest of our lives, to look after the wall. That's how much it means to us.

Note

1 POSCA art pens are highly durable, water-based, permanent marker paint pens.

PART V

What comes next

GO AHEAD, TELL ME

Rita Coleman

I can take it.
I've been around the sun a few times.
Go ahead, tell me all about the deaths,
tell me how they died without caress
in the slipstream between breath and silence
a video call of last words.
Tell me about everyday fear, suspicions,
a sinuous distrust woven in the blood
and guts of many, of most, of me.
I know about the firebelly of injustice.
I will never again utter the words,
'Nobody ever said it would be fair',
to my grandchildren.

Go ahead, tell me one more time
that we're all in this together when we shrink
at the presence of anyone closer than six feet,
at an unmasked face in the near beyond.
Yes, we can wash our hands twelve times
a day and spray disinfectant on our credit card,
on our car keys when we have to go out.
But for all these efforts, this heart is weary,
longs for a day without numbers and spikes,
for a day without idiocy, for a time when
this heart was not broken.

12

Emergency planning is dead

Matthew Hogan

As an emergency manager for the last 17 years, I've spent thousands of hours considering the risk of various apocalypse scenarios. I'm passionate about the work that my profession does, and the incredible people I'm privileged to call colleagues.

Emergency planning. Emergency management. Disaster management. Resilience. Call it what you will, they are terms that get used interchangeably to refer to the process of considering the list of perils that might trouble us, working out how to reduce the risk of that, and considering the response and recovery should those situations occur.

The origins of the profession are hard to place with certainty, and vary with geography, but for as long as there have been people, there have been disasters. And for as long as there have been disasters, people have been responding and recovering. Over time, emergency management approaches have become more organised. This is in response to a changing society and evolving threats. Broadly speaking, all around the world, including in a community near you, there are people whose responsibility it is to consider the worst times, and to work with others to prepare in advance.

Modern emergency management in the UK is largely rooted in Cold War civil defence preparations. In many places the very offices that emergency managers work from are repurposed bunkers and basements from that era. This echoes the largely hidden nature of the field, kept out of sight until our arrangements and expertise are required.

A series of transport and industrial incidents in the late 1980s and early 1990s saw an expansion of the field and a broadening of the skill sets required. To the families and communities that shoulder the weight of the impact it feels brutal to reduce the colossal impact a disaster can have down to a short phrase, but the mention of Chernobyl, Piper Alpha, Three Mile Island, Lockerbie, Marchioness or Grenfell is often sufficient to act as a reminder of the devastating consequences when safety systems fail.

Around the turn of the millennium the UK experienced widespread flooding in many areas, a foot and mouth disease outbreak and fuel strikes. In addition, the cryptic 'Y2k problem' threatened to impact almost every electronic system around the world. Structures and systems in place to respond to transport incidents proved to be suboptimal in response to these scenarios. This is a perennial issue in emergency management; planning for the last incident that just happened instead of being more forward-leaning, anticipating the hazards still coming down the line towards us.

And so we reach the current form of UK emergency management, which is based on 2004 legislation that created a consistent national framework for planning and updated long outdated arrangements. This law, the Civil Contingencies Act, places a set of responsibilities on emergency responder organisations, and enables local risk-based planning through a collaborative structure known as a 'local resilience forum' and multiagency response through a strategic coordination group. The terminology is slightly different in the devolved administrations of the UK.

Whether it's flooding or fires, terrorists or transport incidents, pandemics or power cuts, it's an incredibly wide-ranging and varied field. Emergency managers are just as varied as the range of scenarios we consider. Many have a background in the emergency services or military, but not exclusively. There are fantastic emergency managers with legal backgrounds, or who have managed London hotels, or who decided on a change in career direction from management consultancy. Everyone brings something unique and valuable.

The role of emergency managers is often one of connecting the dots. Whether in the planning or response phase, a lot of time is spent gathering information and translating that into something that is meaningful for their own organisation.

One of my first emergency management roles was in an NHS organisation. I was responsible for the coordination of pandemic planning. Despite our recent experience of COVID-19, pandemics are not new. They've been sat in the top quadrant of the UK National Risk Register since its first publication in 2005.

The National Risk Register was introduced as part of the 2004 reforms in emergency management. The intention was that taking a risk-based approach would provide a proportionate way of responding to a list of around 100 'reasonable worst case scenarios'.

The biggest risks are worked out by rating each situation on a 1 to 5 scale for impact and likelihood. Those scores are combined and assigned to a four-point colour scale, green for the lowest risks, red for the highest and shades of orange in between. The 'reasonable worst case' means that the Risk Register is naturally pessimistic, working on the principle that if you're prepared for a challenging scenario, then response to smaller scale incidents will be included by default.

The National Risk Register informs and is informed by more local assessments, known as Community Risk Registers. The idea of local registers is that risk is not uniform and some places may experience risks differently, or not at all, depending on their circumstances. For instance, the outbreak of a disease may be impacted by demographic and transport factors, and it has to be a very bad day indeed (that is, not a 'reasonable' worst case) for inland areas to experience coastal flooding. Despite the opportunity for local nuance, the top quadrant of most risk registers typically includes pandemics alongside widespread flooding, loss of electricity to a whole region and large-scale malicious attacks using chemical or other contamination sources.

An emergency situation often requires fast-paced decisions over complete analysis of information. However, history can teach us a great deal, and some emergencies occur with surprising regularity. There are, for instance, attributed return periods for flood events of a specific magnitude (which is the often-reported but little understood '100-year flood'). However, some risks are harder to predict, such as the timing, location and nature of future terrorist threats. Pandemics fall somewhere in the middle; there are some known examples, but it's far from a precise calculation of when the next one might strike. Part of the challenge that emergency managers face is the requirement to take decisions in the face of often incomplete or imperfect information.

The flu pandemic of 1918 is relatively well known. We've become more fluent over recent years with the language of pandemics, but there is a longstanding language developed over many years by people who have dedicated their lives to it. Yet, COVID-19 was presented as something unprecedented.

When the Coronavirus Bill, which gave government agencies and public sector bodies powers to issue fines, detain people and ban public gatherings, was introduced, former Health Secretary Matt Hancock stated to the House of Commons, 'the measures I have outlined are unprecedented in peacetime' (Hancock, 2020). Similarly, in response to early criticisms that the UK response was not making best use of available science to guide policy response, the government responded: 'This is an unprecedented global pandemic and we have taken the right steps at the right time to combat it' (Department of Health and Social Care, 2020b). But COVID-19 was not impossible to anticipate.

Emergency managers knew a pandemic was coming. Epidemiologists knew a pandemic was coming. Infectious disease scientists and intensive care specialists knew a pandemic was coming. Together, and with many others, we wrote plans.

Yet the UK government turned their backs on emergency managers and others at the very start of the coronavirus pandemic. Plans that had been written, trained for, shared and tested remained on shelves. Instead, untested approaches for contact tracing or mortuary management were employed. This disregarded local systems and structures, and, crucially, the experience of multiple professions.

Local resilience forums, introduced in 2004 as a planning-only body, found themselves unexpectedly given response duties. This might not sound significant, but for the preceding 18 years they had been instructed that they were bodies purely for planning rather than response, and were consequently not properly resourced to take on this additional role at pace. Lockdowns were instructed, when all previous planning said the priority was to maintain normal activities as far as possible. At flu pandemic exercises since 2006, national bodies gave absolute assurance that stopping public gatherings would be a last resort. As recently as 2011, the UK Influenza Pandemic Preparedness Strategy confirmed that there would be no international travel restrictions (Department of Health and Social Care, [2011] 2014). The desire to 'be seen to be doing something' is highly prevalent in emergency management. On my most cynical days I feel that the desire to remain in sync with other countries took precedence over critically reviewing whether those interventions would be effective in a UK context.

Pre-COVID-19 planning was for a disease with the potential to infect more people and with higher death rates than we have seen since with coronavirus. When measured against how bad a pandemic could theoretically be, we did okay. However, the response that we mustered was woeful. It was infuriating to see years of hard work go ignored, while outrageously ineffective and inefficient responses were improvised in their place. And it's deeply worrying that if we're capable of ignoring those plans, then we're capable of ignoring others for even worse situations.

On multiple occasions through the coronavirus pandemic I questioned my purpose and whether my role was worth it. Had I spent all of my adult life working in a sham field? If nobody bothered to use the plans we developed, then what was the point?

It was a rough ride on the emotional rollercoaster at times, and my confidence took a thorough battering. It was unsettling to see the response go rogue, implementing things outside previous planning.

Previous government guidance noted that health and social care services may, in a moderate or more severe pandemic, 'need to reduce non-urgent activity'. In reality, concerns about extreme pressure on hospital beds saw the construction of seven 'Nightingale Hospitals' in conference venues across the country, without any consideration for where 100,000 staff required to run them might come from. It was an incredible feat from the NHS, military and private sector to build and set up these facilities at extremely short notice. However, knowing in advance that the strategy could include 'build more hospitals' may have allowed staffing issues to have been identified and perhaps resolved before the event.

Emergency planners, like other professions, shouted into the void, our expertise and experience dismissed. But I had a choice – give up or strap in. I choose to strap in, to be the change that I want to see. I hope we're now at the precipice of moving to the next era in how we manage emergencies.

> Emergency planning is dead. Long live emergency planning.

As we emerge into late-stage pandemic, we're presented with a moment for reflection. The uncertainty we've all faced prompts consideration about what we should take from this into the future.

Traditional approaches to 'learning lessons' from disaster involve considering the things that went well, and things that could have gone better. Usually with Post-it notes. That approach rarely results in meaningful change at the best of times. For COVID-19, the learning is too disparate and too expansive for that approach. I don't have the answer to the best way to ensure lessons are captured and acted on. What I do know, however, is that political cycles are short, headlines are ephemeral, organisational memories are fleeting and staff turnover rates are high. So there are plenty of opportunities for the learning to slip away from us.

COVID-19 may get swept under the rug as 'those weird couple of years' with little-to-no learning or isolated to small pockets were there is sufficient energy. My greatest fear is that we may have already passed the point of learning as we lurch from a pandemic into a fractious geopolitical situation and attention is diverted. The next disaster always comes along. In this situation, however, it's possible that those who lead us will see an opportunity to use this as a distraction from examining where and how failings occurred.

To counteract that risk, I think a lot is riding on the stories that we tell about the pandemic. The learning won't be in the form of management speak of action plans and checklists as it usually is; rather it will be in how we collectively choose to commemorate the losses of the pandemic for future generations, and how artists hold a mirror to us and invite us to reflect. Pay attention over the coming years to how films and TV shows find new ways to look back. Read books about a wide variety of COVID-19 experiences, particularly those from marginalised communities.

In the shorter term, if we learn any lessons at all, I suspect they'll be the 'wrong' ones. My prediction is that we'll see huge investments in building up stockpiles of PPE (personal protective equipment). In itself, that's not a terrible thing, but it's short-sighted. It's specific to just one type of disaster, and there are significant challenges in maintaining a stockpile in the longer term after the COVID-19 headlines fade. How do I know that? Because part of the pandemic planning I mentioned previously included building up a considerable stockpile of masks, gloves, gowns and visors, as well as pharmaceuticals. This stockpile was stripped over several years of austerity, with the value reducing by almost half in six years. Reducing the size of the stockpile released cash for investment in other areas, a type of creative accounting to shuffle money around and hide the true impacts of cuts. And it's a complex tension for organisations to grapple with, planning for an uncertain future versus responding to immediate needs.

It's typical that post-disaster investment takes the form of physical assets rather than more complex, but arguably more beneficial and long-lasting, systemic changes.

In the wake of the 9/11 terrorist attacks in the USA, the UK saw a £330 million investment known as New Dimension to enhance the response capacity of the fire service to terrorist attacks involving chemical, biological, radiological or nuclear contaminants or major environmental pollution incidents. The programme provided hundreds of specialist vehicles and equipment and associated training for 10,000 firefighters between 2001 and 2008. A report at the end of the programme by the National Audit Office (NAO, 2008) noted that despite an 'enhanced capacity to respond', there were value-for-money concerns, and improvements were still required to the processes of major incident planning.

Similarly, after the London bombings on 7 July 2005, there was a huge investment in a national strategic stockpile of demountable, temporary mortuary structures. This was a modular facility to construct appropriate facilities in close proximity to a disaster site. This provision has since been withdrawn, with the bits being distributed across the country. The risk of a mass fatality incident where the number of deceased overwhelms local mortuary capacity hasn't gone away. However, turning off the funding to keep this provision means that our responses in the future will be less effective and inconsistent with lessons from previous disasters.

Investing in widgets is another tangible and visible way of 'being seen to do something', but it's the very lowest of the low-hanging fruit when it comes to learning lessons from disaster. We need a new, bolder approach to learning and implementing lessons to bring about meaningful change, not just throwing money at a situation. There needs to be a far greater focus on addressing the root causes of our risks (to work towards preventing emergencies from happening) and in addressing vulnerabilities (so that where prevention is not possible, the needs of the impacted communities and frontline workers are met quickly and effectively). We have the experience and research to do better, but policy makers need to make a choice towards risk reduction rather than reaction.

Emergency planning is dead. Long live emergency planning.

The pandemic shone its light on pre-existing problems. Extreme pressure in the health and social care sector comes as no surprise, and the disproportionate impact on marginalised groups are two examples of COVID-19 exacerbating existing issues. Others in this volume have picked up on just how unfair the pandemic has been for a great many people.

The Civil Contingencies Act provided a much-needed update to outdated legislation. As we approach 20 years on from the passing of the Act, it requires extensive review. It's time to critically analyse the processes and structures developed a generation ago, and redefine what emergency management looks like now.

For me, there are two priorities that require urgent consideration. First, a review the role of local resilience forums as bodies for response coordination. As mentioned previously, a local resilience forum is just the name for a collective of other legal bodies that have formal legal responsibilities. Therefore, giving a local resilience forum a specific role is difficult because it doesn't exist as a legal entity, and so has no authority. Giving it authority is possible, but would require significant resources and a reworking of the responsibilities of other emergency responder organisations.

My second priority would be an extensive review of Part 2 of the Civil Contingencies Act 2004 that concerns the use of 'emergency powers'. It enables a senior government minister to make emergency regulations and amend existing laws. Emergency powers under the Civil Contingencies Act have never been used and are deigned to be a last resort when primary legislation cannot be passed. Therefore, in response to COVID-19, use was made of the Public Health Act 1984. However, this legislation did not contain wide enough powers, and so the government also passed the Coronavirus Act 2020. However, the Civil Contingencies Act also places some greater limits on use of emergency powers, with any regulations lapsing after 30 days and requiring parliamentary approval for every extension. Conversely, the Coronavirus Act required only a report from the secretary of state every other month and a vote by MPs every six months.

We need emergency management to be more representative, more inclusive and more honest with the society we serve, and to reconsider how to measure the value of emergency management beyond pure financial measures. By 'representative', I mean that as a profession, emergency management needs to continue to move towards not just being a place to put people who have already retired from their first career, but also to embrace the diversity, energy and perspectives of new graduates and other people joining the field. To ensure that the arrangements that are developed work for everyone, we need broader engagement with communities to include them in the work we do and take their steer on the aspects that matter most to them. Finally, we need to open up discussion with society about the risks that we face, how people can look after themselves and what they can, and cannot, expect from emergency management.

> Emergency planning is dead. Long live emergency planning.

None of us can know exactly what the future looks like, but it's certain that there will continue to be disasters, emergencies and extreme events. Our future looks set to be riskier by virtue of a changing climate, demographic shifts and complex global economics.

Together, we all go into that riskier future battle-scarred from COVID-19 (and everything else). Emergency planners still have some reserves of energy if we delve deep enough, but like everyone, we also need to allow for time to readjust, to decompress and to make sense of what we have just endured. Emergencies will continue to come along, which will make taking that time difficult, but we need to have more compassion, both in our planning but also for each other.

If you, even in the smallest of ways, are involved in the business of protecting life, protecting property or protecting the continuity of operations, then you are an emergency manager. The work you do is important and your experiences are valid. The formal response systems of the emergency responder organisations need to work better in support of you rather than against you. The profession needs to find ways to broaden our conversations with you, to make new friendships.

Disrupt with kindness. That's the advice of Gill Kernick (2021), a former resident of Grenfell Tower in London, where 72 people lost their lives and many more lives were forever changed in June 2017. I'm taking Kernick's words as my mantra for when this is over and what comes next – to feel assured about the wealth of knowledge and experience in this profession, but also that we should all feel empowered to bring about change.

Emergency planning is dead. Long live emergency planning.

WAITING TO EXHALE

Mehreen Hamdany

In measured breaths
I count the days
In wary inhale
Of air and dust
What was once second nature,
A rhythmic in and out
Becomes a labour,
In ticking clocks
A roll of dice
When wayward wind,
Or blemish untold
A doorknob, a rail, or sheet unfold
Could blow my way, that speck aloft
That arrested humanity in choking cough
A distrust seeps
In leaning in
In holding hands
And gather within
A closed space fogged
A blooming condensation
A latent virulence
Of unbridled respiration
One thoughtless moment
And a deep intake
Could cost sweet scents
And all of taste
Or the ultimate payment
With a mortal soul

A life, extinguished
In stifled withdrawal
So I adorn my face
With mask unyielding
Or submit to seclusion
Of guarded shielding
Let Earth take a breath
Free of Man's smoking fumes
While he is clogged
By what his mistakes exhume
Discard old ways
Or pay the price
Free of greed and excessive vice
But he litters still
That saving grace
Of masks and gloves
And medical waste
The rhythm continues
In plastic pumps
Vents that fill, stunted lungs
Comes a labour
In ticking clocks
Of fractured dreams
There's no waking from
I know your face
But not the colour of your eyes
The moans of your pain
But not the sound of your voice
In wearied breaths
I count the ways
Balanced on knife's edge
Waiting to exhale

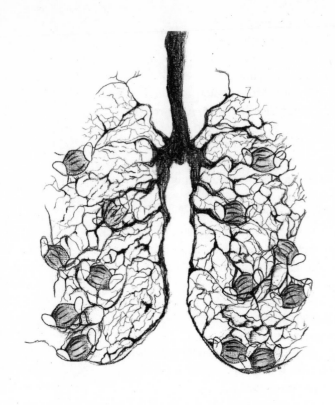

Artwork by Mahwish Hamdany

13

Moving on

Lucy Easthope

Part 1: The plan

I am part of the unwieldy tribe that is emergency planning. It's a tough collective and one that regularly eats its own young. It can feel like we go years without learning the *actual* lessons of terrible tragedy and regularly miss the point. Some planners take the baton for the first few days of the incident, but I found my personal specialism in longer term aftermath (Easthope, 2022b). The centres for the families to wait for news, the mortuaries for the dead and then the much-anticipated and heralded plans for the 20-year rebuild. All of this tends to be wrapped up in a quilt of an international social science called 'disaster recovery' and is reimagined all around the globe. The most likely of all the major disasters was a disease pandemic. For almost two decades it had been placed on the National Risk Register as the UK's most severe risk and was constantly described as 'overdue'. As a hazard it was just so very likely – historically, pandemics have been a fairly regular event (particularly when our metrics might look at likelihood as 1 in 100 years or 1 in 200 years).

I planned for its long-term consequences for 15 years.

One of my roles in the last two decades has been to organise the storytelling workshops, the *debriefs* and the *policy autopsies*, in conference centres and hotels, to replicate the campfires of long ago. Here we pass on, from planner to planner, verbally or through a poorly constructed PowerPoint, our lessons of what worked well when the particular trouble hit. We simplify three years of hard graft into a 200-word template. But some messages are so much harder to capture.

One particular challenge that came before this pandemic was trying to attract the necessary attention for risks that are yet to come to pass – risks that are deemed both highly likely and severe, but even then may seem hard to rigorously plan for. It may come as a shock that a pandemic was the most diligently planned-for risk in UK contingency planning. It is a shock at the end of a volume like this – if we knew of the potential for all of the pain told within these pages, what went wrong? We wrote strategies and ethical frameworks – tools that could be used to decide which patient would get the last ventilator – and lengthy lists of after-shocks. We exercised what life might look like in a pandemic and what choices would need to be made. In 2016 there was a national exercise testing the aftermath of a flu pandemic (Public Health England, 2020b). In the same year the government tested a coronavirus pandemic (Clarke, 2021). It is likely that the details of these exercises and the findings from them will form a major part of any submissions to the COVID-19 public inquiry. We worried long before about the risks to the vulnerable and to already weakened bodies. We worried about healthcare service breakdown. We worried about unequally applied social restrictions that would penalise the marginalised hardest.

So then the question is posed of what do we do with modern-day Cassandras?[1] The small number of us who warn in advance – how do we hear them and 'escalate' accordingly without causing alarm or expending resource unnecessarily? How do we tackle a 'foresight bias' that may come from trying to wrestle with things not yet fully formed? Before – the disaster – is only a series of breathless warnings. Easily ignored, especially if delivered by a woman (Easthope, 2018, 2022b).

Will we listen better next time?

The UK is a nation of disparate wealth and high expectations of local and national government. There is limited recourse to fatalism or God's will. Some parts of society, used to access to privileges and resources, expect and demand that the state not only keeps us safe 24/7, but also responds as fast as the films to any calamity. Other parts of society, used to inequality, know only too well what this failure looks like. Disasters hit people already on the edges hard, and disaster effects are always exacerbated by unfairness and disparity. Children always take a battering, regardless of continent.

If a government fails you in a disaster, then it is quietly failing you all of the time.

So most of all, my toughest and most often-repeated lesson is that disasters always expose harsh political truths and existing cracks within society.

When the pandemic hit, it was as unfair as I had always feared it would be. The *haves* waited for the *have-nots* to deliver their food. Private jet use increased daily. The only safe-ish places for thousands of children were closed to them. The state put tape across swings and park benches.

The final death toll, which will take a decade to shake down, is stapled to that map of inequalities and disparities.

Despite their presentation as neat and bounded, disaster death tolls after large-scale, longitudinal events like these often require many years of further scrutiny. One thing that the pandemic has highlighted is that the public, politicians and even scientists believed that collected data was both rigorous and consistently gathered. In fact, the quality of data can vary hugely:

> Death recording is a complex social process that constructs the eventual output in ways that can introduce systematic biases before comparisons are made. Having introduced these, the output then feeds back and accentuates the biases through the effects on those responsible for defining the cause of death. Mortality is a social and organizational construct and cannot be validly interpreted unless those processes are understood. This applies with particular force to comparisons between national health systems working within very different cultures and with different institutional structures for the recording of deaths. (Dingwall and Vassy, 2015)

And now, as the virus's choke-hold on our health and our society lessens slightly, the time comes for a reckoning.

Part 2: 'Managing expectations'

'Managing expectations' is a phrase that I have come to loathe. In my experience, used by civil servants when talking about bereaved and survivors after disaster, it means that they should try and temper and dilute their quest for justice and truth, and manage what they can expect the process to deliver. As Celia Wells says:

> Major disasters are almost inevitably followed by some sort of inquiry. Inquiries following disasters serve a number of purposes. As well as providing a forum in which those directly affected, whether bereaved or survivors can transact their grief or anger or other emotions in a controlled and public manner, they can also furnish an opportunity to exert pressure for policy changes. (Wells, 1995: 71)

After any UK disaster, so regular and on time that you can set your watch by them, come the calls for a public inquiry. No other government-initiated and defined mechanism is imbued with such faith: that it will, without fear or favour, get to the true causes of the incident and then produce a set of recommendations so forensic that they will redefine public safety forever. Except that history shows they are much more placebo than panacea, even after reform of the law in 2005 (Elliott and McGuinness, 2002). Emergency planners have learned to treat them with caution (Easthope, 2007).

The COVID-19 public inquiry will prove to be one of the more controversial in a tough field. Its terms of reference, however carefully sculpted, will be muddy and divisive. Terms of reference are always the first of many bear traps and can also rapidly become politicised due to ministerial involvement in defining them (Easthope, 2007), and are regularly criticised for omitting key issues, encouraging a focus on a very narrow context and being overly influenced by one particular, dominant worldview of how the event occurred (Easthope, 2007).

One of the most painful frustrations of the inquiry will be temporal. It will simply take too long. An average time for the taking of evidence is five to seven years, with many more years needed for processes of Maxwellisation,[2] editing, further legal checks, proofing, printing and designing the front cover (Whitehall has a preferred style). Even the launch involves months of dedicated planning, embargoes, leaking and briefing. A news bulletin sometime around 2029 might, if we are lucky, carry a series of key points from a weighty three-volume tome accompanied by the narratives of bereaved relatives who gave evidence. There may be charges to receive a copy. The families of soldiers lost in the Iraq War were originally told they would need to pay £767 for their inquiry report. This was later retracted (Mason, 2016).

The other near-insurmountable hurdle for this inquiry will be the lack of a confirmed 'manifest' of survivors and bereaved. Atypically for the majority of major incident inquiries there is a much more complicated, unbounded list of parties with an interest, and problematically *we are all disaster survivors now*. A dying 'with, not of' COVID-19 approach to death certification means the death toll from this disaster reaches into the hundreds of thousands, alongside other tales of co-morbidities, waiting times and neglect. Due to the blanket impact on healthcare, grieving, funeral rites and societal toll, all deaths in the time of this plague were deaths regardless of whether COVID-19 was the certificated cause.

This inquiry cannot logistically offer what some inquiries after disaster within the UK usually offer – to include within their bounds a detailed inquest phase where the demise of all those killed are given an airing.

There are just too many deceased, and the precise details of their demise are just too uncertain. There will be neither capacity nor records to facilitate such things. The inquiry may take the approach of a number of recent health reviews and include illustrative case studies where stories of individuals are formatted into neat little shaded boxes in the report – their story supposed to represent a hundred others. Throughout the time that the inquiry will sit, in an air-conditioned building, with an expensively procured document management system to collate the millions of reports that will be sent to them, people will continue to die with COVID-19 on their death certificate.

In far too many years' time a report will be presented with some muted ceremony, and those who waited patiently, through delays and leaks, will feel empty. I have seen the day of delivery tens of times by now – as one family member bereaved by disaster said to me on *their* day, 'I felt no elation, no resolution, I felt … nothing.'

So what next?

Part 3: Hope and heart

My experience, however, teaches me that all is not lost. Because, with just a few exceptions – the Royal Liverpool Children's Inquiry and Lord Clarke's Public Inquiry into the Identification of Victims following Major Transport Accidents (both in 2001) are examples, the former leading to a fundamental change in the law (Easthope, 2022b) – inquiries are not the change-makers. But other things are. One of the things that I love about my field, that gives me the hope to keep going, is its amazing ability to bend and flex. As Matthew Hogan captures in his writing in Chapter 12, there are many ways to improve our chances of responding to the next inevitable and overdue pandemic as well as expand on a number of safeguards that an inquiry could build into its design to protect a more effective outcome.

The hard work is done on the ground and behind the scenes. And it is important work, with relevance far beyond times of crisis. I am a champion of the emergency planner's *bricolage* (Easthope, 2018), by which I mean the tiny incremental changes that people effect every day in our work. Tweaks that mean health teams in hospitals and local authorities now work together more effectively. The creation of new data dashboards that mean we are readier. Some of the fastest development of drugs and treatments protocols, beyond anything we could have imagined possible. Perhaps even more importantly a generation of social workers and teachers and community safety wardens who have learned that they had it in them to do what was needed when the trouble hit. They were braver and more innovative than they had ever thought possible – and they would do it again.

When the pandemic hit, there was a state-promulgated myth that this was a surprise. That this was unprecedented. That there were neither plans nor planners. As Patricia Tuitt describes in depth in Chapter 6, there are many questions to be asked about the laws passed during this time. Laws were rushed through with a number of un/intended consequences. The idea that this was 'emergency law' for 'emergency times' is simply wrong. The idea that it had to be rushed through without proper democratic scrutiny is wrong. And, as Tuitt points out, it wasn't just the laws. She argues that all of us were subjected to unregulated force during lockdowns – force that was not mandated by law, which always contains the notion of 'reasonableness'. The conflation of law and guidance was rampant, and authorities assumed powers the law had not given them.

When the planners saw the Coronavirus Act (2020), we *knew* that parts of the Act, such as those relating to simplifying bureaucracy and death registration, were direct responses to the problems flagged up in our earlier pandemic exercises. This shows an ability to learn and adapt, albeit with a misstep of which parts were important. Somehow this was more infuriating than anything else. A focus on bureaucratic fixes, but a stubborn, mute silence on all the *other* things we flagged up in the last 15 years. Where were the PPE (personal protective equipment) stockpiles? Where were protocols that should have been co-written by both our top civil servants for health and for education that set out how children would be kept safe from both the virus but also a myriad of other harms? Where was the planning for care home residents? All of these things were known, knowns. And they will still be there next time.

They had time to write this legislation. They had time to do so much more. The government had years to ready generally, then months to respond to the stories emerging from Wuhan, China. That time was wasted.

Now we have one short, finite window to try and remember. To try and pass this on. In other tribes, in other times, I would have travelled from place to place, and campfire to caravan cabal, with my tales of terror and tragedy. Those stories would have served a number of purposes. They would enthral and excite and horrify, and thus pass a cold night more quickly with the other women and their children and frail elders. But my words would have also carried with them a number of other functions. Warnings of future risk and as-yet-unrealised hazards. Suggestions of places to avoid, risky behaviours to cease. Thoughts on balms to use and ways to help.

Words to say, when the worst has happened in front of you. Things to do differently next time. In other times my role would have been understood, protected, even venerated. In other times, understanding that women are particularly good at this would have been more readily accepted.

By the time of the COVID-19 pandemic, in the Western world, there was very little room for a collector, a human quilt, like me. In these modern times, soothsayers and fortune tellers have to find other things to do with their time. Some disasters may be preventable, but not all. It seems anathema that you should experience both the disaster, and then the poor treatment after it. Ask me who I am now, when all is done, and I will tell you that I am the collector of a very specific type of story and the keeper of a very particular type of secret sorrow. I am a noisy *rememberer*, working hard to stop the state from forgetting and moving its lessons into archive, where they will be lost all over again.

The *how* of learning lessons has vexed the emergency planning and management world for as long as we are in it. Planners see inquiry recommendations flutter off into a lost ether on an annual basis, and then we see the near-identical harms repeated somewhere else with a few tweaks to the exact circumstances, and we are tired of it. It could be my quiz show category. Give me one ongoing inquiry and I can give you four earlier inquiries, inquests or reviews that have the same findings.

One of our leading scholars on the politics of inquiries was Eve Coles, who we lost to the pandemic in May 2021. Just a few years earlier she had published yet another impassioned plea that we get better at learning from emergencies (Coles, 2014). She identified a 'myriad of reasons why we don't learn the lessons from emergencies that are routinely identified'. These included a failure to translate policy-level learning to operational practice (big, broad, strategic points that can be hard to make fit into the messy realities of a catastrophe); the loss of an organisational memory, and for this pandemic a whole-state memory; the management of information both within organisations and between organisations that inhibits the dissemination of learning from emergencies; a constant focus in training and education on what to learn rather than how to learn; organisational cultures and deep structures that create an underlying equilibrium in organisations that can be immune to perturbations in the system and thus prevent learning; and a reluctance to commit to change management programmes to embed learning, particularly when the learning comes from an external source.

I am asked if things will be different next time. The lessons more acute and more memorable because we are all disaster survivors now. And because this was just so big. But I think we are just as vulnerable to losing these lessons as we always have been.

When This Is Over is a volume about loss and bereavement. But it is also about what next. My life has taught me that good *will* come. The thing that I have become particularly known for is my recovery planning. I help those who respond to emergencies map out a plan for what next. For the communities, for the places, for the responders themselves.

We all need a compass to navigate the next steps. I think I might just have that. I certainly know that there is life after this, and I think the planners know that there is something that comes after total darkness. But the planners cannot do this alone. We need help with the really big conversations now on how we care for our elderly and those in need of a little extra care and compassion.

We need to return to a place where we understand our frailty and the frailty of those around us. We need to be ready for next time.

In 2023 the highest national risk flagged in the UK National Risk Register will be an influenza pandemic. Planners know that we will need to be ready to go all over again.

Part 4: Moving on

We have been told by our leaders to move on. I have come to know well that cruel phrase, *it's time to move on*. I have seen the air sucked out of a room when civil servants have said it to grieving mothers and still-injured survivors. I have seen it used to flooded communities still living in caravans and friends' back bedrooms (Easthope, 2018).

To veterans relearning how to walk again. To responders who are not eating or sleeping properly yet or ever, whose marriages are falling apart day by day, because they can't find the words to say what they have seen.

Being told to 'move on' is yet another sign of the power relations played out after disaster. I have oft been told to move on – pretty much every time I hand over a lessons document from a scene or a mortuary. I am told that the state has moved on, the public has moved on. Move on. MOVE ON.

And do you know what? They are right. You have to move on. Not to somewhere else, not to a place of forgetting. But like a chess game. You move to the next square. To a place where you hold them to account more effectively. Where you ask them different questions.

There is another reason to move on. Because if you have not yet, then you stay in a place of paralysing pain and anger. That only hurts you and not them. You simply become weaker. For what comes next you are going to need to be stronger than ever.

So – take my advice – move on and give them hell.

Part 5: Giving them hell

One of the things that the indomitable Eve Coles talked about a lot when it came to lessons from emergencies, to improve both our readiness for next time and, more generally, our understanding of what makes society tick *all the time*, was the role of 'double-loop learning'. This was learning that did not lose itself in the finicky minutiae of the specific incident but instead allowed broader lessons and a more expansive analysis of causes. States, agencies and organisations are much more comfortable making neat, operational fixes (new kit, radios or trucks; a change in the person at the top; a new checklist), and simply do not make the necessary cultural changes so that next time really will be different. As Coles said in 2014, this

> is a palliative method that treats the symptoms of failure rather than the cause. Double loop learning on the other hand requires organisations to drill down and look for the recurring, often systemic failures and the

values that govern such behaviour and by changing these before action may be said to have achieved second order or higher learning. (Coles, 2014: 7)

That is the sort of learning that is needed now, and the initiation of such a moment will be the true test of any COVID-19 inquiry.

There is also a further expectation on all of us. The research on public inquiries is near unanimous that the state *will* forget, so it is up to us now to remember – to tell stories and to 'actively archive' – which is what this volume is. To shout a little louder.

There will also be a compassion required from all of us because there is no one truth in life after disaster. There is forgetting, re-remembering, exaggerating, underestimating and hubris. So far the pandemic has been no different, and that can lead to entrenchment of positions – by all of us. Three years after the devastating earthquakes of 2010 and 2011 in Canterbury, New Zealand the Red Cross wrote up their experiences in a companion for communities coming after them. At its centre is this story about seeing through the lenses of multiple parties after disaster:

> The recovery elephant is based on the tale from the Indian subcontinent of six blind men who are asked to touch an elephant to learn what it is like – they then compare notes to find that they are in complete disagreement. If you ask the community they will say recovery feels like a brick wall (the stomach), if you ask a public servant they will say recovery feels like the tightrope between fiscal responsibility, setting national precedent and community needs (the tail), if you ask those who feel swindled by the recovery process they will say it is like a snake (the trunk). Post-disaster, under pressure, our focus narrows and we believe only our 'one truth'. Without listening and collaborating we fail to see the recovery elephant – the many truths and perspectives that make up recovery. This is critical to successful recovery leadership and good planning. (New Zealand Red Cross, 2014)

For disaster, I learn my lessons from those who already live daily with precarity, and in my own life I have been greatly influenced by the words of Gerald Vizenor (2008) who writes about 'survivance' within the Native American experience. The concept and idea of survivance has challenged my understanding of the framing of those living with inequality:

> Survivance throws into relief the dynamic, inventive, and enduring heart of Native cultures well beyond the colonialist trappings of absence, tragedy, and powerlessness ... people in the world are enamored with and obsessed by the concocted images of the Indian – the simulations of indigenous character and cultures as essential victims. Native survivance, on the other hand, is an active sense of presence over historical absence, deracination, and oblivion. The nature of survivance is unmistakable in Native stories, natural reason, active traditions, customs, and narrative resistance and is clearly observable in personal attributes such as humor, spirit, cast of mind, and moral courage. (University of Nebraska Press, 2022)

I read this whenever I need reminding that there must also be room for living alongside the recovering.

That is what comes next.

Notes

[1] In Greek mythology, Cassandra was the daughter of Priam and Hecuba who was endowed with the gift of prophecy but also condemned to the fate of never being believed. Here I use it to mean anyone whose prophecies of doom are shouted out but left unheeded. I give several examples of that throughout my career in Easthope (2022b).

[2] Maxwellisation is the legal process that allows those who are to be criticised in an official report to respond prior to publication.

Afterword

Gary Younge

Just up the stairs from the accident and emergency ward at King's Hospital, London a team of youth workers is on standby to talk to young people who have been admitted with gun or stab wounds. The aim is to intervene in order to break the cycle of youth violence by starting a discussion with the young person about what has brought them to this point of crisis: they are in the hospital because that critical juncture provides the most effective time to engage with them.

They call it the 'teachable moment' – the point at which a person is best positioned to receive a message they have previously been keen to avoid. Talk to an overweight person about their diet on a regular day and they may hear you out only to contemplate your message over an order for burger and fries. Talk to them about it just after they have had a heart attack and you will have a more receptive audience. Similarly, talk to a young person about the dangers of knife crime when they are out with their friends and they may laugh it off; when they are bandaged in a hospital bed, strapped up to an IV, there is a better chance they will hear you out. 'When we can get to someone and talk face to face, especially if they stay overnight, then 80 per cent of them want to have a conversation', a member of the team employed by the charity Redthread told me. 'But if they've left the hospital, only 40 per cent answer the phone.'

The COVID-19 pandemic has provided us with a teachable moment. We have been laid low: it has taken a toll on our physical and mental health, our social networks, economies and human relationships. What might have taken decades to transpire – economically, ecologically, bureaucratically, socially – was condensed into little more than a year. But the pandemic has also introduced a crisis that has given us the opportunity to take stock of the conditions in which we live and the consequences those conditions have engendered. It laid bare our inequalities, vulnerabilities and precarities. The pandemic has illustrated which workers are truly essential, the value of public services and the benefits of progressive state intervention; it has made the case for facts, science and public trust; it has shown us that we are all connected and that we have a collective responsibility for our common wellbeing. It has made the case that there is such a thing as the common good, and it is in all of our interests to pursue it.

In the words of Naomi Klein (2020: xiv), in her Foreword to the paperback edition of *On Fire: The Burning Case for a Green New Deal*:

> If nothing else, [it has] put the lie to the idea that late capitalist societies are incapable of seismic transformations on a deadline. Indeed, from India to Europe to Argentina to the United States, we have witnessed the most aggressive government interventions in the economy since the Second World War. In the US, car manufacturers have started making medical equipment. Spain has nationalized all its private hospitals. And then there have been the shutdowns: deliberate decisions to close down all but essential businesses, as well as schools and other core services, in order to deprive the virus of new opportunities to spread.

It would be a terrible shame to have gone through this much pain, heartache and inconvenience and then not to learn the lessons that have been presented to us. It is only natural that, as the vaccine was rolled out and social spaces start to open, some might celebrate a return to a new normal. But it would be negligent to forget that it was the old normal that got us here. Calls for a 'Great Reset' (World Economic Forum) or even 'Build Back Better' (Joe Biden/Kamala Harris) belie the fact that the foundations on which we stood were shaky at best and unsustainable at worse. Like a young person on the gurney at King's Hospital nursing a knife wound we can either use this experience to turn a corner and change the way we do things, or we can carry on as though nothing happened and endure the predictable consequences.

The most fundamental lesson the pandemic taught us was our common humanity and mutual dependence. That's what made it global. For all the ways we have devised to construct difference – race, nation, class, religion – it foregrounded our common humanity. Notwithstanding variations of shape, size and phenotype, the human body is basically the same everywhere – the virus did not know whether you were Black, white, Christian, Hindu, documented or undocumented. It took you as it found you. Variations in susceptibility for age or medical condition merely prove the point. There is no culture in which people do not get old or sick. In a period of escalating racism and xenophobia you could not build a wall to keep it out, segregate it to trap it in its own laager or simply deport or expel it. It didn't need a passport or papers. Starting in Wuhan and spreading the world over it was a gruesome testament to our desire, capacity and necessity to travel globally and mix socially. There was a brutal irony to the fact that the UK's COVID-19 numbers spiked at precisely the moment it concluded its Brexit negotiations with the European Union: the UK could opt out of Europe, but it could not opt out of the planet.

But it rapidly became clear that while anybody could come down with it and even die from it, some people were more likely to do so than others. The virus may not discriminate, but society does. The last year and a half exposed the fault lines and intersections of racial and economic deprivation, both nationally and internationally. Being Black, Brown or poor was a pre-existing condition. In Britain Black people are up to three times more likely to die from the virus: in the USA they are more than twice as likely to be hospitalised. The same is true, and sometimes even worse, for other minority ethnic groups.

Their vulnerability was not biological, but societal. Racial minorities were most likely to live in crowded conditions, to have to work, to be employed in sectors such as care work, nursing, security, public transport, taxi driving and the gig economy, where transmission was most common. As such they fell foul not of the laws of biology but probabilities. This is what systemic discrimination looks like: not bad people doing bad things to good people (although there is plenty of that too), but a series of processes that ensure that wherever there is a pile of deprivation, minorities will be at the bottom of it.

Awareness of this reality became particularly acute following the murder of George Floyd in the USA, sparking worldwide anti-racist protests that saw resistance pollinate as each country and region translated the issue to its own context. The video of George Floyd going viral in the midst of the broader virus allowed the connection to be made between the brazen racism of murderous police violence and the more banal, quotidian experience of racism that was blighting communities across the West. Whether it was a knee on the neck or a ventilator in an emergency ward, too many of us could not breathe.

It also became clear, as our labour forces were stripped down to just key workers – the nurses, bus and train drivers, sanitation workers and Deliveroo deliverers – just who was keeping late-stage capitalism on the road. Over-represented among those who kept us well, fed, mobile and clean were those migrant and non-white communities who had been demonised as scroungers, pilferers and criminals. (The two nurses that UK Prime Minister Boris Johnson singled out for praise were from Portugal and New Zealand. The New Zealander has since gone back: 'We're not getting the respect and now pay that we deserve', she said. 'I'm just sick of it. So, I've handed in my resignation.') The notion that they were critical to Western economies was no longer simply a rhetorical point. The fact that they were essential was a literal and quasi-legal designation. The country couldn't function without them.

As such COVID-19 did not affect non-white people disproportionately because of their race but because their race makes them disproportionately poor, with poverty being one of the key consequences of racism. And it was the poor of all races who found themselves at risk. In the UK, the age-adjusted death rate in the most deprived tenth of areas has been double that of the least deprived areas.

What is true within nations has also been replicated between them. The poorest countries, which, thanks to the legacy of colonialism and imperialism, also tend to be overwhelmingly populated by Black and Brown people, are being actively prevented from emerging from the threat of COVID-19 in a timely manner because they are struggling to acquire the vaccine in sufficient quantities to make an impact. According to Our World in Data, at the time of writing (2022), 73.9 per cent of the UK and 91.4 per cent of Portugal was fully vaccinated compared to just 1.1 per cent of Haiti and 2.9 per cent of Papua New Guinea (Ritchie et al, 2020).

So we have a global pandemic but no global solution, which is the same as having no solution at all. The pandemic did not invent these disparities; it simply clarified, amplified and accelerated them.

Closer to home, the very lockdowns that were supposed to make us safe left some of us more vulnerable. The United Nations organisation UN Women and the *American Journal of Emergency Medicine* reported a spike in domestic violence of 300 per cent in Hubei, China, 50 per cent in Brazil, 33 per cent in Singapore, 30 per cent in Cyprus and 25 per cent in Argentina. Several US cities, like San Antonio, Texas and Portland, Oregon, showed similar spikes in domestic violence.

Once again, COVID-19 did not create this situation; it inflamed it. Jacky Mulveen, project manager of Women's Empowerment and Recovery Educators (WE:ARE), an advocacy and support group in Birmingham, England, told *Time* magazine: 'Covid doesn't make an abuser. But Covid exacerbates it. It gives them more tools, more chances to control you. The abuser says, "You can't go out; you're not going anywhere," and the government also is saying, "You have to stay in."'

But if COVID-19 outlined what the longstanding problems were, it also indicated what the solutions might be. In a period of escalating political cynicism and the primacy of individualism it was good governance, trust and collective engagement that made the difference. The countries that proved most successful at containing the spread provided generous furlough packages, sick pay entitlements and other support to assist people who couldn't work, either because of lockdown or sickness. The more citizens were likely to trust the government, the more likely they were to follow the rules.

The UK ranks particularly low on the Organisation for Economic Co-operation and Development (OECD) survey for trust in government, with a lower percentage of people saying they have confidence in their own national government than in Brazil, Italy and Russia. This is hardly surprising when it emerged that the highest levels of government, including the prime minister, had repeatedly and flagrantly broken the very lockdown laws they had imposed, hosting several alcohol-fuelled parties, and were consequently fined by the police.

It should be no surprise that the countries where the pandemic was most likely to spiral out of control – the UK, Brazil, the USA, India – were the ones with the most vicious, right-wing leaders who had come to power by capitalising on public cynicism, shameless lying and recklessly scapegoating minorities. (The US states with the highest death rates all have Republican governors who resisted mask mandates, among other things.) Their inflammatory rhetoric had no purchase on a genuine crisis that demanded strategic planning and organisational competence.

In his essay 'In front of your nose', George Orwell (1946) wrote:

> We are capable of believing things which we know to be untrue. And then, when we are finally proved wrong, impudently twisting the facts so as to show that we were right. Intellectually, it is possible to carry on this process for an indefinite time: the only check on it is that sooner or later a false belief bumps up against solid reality, usually on a battlefield.

COVID-19 was the battlefield. And thousands died in these countries because of their leaders' denial, scepticism and callous incompetence. Indeed, in a range of ways, from wearing masks to locking down, COVID-19 presented a challenge to the hard right because there was no individual response to it that could be meaningful. It demanded that you care about people you didn't know and act not just for yourself, but also in the interests of society as a whole. It forced a reckoning with who and what an economy is for – what is the point of having a healthy economy if the people in it are unhealthy?

At a time when people found it easier to imagine the end of the world than the end of capitalism, here was a moment of comprehensive state intervention that expanded our imagination of what is possible. What was true for COVID-19 could also be true for climate change, argues Klein (2020: xvi):

> Clearly, when societies decide to treat an emergency as an emergency all manner of possibilities instantly bloom. And when governments are genuinely understood to be making changes in the interest of protecting life and keeping people safe, and when these changes are imposed on individuals and big business alike, most of us are willing – even eager – to do our part.

So we have a choice. For all the trauma, COVID-19 has gifted us with an opportunity to rethink the way we do things. History does not repeat itself but, as Mark Twain is credited with saying, 'it often rhymes'. As the Depression in the USA gave way to the New Deal, or the end of the Second World War heralded the beginning of a welfare state in Europe, we have the chance to reform our economies and societies with the lessons we have learned in mind. We can go back to a system that marginalises and a parochial culture that scapegoats, or we can go forward to a set of new priorities that values people and the public sphere differently.

'You already know enough', wrote the late Sven Lindqvist in his book about European imperialism in Africa, *Exterminate All the Brutes* (1996: 2). 'So do I. It is not knowledge that we lack. What is missing is the courage to understand what we know and to draw conclusions.'

We have been here before. After the financial crisis we knew that the economic system on which our lives and livelihoods were dependent was unsustainable, its future precarious and the ramifications devastating. But we did not have the courage to draw the conclusions that would liberate us from its clutches. Not long after, the bankers' bonuses were back and the public sector was paying the price for their venality.

The omens this time are not great either. There has been significant strain on our economies. The question is, who will shoulder the burden? 'Capitalists', argued Lenin, 'can buy themselves out of any crisis so long as they make the workers pay.'

This, once again, has been the story so far. COVID-19 has created greater disparities between rich and poor and between white people and racialised minorities than before. During the pandemic, the chief executive of Norwegian Cruise Line doubled his salary to US$36.4 million, even as his company lost US$4 billion and furloughed 20 per cent of its staff. Boeing's chief executive enjoyed a US$21.1 million salary, even as his company reported a US$12 billion loss and laid off 30,000 workers. In the USA Black people were 4.5 times more likely to be policed or punished for coronavirus orders than white people; in London Black people were twice as likely to be fined for breaching COVID-19 orders. The prolific partying taking place in Downing Street was the most emblematic illustration that those demanding sacrifice clearly did not believe those demands applied to themselves.

Meanwhile, in the absence of a patent waiver, the West is set to respond to COVID-19 in the Global South in much the same way that it has responded to poverty and war there – by pulling up the drawbridge and criminalising the very migrants on which they depend (unless the migrants are from Ukraine). These measures will likely be as effective for the pandemic as they have been for migration. So long as COVID-19 is a problem for some people somewhere in the world, it will be a problem for everyone on the planet.

So the risk that we will repeat the same mistakes is real and should not be ducked. 'If you beat your head against the wall,' the Italian Marxist Antonio Gramsci once wrote, 'it is your head which breaks, and not the wall.' Yet again we stand on the verge of an enormous headache of our own making.

None of this is inevitable; much of it is in play. Wherever a better world is possible, the threat of a worse one lurks too. The political volatility that was evident when we entered this crisis has, if anything, grown with the pandemic. The challenge is essentially ideological, if not philosophical. In this pivotal and unprecedented moment the prize will go to whoever, or whatever, can both rally the most people and marshal the most power behind its idea of the future.

As we have seen, it needn't be the best idea that helps the most people. But it could be. In this progressives must practise the basic rule of jujitsu and use the weight of our opponents against them. For the last two years we have been told to forget our differences because we were all in this together – even when those very differences illustrated why and how we weren't all in it together. We were lectured on the importance of sacrifice and mutual consideration so that we might be encouraged to accept extraordinary measures – unthinkable prior to the pandemic – in the common good.

We can leverage all of those notions, which neoliberal disdain had previously left atrophying, and put them to use. Nobody can say it cannot be done because it has been done. We can and must demand more, better and equitable service from the state. In the past we might have advocated for the provision of laptops for working-class children at school, a living wage when people were out of work, and putting public health before private profit, and been dismissed as dreamers. Now, nobody can say it cannot be done, because it has been done.

In the past we might have pointed to the inequalities and inequities of race, gender and class discrimination, health outcomes and housing needs, and been dismissed as whiners. Now nobody can say that they didn't know. We might have pointed out how our common humanity was undermined by global inequalities that informed issues such as trade, migration and climate change, and been dismissed as unpatriotic cosmopolitans. Now, nobody can say that they didn't know.

We should not expect these arguments to be accepted, these precedents followed or this knowledge to be acknowledged. There are vested interests at stake in forgetting what we know and ignoring what has been done. The old normal worked for some, and almost by definition, the redistribution of wealth, resources and power is not in the interests of everyone.

There has rarely been a more propitious and clarifying moment to make the case that the path we were on was not just undesirable, but unsustainable, and that it is within our ability to shift course. If politics is the art of the possible, then radicalism must entail the capacity to imagine new possibilities. For better, and for worse, COVID-19 has already made so much happen that we didn't think was possible. Imagine what could happen next?

Acknowledgements

An earlier version of this Afterword was published in Dutch in *One World* magazine on 23 July 2021, available from: www.oneworld.nl/lezen/essay/ waarom-we-verandering-moeten-eisen-nu-de-samenleving-opengaat

Notes on contributors

Amna Abdul-Latif, Manchester City Councillor and Associate Director for Youth Empowerment: Anne Frank Trust.

Dipali Anumol, PhD candidate and artist, The Fletcher School of Law and Diplomacy, Tufts University.

Manca Bajec, artist, writer and researcher, Manca has presented her work worldwide including in Kaunas, London, Sarajevo, New York and Cape Town. She is Managing Editor for the *Journal of Visual Culture*.

Sue Black, Baroness Black of Strome, DBE, OBE, President of St John's College, University of Oxford and Visiting Professor of Forensic Anatomy. Author of *All that Remains: A Life in Death* (Penguin, 2019). Professor Black is one of the world's leading forensic scientists and has most recently been the Pro-Vice-Chancellor for Engagement at Lancaster University, tasked with raising the university's profile locally, regionally and nationally while championing the economic growth and regeneration of northwest England.

Gracie Mae Bradley, a writer and campaigner working across abolition, civil liberties, state racism and surveillance. She is co-author of *Against Borders* (Verso 2022), and directed the civil liberties NGO Liberty from 2020–21.

Mark Brown, Development Director of Social Spider CIC. Mark was shortlisted for the Mind Champion of the Year Award in 2010.

Sue Bryant, Registered General Nurse, Royal Hampshire County Hospital, Winchester, NHS. Sue is also an artist.

Rita Coleman writes poetry, prose, memoirs and stories for children in rural Greene County, Ohio, USA. She has written two books of poetry, *And Yet* (Finishing Line Press, 2017) and *Mystic Connections* (Booksurge Publishing, 2009). Her first full-length poetry collection, *In the Near Distance*, has been accepted for publication.

Amy Cortvriend, Lecturer in Criminology, University of Northampton; her PhD in criminology, from the University of Manchester, focuses on Criminology. Amy is also an activist, advocating for the rights of people seeking safety.

Lucy Easthope, Professor in Practice of Risk and Hazard at Durham University and Fellow in Mass Fatalities and Pandemics at the Centre for Death and Society, University of Bath. Author of *When the Dust Settles* (Hodder & Stoughton, 2022).

Jenny Edkins, Honorary Professor of Politics, University of Manchester and Emeritus Professor in the Department of International Politics, Aberystwyth University. Author of *Change and the Politics of Certainty* (Manchester University Press, 2019); *Missing: Persons and Politics* (Cornell University Press, 2011); and *Trauma and the Memory of Politics* (Cambridge University Press, 2003); co-editor of *After Grenfell: Violence, Resistance and Response* (Pluto Press, 2019).

Paul Famosaya, Lecturer in Criminology, University of Northampton, Paul specialises in policing and criminological theories. He is the 2021 winner of the Emerald Literati Award as the outstanding reviewer of the year.

Fran Hall, Founder of Friends of the National Covid Memorial Wall and CEO of the Good Funeral Guide CIC. Fran joined Covid-19 Bereaved Families for Justice in November 2020, after the death of her husband from COVID-19.

Mehreen Hamdany, a writer and journalist based in the UK.

Matthew Hogan, an emergency planning professional in London, and Deputy Head of London Resilience at London Fire Brigade.

Mark Honigsbaum, Senior Lecturer, Department of Journalism, City, University of London, is a writer and academic specialising in the history and science of infectious disease. His books include a global history of malaria and a social history of the 1918–19 influenza pandemic.

Danielle House, Senior Research Associate in the School for Policy Studies, University of Bristol, previously Postdoctoral Researcher at the University of Reading on a project exploring experiences of death for migrants and minorities.

Lara-Rose Iredale, a Senior Anatomical Pathology Technologist (APT) who lived and worked in London as an APT in the NHS for nine years, and is now living and working as an APT in Yorkshire.

Farjana Islam has recently completed a PhD at Heriot Watt University, Edinburgh in Urban Studies.

Safina Islam, Head, Ahmed Iqbal Ullah Race Archives and Community Engagement (RACE) Centre and Education Trust, and Chair of Ananna, Manchester Bangladeshi women's organisation.

Led By Donkeys, an artist and activist collective created by Ben Stewart, James Sadri, Oliver Knowles and Will Rose.

Avril Maddrell, Professor of Social and Cultural Geography, University of Reading. Her recent research projects include 'Cemeteries and crematoria as public spaces of belonging in Europe: A study of migrant and minority cultural inclusion, exclusion and integration' (CeMi) (HERA).

Herbert Woodward Martin, poet, librettist for 'Pity these ashes, pity this dust, Tulsa, 1921: A concert aria' and 'A knee on the neck: A cantata in memory of George Floyd'. Author of *The Shape of Regret* (Wayne State University Press, 2019) and *Sometimes, Say My Name* (Poets Choice Publishing, 2020).

Jennifer Mustapha, Assistant Professor of Political Science at Huron University College in London, Ontario, Canada.

Anjana Nair, poet, creator @tinyearths. Author of *Stripped: A Collection of Poems* (Authorspress, 2019), and former Editor of *Agriculture Today* (India).

Kandida Purnell, Associate Professor of International Relations, Richmond, The American International University in London. Author of *Rethinking the Body in Global Politics* (Routledge, 2021).

Yvonne Edouke Riley, CEO, Dynamic Support of Greater Manchester.

Jo Robson, archivist for the COVID-19 collecting project and freelance archivist for the Ahmed Iqbal Ullah Education Trust (AIUET).

Michael Rosen, poet and former Children's Laureate. Author of *Many Different Kinds of Love: Life, Death, and the NHS* (Ebury, 2021).

Hannah Rumble, Research Fellow at the Centre for Death and Society, University of Bath, and member of the Editorial Board for the journal *Mortality: Promoting the Interdisciplinary Study of Death and Dying.*

Sandhya Sharma, VAWG (Violence Against Women and Girls) specialist and previous Co-Director of Safety4Sisters.

Irene Naikaali Ssentongo was born and raised in one of the famous ghettos of Kampala, Uganda, in the early 1980s. She uses her voice and the power of words to challenge vulnerable women to take self-reliant action.

Circle Steele, CEO, Wai Yin Chinese Society.

Marvin Thompson was born in London to Jamaican parents and now lives in mountainous South Wales. His poem 'The fruit of the spirit is love' won the National Poetry Competition in 2020.

Patricia Tuitt, a Legal Academic, formerly Professor and Dean of the School of Law at Birkbeck, University of London (2009–17). See patriciatuitt.com

Karen West, Professor of Social Policy and Ageing, University of Bristol and Senior Research Fellow at the NIHR School for Social Care Research.

Gary Younge, an award-winning journalist, author, broadcaster and academic, as well as Professor of Sociology at the University of Manchester.

References

Adam, David (2022) 'The pandemic's true death toll: Millions more than official counts', *Nature*, 601: 312–15. https://doi.org/10.1038/d41586-022-00104-8

Agamben, Giorgio (2021) *Where Are We Now? The Epidemic as Politics* (2nd edn), translated by Valeria Dani, London: Eris Press.

Ahearne, Gemma (2021) 'Long read: The war on dissent during the state of exception', *plasticdollheads*, 25 July. Available from: https://plasticdollheads.wordpress.com/2021/07/25/long-read-the-war-on-dissent-during-the-state-of-exception

Ahearne, Gemma (2022) 'Partygate: A lockdown of justice?', School of Law and Social Justice, University of Liverpool [Blog], 10 February. Available from: www.liverpool.ac.uk/law-and-social-justice/blog/partygate-lockdown-justice

Ahmed, Sara (2014a) *Wilful Subjects*, Durham, NC: Duke University Press.

Ahmed, Sara (2014b) 'Atmospheric walls', *Feministkilljoys* [Blog], 15 September. Available from: https://feministkilljoys.com/2014/09/15/atmospheric-walls

Akhtar, Smina (2020) 'When state racism and austerity meet the pandemic: The death of a Syrian refugee in hotel detention', *Discover Society* [Blog], 14 May. Available from: https://archive.discoversociety.org/2020/05/14/when-state-racism-and-austerity-meet-the-pandemic-the-death-of-a-syrian-refugee-in-hotel-detention

Aliverti, Ana (2012) 'Making people criminal: The role of the criminal law in immigration enforcement', *Theoretical Criminology*, 16(4): 417–34. https://doi.org/10.1177/1362480612449779

Amnesty International (2020) 'UK: Older people in care homes abandoned to die amid Government failures during coronavirus pandemic – New report', Press release, 4 October. Available from: www.amnesty.org.uk/press-releases/uk-older-people-care-homes-abandoned-die-amid-government-failures-during-coronavirus

Anonymous (2020) 'First person', *Positive Action in Housing* [News story], 27 November. Available from: www.paih.org/first-person-2

Ansari, Humayun (2007) 'Burying the dead: Making Muslim space in Britain', *Historical Research*, 80(210): 545–66. https://doi.org/10.1111/j.1468-2281.2007.00432.x

APPGDC (All-Party Parliamentary Group on Democracy and the Constitution) (2021) *An Inquiry into Police Conduct at the Clapham Vigil and Bristol Protests and the Implications for the Police Crime Sentencing and Courts Bill by the All Party Parliamentary Group on Democracy and the Constitution, Funded by the Joseph Rowntree Reform Trust.*

Aradau, Claudia and Tazzioli, Martina (2021) 'Covid-19 and rebordering the world', *Radical Philosophy*, 2(10): 8.

Auer, Peter (1998) *Code-Switching in Conversation: Language, Interaction and Identity*, Cambridge: Cambridge University Press.

Bajaj, Simar-Singh, Maki, Lwando and Cody Stanford, Fatima (2022) 'Vaccine apartheid: Global cooperation and equity', *The Lancet*, 399(10334): 1452–3. https://doi.org/10.1016/S0140-6736(22)00328-2

Baldassar, Loretta (2014) 'Too sick to move: Distant "crisis" care in transnational families', *International Review of Sociology*, 24(3): 391–405. https://doi.org/10.1080/03906701.2014.954328

Barahona de Brito, Alexandra, González-Enríquez, Carmen and Aguilar, Paloma (2001) *The Politics of Memory and Democratization*, Oxford: Oxford University Press.

Barnard, Helen and Turner, Claire (2011) *Poverty and Ethnicity: A Review of Evidence*, York: Joseph Rowntree Foundation, 18 May. Available from: www.jrf.org.uk/report/poverty-and-ethnicity-review-evidence

Barr, Damian (2020) 'We are not all in the same boat.' Available from: www.damianbarr.com/same-storm

Baudrillard, Jean (1998) *America*, London and New York: Verso.

BBC (2021) *Disclosure: Desperately Seeking Asylum* [Television], 12 July. Available from: www.bbc.co.uk/iplayer/episode/m000x4lv/disclosure-series-4-1-desperately-seeking-asylum

BBC News (2020a) 'Coronavirus: Body in "industrial fridge for six days"', 24 April. Available from: www.bbc.co.uk/news/uk-england-birmingham-52368827

BBC News (2020b) 'Coronavirus: UK holds minute's silence for key workers who died', 28 April. Available from: www.bbc.co.uk/news/uk-52450138

BBC News (2020c) 'Black Lives Matter protests: March held in Liverpool', 13 June. Available from: www.bbc.co.uk/news/uk-england-merseyside-53033810

BBC News (2020d) 'London protests: Demonstrators clash with police', 13 June. Available from: www.bbc.co.uk/news/uk-53031072

BBC Politics (2019) 'Parliament is like a "blocked artery at the heart of the British body politic" – PM Boris Johnson says the majority of the UK can see that it's time to deliver the "will of the people" and sort out Brexit', Tweet, 15 November. Available from: https://twitter.com/BBCPolitics/status/1195323258242883584

BBC Two (2021) 'Covid: Where is the anti-lockdown movement headed?', BBC *Newsnight*, 30 June. Available from: www.youtube.com/watch?v=EqYfTw90sBU

BBC Two (2022) '*Newsnight* with Kirsty Wark', 10:30 pm, 26 January. Available from: www.bbc.co.uk/iplayer/episode/m0013wzq/newsnight-26012022?page=1

Beebeejaun, Yasminah, McClymont, Katie, Maddrell, Avril, Mathijssen, Brenda and McNally, Danny (2021) 'Death in the peripheries: Planning for minority ethnic groups beyond "the city"', *Journal of Planning Education and Research*, 1–14. https://doi.org/10.1177/0739456X211043275

Beiner, Guy (2018) *Forgetful Remembrance: Social Forgetting and Vernacular Historiography of a Rebellion in Ulster*, Oxford: Oxford University Press.

Beiner, Guy (2022a) 'The great flu: Between remembering and forgetting', in Guy Beiner (ed) *Pandemic Re-Awakenings*, Oxford: Oxford University Press, pp 1–48.

Beiner, Guy (ed) (2022b) *Pandemic Re-Awakenings: The Forgotten and Unforgotten 'Spanish' Flu of 1918–1919*, Oxford: Oxford University Press.

Benjamin, Walter (1996 [1921]) 'Critique of violence', in Marcus Bullock and Michael W. Jennings (eds) *Walter Benjamin: Selected Writings*, Volume 1, *1913–1926*, Cambridge: Harvard University Press, pp 236–52.

Bhatia, Monish (2021) 'Racial surveillance and the mental health impacts of electronic monitoring on migrants', *Race & Class*, 62(3): 18–36. https://doi.org/10.1177/0306396820963485

Bhatia, Shekha (2020) '"He is optimistic, determined and resilient": Boris Johnson's father Stanley believes PM has the strength to beat coronavirus as he reveals he is being kept in the dark about his son's condition', *Mail Online*, 7 April. Available from: www.dailymail.co.uk/news/article-8197073/Boris-Johnsons-father-Stanley-believes-PM-strength-beat-coronavirus.html

Bilton, Richard (2020) 'Has the Government failed the NHS?', *Panorama*, BBC One, 27 April. Available from: www.youtube.com/watch?v=tSuHp-FVJsQ

Blanchot, Maurice (1995) *The Writing of the Disaster* [*L'écriture du désastre*], translated by Ann Smock, Lincoln, NE: University of Nebraska Press.

Booth, Robert (2020) 'Uber driver dies from Covid-19 after hiding it over fear of eviction', *The Guardian*, 17 April. Available from: www.theguardian.com/world/2020/apr/17/uber-driver-dies-from-covid-19-after-hiding-it-over-fear-of-eviction

Booth, Robert (2021) 'Justin Welby calls for start to public inquiry into handling of Covid', *The Guardian*, 21 April. Available from: www.theguardian.com/world/2021/apr/21/justin-welby-calls-for-start-to-public-inquiry-into-handling-of-covid

Boss, Pauline (1999) *Ambiguous Loss: Learning to Live with Unresolved Grief*, Cambridge, MA: Harvard University Press.

Bosworth, Mary and Vannier, Marion (2016) 'Comparing immigration detention in Britain and France: A matter of time?', *European Journal of Migration and Law*, 18(2): 157–76. https://doi.org/10.1163/15718166-12342097

Bourdieu, Pierre (2000) *Pascalian Meditations*, Stanford, CA: Stanford University Press.

Bowling, Ben and Westenra, Sophie (2020) '"A really hostile environment": Adiaphorization, global policing and the crimmigration control system', *Theoretical Criminology*, 24(2): 163–83. https://doi.org/10.1177/1362480618774034

Brand, Dionne (2020) 'On narrative, reckoning and the calculus of living and dying', *Toronto Star*, 4 July. Available from: www.thestar.com/entertainment/books/2020/07/04/dionne-brand-on-narrative-reckoning-and-the-calculus-of-living-and-dying.html

Bravo, Vanessa (2017) 'Coping with dying and deaths at home: How undocumented migrants in the United States experience the process of transnational grieving', *Mortality*, 22: 33–44. https://doi.org/10.1080/13576275.2016.1192590

Brooks, Libby (2020) 'Glasgow asylum seekers moved into hotels where distancing is "impossible"', *The Guardian*, 22 April. Available from: www.theguardian.com/uk-news/2020/apr/22/glasgow-asylum-seekers-told-to-pack-up-with-an-hours-notice

Brown, Jennifer and Horvath, Miranda (2022) 'Sarah Everard: The tipping point to take violence against women and girls seriously?', British Politics and Policy at LSE [Blog]. Available from: http://eprints.lse.ac.uk/112889/1/politicsandpolicy_sarah_everard.pdf

Budgeon, Shelley (2003) 'Identity as an embodied event', *Body & Society*, 9(1): 35–55.

Buncombe, Andrew, Sengupta, Kim and Comerford, Cathy (1998) '"It's like having Hitler move in", say the General's new neighbours in the Gin Belt', *The Independent*, 2 December. Available from: www.independent.co.uk/news/uk/crime/its-like-having-hitler-move-in-say-the-generals-new-neighbours-in-the-gin-belt-739575.html

Butler, Judith (2004) *Precarious Life: The Power of Mourning and Violence*, London and New York: Verso.

Butler, Judith (2009) *Frames of War: When Is Life Grievable?*, London and New York: Verso.

Butler, Judith and Yancy, George (2020) 'Interview: Mourning is a political act amid the pandemic and its disparities' (Republication), *Journal of Bioethical Inquiry*, 17: 483–7.

Canning, Victoria (2017) *Gendered Harm and Structural Violence in the British Asylum System*, London: Taylor & Francis.

Carr, Nicola (2021) 'Probation in a pandemic', *Probation Journal*, 68(1): 3–7. https://doi.org/10.1177/0264550521991388

Carrell, Severin (2022) 'Sudanese refugee made 72 calls seeking help before Glasgow hotel stabbings', *The Guardian*, 12 April. Available from: www.theguardian.com/uk-news/2022/apr/12/sudanese-refugee-made-72-calls-seeking-help-before-glasgow-hotel-stabbings

Centre for Ageing Better (2020) *The Experience of People Approaching Later Life in Lockdown: The Impact of COVID-19 on 50–70-Year-Olds in England*, July. Available from: https://ageing-better.org.uk/sites/default/files/2020-07/experience-of-people-approaching-later-life-lockdown.pdf

CGTN (China Global Television Network) (2021) 'Thousands of anti-lockdown protesters clash with London police', 25 April. Available from: www.youtube.com/watch?v=QvSrfl72Uac

Clarke, Martin V. (2021) 'The long haul: Stages of grief following a family bereavement', in Erica Borgstrom and Shannon Mallon (eds) *Narratives of Covid: Loss, Dying, Death and Grief During Covid-19*, Milton Keynes: The Open University, pp 114–17.

Cockroft, Stephanie and Speare-Cole, Rebecca (2020) 'Trafalgar Square antilock down protest shutdown by police after thousands of maskless demonstrators ignore social distancing', *Evening Standard*, 26 September. Available from: www.standard.co.uk/news/london/trafalgar-square-antilockdown-protest-thousands-a4556931.html

Cohen, Stanley (2013) *States of Denial: Knowing about Atrocities and Suffering*, Cambridge: Polity Press.

Coles, Eve (2014) *Learning the Lessons from Major Incidents: A Short Review of the Literature*, Emergency Planning College, Occasional Papers, New Series No 10, Easingwold. Available from: www.epcresilience.com/application/files/4916/5236/8945/Occ10-Paper.pdf

Coronavirus Act (2020) 'Registration of deaths and still-births etc.' Available from: www.legislation.gov.uk/ukpga/2020/7/part/1/crossheading/registration-of-deaths-and-stillbirths-etc/enacted

Cortvriend, Amy (2020) 'Coping with vulnerability: The limbo created by the UK asylum system', *International Journal for Crime, Justice and Social Democracy*, 9(3): 61–74. https://doi.org/10.5204/ijcjsd.v9i3.1586

Cover, Robert (1986) 'Violence and the word', *The Yale Law Journal*, 95(8): 1601–29. https://doi.org/10.2307/796468

Covid-19 Bereaved Families for Justice (2021a) 'Archbishop of Canterbury Justin Welby on his visit to the National Covid Memorial Wall', 21 April. Available from: www.facebook.com/CovidJusticeUK/videos/archbishop-of-canterbury-justin-welby-on-his-visit-to-the-national-covid-memoria/451477262750229

Covid-19 Bereaved Families for Justice (2021b) Tweet, 29 March. https://twitter.com/CovidJusticeUK/status/1508746635668561920

Covid-19 Bereaved Families for Justice (2021c) Tweet, 25 April. https://twitter.com/CovidJusticeUK/status/1386448840576970753

Covid-19 Bereaved Families for Justice (2022a) Tweet, 21 February. https://twitter.com/CovidJusticeUK/status/1495813572403814402

Covid-19 Bereaved Families for Justice (2022b) Twitter thread, 31 January. https://twitter.com/CovidJusticeUK/status/1488225536304427012

Coward, Ruth (2021) 'A grief denied', in Erica Borgstrom and Shannon Mallon (eds) *Narratives of Covid: Loss, Dying, Death and Grief During Covid-19*, Milton Keynes: The Open University, pp 49–53.

Cruse Bereavement Care (2022) 'Bereavement Supporter Project.' Available from: www.cruse.org.uk/about/our-work/bereavement-supporter-project

Danto, Arthur (1985) 'The Vietnam Veterans Memorial', *The Nation*, 31 August. Available from: http://hettingern.people.cofc.edu/Aesthetics_Fall_2010/Danto_Vietnam_Veteran%27s_Memorial.pdf

de Londras, Fiona and Lock, Daniela (2021) Written evidence to the Joint Committee on Human Rights, 11 January. Available from: https://committees.parliament.uk/writtenevidence/21159/pdf

Dean, Robert D. (2002) 'Masculinity as ideology: John F. Kennedy and the domestic politics of foreign policy', *Diplomatic History*, 22(1): 29–62.

della Porta, Donatella, Reiter, Herbert and Marx, Gary T. (1998) 'Introduction: The policing of protest in Western democracies', in Donatella della Porta and Herbert Reiter (eds) *Policing Protest: The Control of Mass Demonstrations in Western Democracies*, Minneapolis, MN: University of Minnesota Press, pp 1–32.

Department of Health and Social Care ([2011] 2014) *UK Influenza Pandemic Preparedness Strategy: Guidance on Preparing for and Responding to an Influenza Pandemic*. Available from: www.gov.uk/government/publications/review-of-the-evidence-base-underpinning-the-uk-influenza-pandemic-preparedness-strategy

Department of Health and Social Care (2020a) 'Emergency bill to strengthen coronavirus (COVID-19) response plans', News story, 17 March. Available from: www.gov.uk/government/news/emergency-bill-to-strengthen-coronavirus-covid-19-response-plans

Department of Health and Social Care (2020b) 'Response to Sunday Times Insight article', Press Office, 19 April. Available from: https://healthmedia.blog.gov.uk/2020/04/19/response-to-sunday-times-insight-article

Derrida, Jacques (1992) 'Force of law: The mystical foundations of authority', in Drucilla Cornell, Michel Rosenfeld and David Gray Carlton (eds) *Deconstruction and the Possibility of Justice*, London: Routledge, pp 3–67.

Dingwall, Robert and Vassy, Carine (2015) *The Social Construction of Mortality Data*. Available from: https://chpi.org.uk/blog/social-construction-mortality-data

Disaster Action (2022) 'Reflections on personal experience of disaster' [Leaflet]. Available from: www.disasteraction.org.uk/leaflets/reflections_on_personal_experience_of_disaster

Doctors of the World, Helen Bamber Foundation, Forrest Medico-Legal Services and Freedom From Torture (2021) *Asylum Accommodation: Clinical Harm Caused by the Use of Barracks as Housing for Asylum Seekers*. Available from: www.freedomfromtorture.org/sites/default/files/2021-02/Submission%20to%20HASC%20on%20barracks_HBF_Forrest_DOTW_FfT_FINAL.pdf

Dodsworth, Laura (2020) 'Counting the dead', *The Critic*, 11 September. Available from: https://thecritic.co.uk/counting-the-dead

Dutton, Rachael (2021) *Retirement Village and Extra Care Housing in England: Operators' Experience during the COVID-19 Pandemic*, RE-COV Study, Full Report, April. Available from: www.stmonicatrust.org.uk/resources/files/RE-COV-Study-FULL-REPORT-29-Apr-2021-final-version.pdf

Easthope, Lucy (2007) *Public Inquiries after Disaster: A Thematic Review*, Project Report, Cabinet Office Emergency Planning College. Available from: https://eprints.lincoln.ac.uk/id/eprint/26828

Easthope, Lucy (2018) *The Recovery Myth: The Plans and Situated Realities of Post-Disaster Response*, Cham: Palgrave Macmillan.

Easthope, Lucy (2022a) Tweet, 20 January. Available from: https://twitter.com/LucyGoBag/status/1484092993393070080

Easthope, Lucy (2022b) *When the Dust Settles: Stories of Love, Loss and Hope from an Expert in Disaster*, London: Hodder & Stoughton.

Easthope, Lucy (2022c) 'Out of the dust: Britain's leading disaster expert on coping with crisis', *The Observer*, 20 March. Available from: www.theguardian.com/books/2022/mar/20/out-of-the-dust-lucy-easthope-britains-leading-disaster-expert-on-coping-with-crisis

Edkins, Jenny (2003) *Trauma and the Memory of Politics*, Cambridge: Cambridge University Press.

Edkins, Jenny (2011) *Missing: Persons and Politics*, Ithaca, NY: Cornell University Press.

Elliott, Dominic and McGuinness, Martina (2002) 'Public inquiry: Panacea or placebo?', *Journal of Contingencies and Crisis Management*, 10(1): 14–25. https://doi.org/10.1111/1468-5973.00177

Enloe, Cynthia (2020) 'COVID-19: "Waging war" against a virus is NOT what we need to be doing', WILPF (Women's International League for Peace and Freedom), Analysis, 23 March. Available from: www.wilpf.org/covid-19-waging-war-against-a-virus-is-not-what-we-need-to-be-doing

Epstein, Steven (2016) *Impure Science: Aids, Activism, and the Politics of Knowledge*, Oakland, CA: University of California Press.

Erll, Astrid (2009) 'Remembering across time, space, and cultures: Premediation, remediation and the "Indian Mutiny"', in Astrid Erll and Ann Rigney (eds) *Mediation, Remediation, and the Dynamics of Cultural Memory*, Berlin and New York: Walter de Gruyter, pp 109–38.

Erll, Astrid (2020) 'Afterword: Memory worlds in times of corona', *Memory Studies*, 13(5): 861–74. doi:10.1177/1750698020943014.

EVAW (End Violence Against Women) (2021) 'Almost half of women have less trust in police following Sarah Everard Murder', Press release, 18 November. Available from: www.endviolenceagainstwomen.org.uk/almost-half-of-women-have-less-trust-in-police-following-sarah-everard-murder

Evening Standard (2021) 'Arrests as police clash with protesters at Sarah Everard vigil in Clapham Common' [video], 13 March. Available from: www.youtube.com/watch?v=fFdJMbmX4Hg

Famosaya, Paul (2020) 'Police–citizen interactions in Nigeria: The "ordinary" aspects', *Policing & Society*, 31(8): 936–49. doi: 10.1080/10439463.2020.1798953.

Farrow, Kathryn (2020) 'Policing the pandemic in the UK using the principles of procedural justice', *Policing: A Journal of Policy and Practice*, 14(3): 587–92. https://doi.org/10.1093/police/paaa031

Finlay, Robin, Hopkins, Peter and Benwell, Matthew (2021) *'It's Like Rubbing Salt on the Wound': The Impacts of Covid-19 and Lockdown on Asylum Seekers and Refugees*. Newcastle upon Tyne: Newcastle University. Available from: https://eprints.ncl.ac.uk/file_store/production/278292/9CA31F73-22E2-4362-B45B-1EC82308EA7E.pdf

Fisher, Pip (2020) 'How was lockdown for you? Asylum seekers' mental health during the pandemic', *British Journal of General Practice*, 70(698): 434. https://bjgp.org/content/bjgp/70/698/434.2.full.pdf

Fletcher, Erica (2021) 'Gender inequality in the gig economy', *Autonomy*, 1 June. Available from: https://autonomy.work/portfolio/fletcher-gig-economy

Foucault, Michel (1976) *The History of Sexuality: Volume 1. An Introduction*, London and New York: Penguin Books.

France, David (2016) *How to Survive a Plague: The Story of How Activists and Scientists Tamed Aids*, London: Picador.

Fu, Lin, Lindenmeyer, Antje, Phillimore, Jenny and Lessard-Phillips, Laurence (2022) 'Vulnerable migrants' access to healthcare in the early stages of the COVID-19 pandemic in the UK', *Public Health*, 203: 36–42. https://doi.org/10.1016/j.puhe.2021.12.008

Gamlin, Jennie, Gibbon, Sahra and Calestani, Melania (2021) 'The biopolitics of COVID-19 in the UK: Racism, nationalism and the afterlife of colonialism', in Lenore Manderson, Nancy J. Burke and Ayo Wahlberg (eds) *Viral Loads: Anthropologies of Urgency in the Time of COVID-19*, London: UCL Press, pp 108–27.

Gardner, Katy (2002) 'Death of a migrant: Transnational death rituals and gender among British Sylhetis', *Global Networks*, 2(3): 191–204.

Gayle, Damien, Busby, Mattha and Quinn, Ben (2020) 'Coronavirus: Police break up anti-lockdown protest in London', *The Guardian*, 26 September. Available from: www.theguardian.com/world/2020/sep/26/london-lockdown-protesters-urged-to-follow-covid-rules

Gentleman, Amelia (2018) 'Windrush scandal: Albert Thompson gets cancer treatment date', *The Guardian*, 24 April. Available from: www.theguardian.com/uk-news/2018/apr/24/windrush-scandal-albert-thompson-gets-cancer-treatment-date

Gentleman, Amelia (2019) *The Windrush Betrayal: Exposing the Hostile Environment*, London: Guardian Faber.

Gerbaudo, Paulo (2020) 'The pandemic crowd: Protest in the time of Covid-19', *Journal of International Affairs*, 73(2): 61–76. Available from: www.jstor.org/stable/26939966

Gillis, John R. (1994) 'Introduction. Memory and identity: The history of a relationship', in John R. Gillis (ed) *Commemorations: The Politics of National Identity*, Princeton, NJ: Princeton University Press, pp 1–24.

Gilmore, Joanna (2010) 'Policing protest: An authoritarian consensus', *Criminal Justice Matters*, 82(1): 21–3. doi:10.1080/09627251.2010.525926.

Global News (2020) 'Coronavirus: Anti-lockdown protesters clash with police in London's Trafalgar Square', 26 September. Available from: www.youtube.com/watch?v=gf-cJ5n8JvY

Goffman, Erving (1961) *Asylums: Essays on the Social Situation of Mental Patients and Other Inmates*, London: Penguin.

Goffman, Erving (1963) *Stigma: Notes on the Management of Spoiled Identity*, London: Penguin.

Gold Jennings Solicitors (2021) 'High Court challenge to Home Secretary's unlawful imposition of 23-hour daily curfew on those in asylum support accommodation', News story, 19 February. Available from: www.matthewgold.co.uk/high-court-challenge-to-home-secretarys-unlawful-imposition-of-23-hour-daily-curfew-on-those-in-asylum-support-accommodation

Goodall, Lewis (2022) Tweet, 27 January. https://twitter.com/lewis_goodall/status/1486703484212756484

Good Morning Britain (2021) 'Sarah Everard vigil protester explains "terror" of being held by police in emotional interview', 15 March. Available from: www.youtube.com/watch?v=LYml7Vy_Ooo&list=LL&index=8

Grace, Jamie (2021) 'From statues to statute: Protests and vigils in the time of COVID-19', SSRN, 30 March. Available from: http://dx.doi.org/10.2139/ssrn.3814145

Grayson, John (2020) 'Asylum in the time of Covid-19', Institute of Race Relations, News story, 26 March. Available from: https://irr.org.uk/article/asylum-in-the-time-of-covid-19

greenspace scotland (2021) 'Scotland's Covid memorial'. Available from: www.greenspacescotland.org.uk/national-covid-memorial

Gregory, Adrian (1994) *The Silence of Memory: Armistice Day 1919–1946*, Oxford and Providence: Berg.

Griffin, Shaun (2020) 'Covid-19: England comes into line with rest of UK on recording deaths', *BMJ*, 370: m3220. https://doi.org/10.1136/bmj.m3220

Haddad, Amy (2020) 'Metaphorical militarisation: Covid-19 and the language of war', *The Strategist*, 13 May. Available from: www.aspistrategist.org.au/metaphorical-militarisation-covid-19-and-the-language-of-war

Han, Yuna, Millar, Katharine M. and Bayley, Martin J. (2021) 'COVID-19 as a mass death event', *Ethics and International Affairs*, 35(1): 5–17. https://doi.org/10.1017/S0892679421000022

Hancock, Matt (2020) 'Controlling the spread of COVID-19: Health Secretary's Statement to Parliament', UK Government, 16 March. Available from: www.gov.uk/government/speeches/controlling-the-spread-of-covid-19-health-secretarys-statement-to-parliament

Harris, Scarlet, Joseph-Salisbury, Remi, Williams, Patrick and White, Lisa (2022) 'Notes on policing, racism and the Covid-19 pandemic in the UK', *Race & Class*, 63(3): 92–102. doi:10.1177/03063968211063436.

Ho, Elaine Lynn-Ee and Maddrell, Avril (2020) 'Intolerable intersectional burdens: A COVID-19 research agenda for social and cultural geographies', *Social & Cultural Geography*, 22(1): 1–10. https://doi.org/10.1080/14649365.2020.1837215

Hockey, Jenny, Komaromy, Carol and Woodthorpe, Kate (eds) (2010) *The Matter of Death: Space, Place and Materiality*, Basingstoke: Palgrave Macmillan.

Hockey, Jenny, Penhale, Bridget and Sibley, David (2001) 'Landscapes of loss: Spaces of memory, times of bereavement', *Ageing & Society*, 21(6): 739–57. doi:10.1017/S0144686X01008480.

Home Office (2020) 'The use of temporary hotels to house asylum seekers during Covid-19', Home Office in the Media [Blog], 8 August. Available from: https://homeofficemedia.blog.gov.uk/2020/08/08/the-use-of-temporary-hotels-to-house-asylum-seekers-during-covid-19

Home Office (2021) 'How many people are detained or returned?' GOV.UK [Data]. Available from: www.gov.uk/government/statistics/immigration-statistics-year-ending-september-2021/how-many-people-are-detained-or-returned

Honigsbaum, Mark (2009) *Living With Enza: The Forgotten Story of Britain and the Great Flu Pandemic of 1918*, Basingstoke: Palgrave Macmillan.

Honigsbaum, Mark (2017) 'Through a glass brightly: Whitechapel's pandemic window', *The Historian*, 6 October, Queen Mary University of London. Available from: https://projects.history.qmul.ac.uk/thehistorian/2017/10/06/through-a-glass-brightly-whitechapels-pandemic-window

Honigsbaum, Mark (2021a) 'Commemorating Covid', *Going Viral*, Libsyn, 6 July. Available from: https://directory.libsyn.com/shows/view/id/goingviralthepod

Hoskins, Andrew (2011) '7/7 and connective memory: Interactional trajectories of remembering in post-scarcity culture', *Memory Studies*, 4(3): 269–80. doi:10.1177/1750698011402570.

Hossein-Pour, Anahita (2019) 'Vote Leave boss Dominic Cummings blasts Tory Eurosceptics as "metastasising tumour" in call for new Brexit Party', *PoliticsHome*, 27 March. Available from: www.politicshome.com/news/article/vote-leave-boss-dominic-cummings-blasts-tory-eurosceptics-as-metastasising-tumour-in-call-for-new-brexit-party

House of Commons Home Affairs Committee (2017) *Asylum Accommodation*. Available from: https://publications.parliament.uk/pa/cm201617/cmselect/cmhaff/637/637.pdf

House of Commons Select Committee (2020) *Home Office Preparedness for COVID-19 (Coronavirus): Institutional Accommodation*. Available from: https://publications.parliament.uk/pa/cm5801/cmselect/cmhaff/562/56204.htm

House of Commons and House of Lords Joint Committee on Human Rights (2021) *The Government Response to Covid-19: Freedom of Assembly and the Right to Protest*, HC 1328, HL Paper 252, 19 March. Available from: https://committees.parliament.uk/publications/5153/documents/50935/default

Howard, Mark (2022) 'The necropolice economy: Mapping biopolitical priorities and human expendability in the time of COVID-19', *Societies*, 12(2). https://doi.org/10.3390/soc12010002

Hynes, Patricia (2011) *The Dispersal and Social Exclusion of Asylum Seekers*, Bristol: Policy Press.

Hynes, Patricia and Sales, Rosemary (2009) 'New communities: Asylum seekers and dispersal', in Alice Bloch and John Solomos (eds) *Race and Ethnicity in the 21st Century*, Basingstoke: Palgrave Macmillan, pp 39–61.

Inayatullah, Naeem (2020) 'Virus, vaccine, and value in a curved universe', *Review of Human Rights*, 6(1): xxxvii–xlii. https://doi.org/10.35994/rhr.v6i1.112

Inkpen, Robert, Ghaemmaghami, Aram, Newiss, Geoff, et al (2022) '"Othering" by consent? Public attitudes to Covid-19 restrictions and the role of the police in managing compliance in England', *The Sociological Quarterly*. doi:10.1080/00380253.2022.2066030.

Irving, Henry (2020) 'Blitz spirit won't help "win the fight" against Covid-19', *History & Policy*, 20 March. Available from: www.historyandpolicy.org/opinion-articles/articles/blitz-spirit-wont-help-win-the-fight-against-covid-19

Islam, Farjana and Netto, Gina (2020) '"The virus does not discriminate": Debunking the myth: The unequal impact of COVID-19 on ethnic minority groups', *Radical Statistics*, 126. www.radstats.org.uk/journal/issue126

ITV News (2022) 'Daughter whose mother died alone "furious" at Downing Street drinks party at height of lockdown', 10 January. Available from: www.itv.com/news/2022-01-10/bereaved-families-furious-and-sick-at-downing-st-drinks-party-in-may-2020

JCHR (Joint Committee on Human Rights) (2020) *Chair's Briefing Paper: The Health Protection (Coronavirus Restrictions) (England) Regulations 2021 & The Lockdown Restrictions*, 8 April, pp 1–16. Available from: https://publications.parliament.uk/pa/jt5801/jtselect/jtrights/correspondence/Chairs-briefing-paper-regarding-Health-Protection-Coronavirus-Restrictions-England-Regulation-2020.pdf

JCHR (2021) *The Government Response to COVID-19: Fixed Penalty Notices. Fourteenth Report of Session 2019–21*. HC 1364; HL Paper 272. Available from: https://committees.parliament.uk/publications/5621/documents/55581/default

Jenkins, Ciaran (2020a) 'Can we rely on Covid-19 death figures?', Channel 4 News, 13 April. Available from: www.channel4.com/news/can-we-rely-on-covid-19-death-figures

Jenkins, Ciaran (2020b) Twitter thread, 13 April. https://twitter.com/c4ciaran/status/1249787270292480000

Johnson, Boris (2020a) Facebook post, 22 March. Available from: www.facebook.com/borisjohnson/posts/we-will-get-through-this-together-and-we-will-beat-the-virus-to-win-this-fight-w/10157264938451317

Johnson, Boris (2020b) 'Prime Minister's statement on coronavirus (COVID-19): 23 March 2020', Gov.uk, 23 March. Available from: www.gov.uk/government/speeches/pm-address-to-the-nation-on-coronavirus-23-march-2020

Johnson, Boris (2020c) 'PM video message on coronavirus: 27 March 2020,' Gov.uk, 27 March. Available from: www.gov.uk/government/speeches/pm-video-message-on-coronavirus-27-march-2020

Jones, Fay (2021) 'Policing and prevention of violence against women', *Parallel Parliament*, 15 March. Available from: www.parallelparliament.co.uk/mp/fay-jones/debate/2021-03-15/commons/commons-chamber/policing-and-prevention-of-violence-against-women

Joyce, Peter (2009) 'The policing of protest: In the light of recent events, Peter Joyce examines the evolution of the police's approach to handling demonstrations and disorder', *Policing Today*, 15(3): 31–3.

Jubany, Olga (2017) *Screening Asylum in a Culture of Disbelief*, Basingstoke: Palgrave Macmillan.

Judiciary of England and Wales (2022) 'Leigh v The Commissioner of Police of the Metropolis', Press statement, [2022] EWHC 527 (Admin) Lord Justice Warby & Mr Justice Holgate, 11 March. Available from: www.judiciary.uk/wp-content/uploads/2022/07/Leigh-v-MPS.Press-Summary.pdf

Kantorowicz, Ernst (1957) *The King's Two Bodies: A Study on Medieval Political Theology*, Princeton, NJ: Princeton University Press.

Kernick, Gill (2021) *Catastrophe and Systemic Change: Learning from the Grenfell Tower Fire and Other Disasters*, London: London Publishing Partnership.

Khan, Sadiq (2021) Twitter, 13 March. Available from: https://twitter.com/sadiqkhan/status/1370855110088257538

Kirkup, James and Winnett, Robert (2012) 'Theresa May interview: "We're going to give illegal migrants a really hostile reception"', *The Telegraph*, 19 June. Available from: www.telegraph.co.uk/news/0/theresa-may-interview-going-give-illegal-migrants-really-hostile

Klein, Naomi (2020) *On Fire: The Burning Case for a Green New Deal*, London: Penguin Books.

Knight, Sam (2021) 'The bodies piled high, whatever Boris Johnson said', *The New Yorker*, 30 April. Available from: www.newyorker.com/news/letter-from-the-uk/the-bodies-piled-high-whatever-boris-johnson-said

Laing, Heather and Tierney, Abi (2020) *Evaluation of Accommodation and Support Services Experienced by Asylum Seekers in Glasgow During COVID-19: Key Findings and Recommendations*. Available from: https://theferret.scot/soaring-suicide-harm-asylum-linked-accommodation

Lammy, David (2017) *The Lammy Review: An Independent Review into the Treatment of, and Outcomes for, Black, Asian and Minority Ethnic Individuals in the Criminal Justice System*, London. Available from: www.gov.uk/government/publications/lammy-review-final-report

Lavalley, Ryan and Johnson, Khalilah Robinson (2020) 'Occupation, injustice, and anti-Black racism in the United States of America', *Journal of Occupational Science*, 29(4): 487–99. doi:10.1080/14427591.2020.1810111.

Laville, Sandra (2020) 'London woman dies of suspected Covid-19 after being told she was "not priority"', *The Guardian*, 25 March. Available from: www.theguardian.com/world/2020/mar/25/london-woman-36-dies-of-suspected-covid-19-after-being-told-she-is-not-priority

Lindqvist, Sven (1996) *Exterminate All the Brutes*, translated by Joan Tate, New York: The New Press.

Lister, Kat (2022) '"I feel your country's anger" – Why the memorial to Britain's Covid dead will be set ablaze', *The Guardian*, 17 May. Available from: www.theguardian.com/artanddesign/2022/may/17/anger-memorial-britain-covid-dead-ablaze-david-best-burning-man

London SE1 (2016) '"Mad cow disease" memorial should be moved, say Lambeth planners', London SE1 Community Website, 23 January. Available from: www.london-se1.co.uk/news/view/8615

Lynskey, Dorian (2021) 'Wall of love: The incredible story behind the national Covid memorial', *The Observer*, 18 July. Available from: www.theguardian.com/world/2021/jul/18/wall-of-love-the-incredible-story-behind-the-national-covid-memorial-led-by-donkeys

Maddrell, Avril (2016) 'Mapping grief: A conceptual framework for understanding the spatial dimensions of bereavement, mourning and remembrance', *Social and Cultural Geography*, 17(2): 166–88. doi:10.1080/14649365.2015.1075579.

Maddrell, Avril (2020) 'Bereavement, grief, and consolation: Emotional-affective geographies of loss during COVID-19', *Dialogues in Human Geography*, 10(2): 107–11. doi.org/10.1177/2043820620934947.

Maddrell, Avril, McNally, Danny, Beebeejaun, Yasminah, McClymont, Katie and Mathijssen, Brenda (2021) 'Intersections of (infra)structural violence and cultural inclusion: The geopolitics of minority cemeteries and crematoria provision', *Transactions of the Institute of British Geographers*, 46: 675–88. http://doi.org/10.1111/tran.12437

Manhire, Toby (2022) 'Boris Johnson's partygate buffet from hell: a beginner's guide', *The Spin Off*, 26 January. Available from: https://thespinoff.co.nz/politics/26-01-2022/boris-johnsons-partygate-buffet-from-hell-a-beginners-guide

Mannergren Selimovic, Johanna (2020) 'Remembering corona: The politics of memory and the pandemic', *Utrikesmagasinet*, 22 May. Available from: www.ui.se/utrikesmagasinet/kronikor/2020/remembering-corona-the-politics-of-memory-and-the-pandemic

Mannergren Selimovic, Johanna (2021) 'Articulating presence of absence: Everyday memory and the performance of silence in Sarajevo', in Olivette Otele, Luisa Gandolfo and Yoav Galai (eds) *Post-Conflict Memorialization: Missing Memorials, Absent Bodies*, Basingstoke: Palgrave Macmillan, pp 15–34.

Manzoor-Khan, Suhaiymah (2020) 'Breathlessness is not a momentary condition' [Video of an original poem commissioned by The Centre for Research on Race and Law at Birkbeck School of Law, August 2020]. Available from: www.youtube.com/watch?v=0Jwy-zaY4Zk

Maravia, Usman (2020) 'Rationale for suspending Friday prayers, funerary rites, and fasting Ramadan during COVID-19: An analysis of the fatawa related to the coronavirus', *Journal of the British Islamic Medical Association*, 4(2): 1–6. Available from: www.jbima.com/article/rationale-for-suspending-friday-prayers-funerary-rites-and-fasting-ramadan-during-covid-19-an-analysis-of-the-fatawa-related-to-the-coronavirus

Mason, Rowena (2016) 'Families to get free copy of Chilcot report after Cameron intervenes', *The Guardian*, 3 June. Available from: www.theguardian.com/uk-news/2016/jun/03/chilcot-report-iraq-war-soldiers-families-free-copy-david-cameron-intervenes

Mason, Rowena (2020) 'Boris Johnson boasted of shaking hands on day Sage warned not to,' *The Guardian*, 5 May. Available from: www.theguardian.com/politics/2020/may/05/boris-johnson-boasted-of-shaking-hands-on-day-sage-warned-not-to

Mbembe, Achille (2003) 'Necropolitics', *Public Culture*, 15(1): 11–40.

Mbembe, Achille (2013) *Critique of Black Reason*, Durham, NC and London: Duke University Press.

Mbembe, Achille (2018) 'On Afrofuturism and the "genealogies of the object"', *Copyriot*, 14 December. Available from: https://non.copyriot.com/achille-mbembe-on-afrofuturism-and-the-genealogies-of-the-object

Mbembe, Achille (2020a) 'The universal right to breathe', *Critical Inquiry*, 13 April. Available from: https://critinq.wordpress.com/2020/04/13/the-universal-right-to-breathe

Mbembe, Achille (2020b) 'Achille Mbembe: The necropolitics of a pandemic', *Autonomies*, 24 April. Available from: http://autonomies.org/2020/04/achille-mbembe-the-necropolitics-of-a-pandemic

Mendick, Robert and Yorke, Harry (2020) 'The inside story of Boris Johnson's coronavirus battle', *The Telegraph*, 6 April. Available from: www.telegraph.co.uk/politics/2020/04/06/inside-story-boris-johnsons-coronavirus-battle

Miller, Daniel and Parrot, Fiona (2009) 'Loss and material culture in Southeast London', *Journal of the Royal Anthropological Institute*, 15: 502–19. doi:10.1111/j.1467-9655.2009.01570.x.

Milne, Amber (2020) 'UK under fire for suggesting coronavirus "great leveller"', *Reuters*, 9 April. Available from: www.reuters.com/article/us-health-coronavirus-leveller-trfn-idUSKCN21R30P

Mitha, Karim, Qureshi, Kaveri, Adatia, Shelina and Dodhia, Hiten (2020) 'Racism as a social determinant: COVID-19 and its impacts on racial/ethnic minorities', *Discover Society* [Blog], 22 December. Available from: https://archive.discoversociety. org/2020/12/22/racism-as-a-social-determinant-covid-19-and-its-impacts-on-racial-ethnic-minorities

Musu, Andrea (2020) 'War metaphors used for COVID-19 are compelling but also dangerous', *The Conversation*, 8 April. Available from: https://theconversation.com/war-metaphors-used-for-covid-19-are-compelling-but-also-dangerous-135406

Myhill, Andy and Quinton, Paul (2011) *It's a Fair Cop? Police Legitimacy, Public Cooperation, and Crime Reduction: An Interpretative Evidence Commentary*, London: National Policing Improvement Agency.

NAO (National Audit Office) (2008) *New Dimension – Enhancing the Fire and Rescue Services' Capacity to Respond to Terrorist and Other Large-Scale Incidents*. Available from: www.nao.org.uk/ report/new-dimension-enhancing-the-fire-and-rescue-services-capacity-to-respond-to-terrorist-and-other-large-scale-incidents

National AIDS Memorial (2022) 'Search the AIDs Memorial Quilt.' Available from: www.aidsmemorial.org/interactive-aids-quilt

National Covid Memorial Wall, The (2021) Tweet, 4 April. Available from: https://twitter.com/CovidMemorialUK/ status/1511055241885716484

National Covid Memorial Wall, The (2022) 'Walk the National Covid Memorial Wall.' Available from: https://nationalcovidmemorial wall.org

Neal, David (2021) *A Short Inspection of Reporting Events at Becket House Immigration Reporting Centre Based on Onsite Observations.* Available from: www.gov.uk/government/news/inspection-report-published-a-short-inspection-of-reporting-events-at-becket-house-immigration-reporting-centre-based-on-onsite-observations

Netpol (Network for Police Monitoring) (2020) *Britain is Not Innocent: A Netpol Report on the Policing of Black Lives Matter Protests.* Available from: https://netpol.org/black-lives-matter

New Zealand Red Cross (2014) *Leading in Disaster Recovery. A Companion through the Chaos.* Available from: https://media. redcross.org.nz/media/documents/Leading_in_Disaster_ Recovery_A_Companion_Through_the_Chaos.pdf

Newton Dunn, Tom (2020) Coronovirus Press Conference, 10 Downing Street [video, from 38:35 on], 14 April. Available from: www.youtube.com/watch?v=ANYGCXpU9hM

NHS England (2020) 'New NHS nightingale hospital to fight coronavirus', News, 24 March. Available from: www.england. nhs.uk/2020/03/new-nhs-nightingale-hospital-to-fight-coronavirus

NHS Providers (2020) 'Same storm, different boats: Inequalities in the COVID-19 pandemic.' Available from: https://nhsproviders. org/same-storm-different-boats

Nuila, Ricardo (2020) 'To fight the coronavirus you need an army', *The New Yorker*, 17 July. Available from: www.newyorker. com/science/medical-dispatch/to-fight-the-coronavirus-you-need-an-army

O'Carroll, Lisa (2020) 'Iain Duncan Smith, a friend and colleague of the Prime Minister, has said he is "shocked with the news", he has told the BBC', *The Guardian* Coronavirus Live [Blog], 6 April, 15:44. Available from: www.theguardian.com/world/ live/2020/apr/06/coronavirus-live-news-boris-johnson-admitted-to-hospital-as-trump-again-touts-hydroxychloroqui ne?page=with:block-5e8b86348f08c35a1d11b2b6

ONS (Office for National Statistics) (2021a) 'Coronavirus (COVID-19) related deaths by occupation, England and Wales: deaths registered between 9 March and 28 December 2020', 25 January. Available from: www.ons.gov.uk/peoplepopulation andcommunity/healthandsocialcare/causesofdeath/bulletins/ coronaviruscovid19relateddeathsbyoccupationenglandandwales/ deathsregisteredbetween9marchand28december2020

ONS (2021b) 'Alcohol-specific deaths in the UK: registered in 2020', 7 December. Available from: www.ons.gov.uk/people populationandcommunity/healthandsocialcare/causesofdeath/ bulletins/alcoholrelateddeathsintheunitedkingdom/registered in2020

ONS (2021c) 'Updating ethnic contrasts in deaths involving the coronavirus (COVID-19), England: 24 January 2020 to 31 March 2021.' Available from: www.ons.gov.uk/peoplepopulation andcommunity/birthsdeathsandmarriages/deaths/articles/ updatingethniccontrastsindeathsinvolvingthecoronaviruscovid19 englandandwales/24january2020to31march2021

ONS (2022) 'Updating ethnic contrasts in deaths involving the coronavirus (COVID-19), England: 8 December 2020 to 1 December 2021', 26 January. Available from: www.ons.gov.uk/ peoplepopulationandcommunity/birthsdeathsandmarriages/ deaths/articles/updatingethniccontrastsindeathsinvolvingthe coronaviruscovid19englandandwales/8december2020to1 december2021

Orwell, George (1946) 'In front of your nose', *Tribune*, 22 March.

Otele, Olivette, Gandolfo, Luisa and Galai, Yoav (2021) 'Afterword: Mourning, memorialising, and absence in the Covid-19 era', in Olivette Otele, Luisa Gandolfo and Yoav Galai (eds) *Post-Conflict Memorialization: Missing Memorials, Absent Bodies*, Basingstoke: Palgrave Macmillan, pp 241–52.

Owen, Wilfred (1920) 'Dulce et Decorum Est' [originally published in Wilfred Owen, *Poems*, London, Chatto & Windus]. Available from: www.poetryfoundation.org/poems/46560/ dulce-et-decorum-est

Patel, Priti (2020) Public Order, Volume 677: debated on Monday 8 June, *Hansard*. Available from: https://hansard.parliament. uk/commons/2020-06-08/debates/212DD2A6-B810-4FDE-B3BD-1642F5BA1E86/PublicOrder

Patterson, Laura (2021) 'TTFN', in Erica Borgstrom and Shannon Mallon (eds) *Narratives of Covid: Loss, Dying, Death and Grief During Covid-19*, Milton Keynes: The Open University, pp 132–7.

Pearl, Martyn and Zetter, Roger (2001) 'From refuge to exclusion: Housing as an instrument of social exclusion for refugees and asylum seekers in the UK', in Peter Somerville and Andy Steele (eds) *'Race', Housing and Social Exclusion*, London: Jessica Kingsley Publishers, pp 226–44.

Pemberton, Simon (2015) *Harmful Societies: Understanding Social Harm*, Bristol: University of Bristol Press.

Percival, Richard (2020) 'Plan to dig mass graves in UK to hold coffins of hundreds of coronavirus victims', *Mirror*, 20 May. Available from: www.mirror.co.uk/news/uk-news/first-mass-graves-could-dug-22059276

Philp, Chris (2020) 'Covid-19: Asylum seeker services in Glasgow', *Hansard*, UK Parliament, 677. Available from: https://hansard.parliament.uk//commons/2020-06-17/debates/3D0E2AD4-B458-4769-87EB-05ECB355868A/Covid-19AsylumSeekerServicesInGlasgow

Platt, Lucinda and Warwick, Ross (2020) *Are Some Ethnic Groups More Vulnerable to COVID-19 than Others?*, Inequality: The IFS Deaton Review, London: Institute for Fiscal Studies. Available from: www.ifs.org.uk/inequality/wp-content/uploads/2020/04/Are-some-ethnic-groups-more-vulnerable-to-COVID-19-than-others-IFS-Briefing-Note.pdf

Politico (2022) 'United Kingdom: National parliament voting intention.' Poll of Polls. Available from: www.politico.eu/europe-poll-of-polls/united-kingdom

Power, Gabriel (2020) 'The most expensive towns outside London in the UK', *The Week, Portfolio*, 18 February. Available from: www.theweek.co.uk/80569/the-most-expensive-uk-towns-outside-london

Public Health England (2020a) 'Disparities in the risk and outcomes of COVID-19.' Available from: https://assets.publishing.service.gov.uk/government/uploads/system/uploads/attachment_data/file/908434/Disparities_in_the_risk_and_outcomes_of_COVID_August_2020_update.pdf

Public Health England (2020b) *Exercise Cygnus Report*. Available from: www.gov.uk/government/publications/uk-pandemic-preparedness/exercise-cygnus-report-accessible-report

Purnell, Kandida (2015) 'Body politics and boundary work nobodies on hunger strike at Guantánamo (2013–2015)', *Alternatives: Global, Local, Political*, 39(4): 271–86.

Purnell, Kandida (2018) 'Grieving, valuing and viewing differently: The global war on terror's American toll', *International Political Sociology*, 12(2): 156–71.

Purnell, Kandida (2020a) 'From PhD to pandemic', *COVID-19 Global Health Diaries*, 29 April. Available from: https://covid19healthdiaries.com/diary?did=170

Purnell, Kandida (2020b) 'Calm the fuck down!', *Global Public Health COVID-19 Diaries*, 3 May. Available from: https://covid19healthdiaries.com/diary?did=180

Purnell, Kandida (2020c) 'On numbers and numbness', *Global Public Health COVID-19 Diaries*, 19 July. Available from: https://covid19healthdiaries.com/diary?did=306

Purnell, Kandida (2021a) *Rethinking the Body in Global Politics: Bodies, Body Politics, and the Body Politic in a Time of Pandemic*, London and New York: Routledge.

Purnell, Kandida (2021b) 'Out of touch, out of tune', *Emotions and Society*, 3(2): 277–93. doi:10.1332/26316902 1X16171227433111.

Purnell, Kandida (2021c) 'Bodies coming apart and bodies becoming parts: Widening, deepening, and embodying ontological (in)security in the context of the COVID-19 pandemic', *Global Studies Quarterly*, 1(4), December, ksab037. Available from: ehttps://doi.org/10.1093/isagsq/ksab037

Pyman, Tom (2020) 'Government is accused of underplaying coronavirus death toll at height of crisis as it is revealed more than 1,000 people died every day in the UK for 22 consecutive days', *Daily Mail*, 20 June. Available from: www.dailymail.co.uk/news/article-8441651/More-1-000-people-died-day-UK-22-consecutivedays.html

Radebe, Patrick (2021) 'Derek Chauvin: Racist cop or product of a racist police academy?', *Journal of Black Studies*, 52(3): 231–47. doi:10.1177/0021934720983501.

Reesp, Susan (2003) 'Refuge or retrauma? The impact of asylum seeker status on the wellbeing of East Timorese women asylum seekers residing in the Australian community', *Australasian Psychiatry*, 11: S96–101. https://doi.org/10.1046/j.1038-5282.2003.02022.x

Reicher, Stephen, Stott, Clifford, Drury, John, Adang, Otto, Cronin, Patrick and Livingstone, Andrew (2007) 'Knowledge-based public order policing: Principles and practice', *Policing: A Journal of Policy and Practice*, 1(4): 403–15. https://doi.org/10.1093/police/pam067

Reiner, Robert (1998) 'Policing, protest, and disorder in Britain', in Donatella della Porta and Herbert Reiter (eds) *Policing Protest: The Control of Mass Demonstrations in Western Democracies*, Minneapolis, MN: University of Minnesota Press, pp 35–48.

Richardson, Therese (2014) 'Spousal bereavement in later life', *Mortality*, 19(1): 61–79. doi:10.1080/13576275.2013.867844.

Ritchie, Hannah, Mathieu, Edouard, Rodés-Guirao, Lucas, et al (2020) 'Coronavirus (COVID-19) vaccinations.' Available from: https://ourworldindata.org/covid-vaccinations?country=OWID_WRL

Rosen, Michael (2022) Tweet and replies, 10 January. https://twitter.com/MichaelRosenYes/status/1480664420946780164

Rossner, Meredith, Tait, David and McCurdy, Martha (2021) 'Justice reimagined: Challenges and opportunities with implementing virtual courts', *Current Issues in Criminal Justice*, 33(1): 94–110, doi:10.1080/10345329.2020.1859968.

Sabbagh, Dan and Dodd, Vikram (2020) 'BLM organisers call off London event to avoid clash with far right', *The Guardian*, 11 June. Available from: www.theguardian.com/uk-news/2020/jun/11/blm-organisers-call-off-london-event-to-prevent-clashes-with-far-right

Sabbagh, Dan and Mason, Rowena (2020) 'The strange lead-up to Boris Johnson's admission to hospital', *The Guardian*, 6 April. Available from: www.theguardian.com/uk-news/2020/apr/06/the-strange-lead-up-to-boris-johnsons-admission-to-hospital

Sanchez Taylor, Jacqueline (2020) 'Life interrupted: Covid-19 and Black Lives Matter', *Discover Society* [Blog], 25 June. Available from: https://archive.discoversociety.org/2020/06/25/life-interrupted-covid-19-and-black-lives-matter

Scheper-Hughes, Nancy and Wacquant, Loic (2002) *Commodifying Bodies*, London: SAGE Publications.

Schofield, Kevin and Honeycombe-Foster, Matt (2020) 'Dominic Raab says he is confident that "fighter" Boris Johnson will beat the coronavirus', *PoliticsHome*, 7 April. Available from: www.politicshome.com/news/article/dominic-raab-says-he-is-confident-that-fighter-boris-johnson-will-beat-the-coronavirus

Shaw, Neil (2020) 'New food laws unveiled on Monday in bid to cut obesity', *Essex Live*, 27 July. Available from: www.essexlive.news/news/uk-world-news/new-food-laws-unveiled-monday-4366617

Sheptycki, James (2000) *Issues in Transnational Policing*, London: Routledge.

Sherwood, Harriet (2020) 'UK councils begin to ban funeral ceremonies due to coronavirus', *The Guardian*, 4 April. Available from: www.theguardian.com/world/2020/apr/04/uk-councils-begin-to-ban-funeral-ceremonies-due-to-coronavirus

Shilling, Chris (1993) *The Body and Social Theory*, London: SAGE Publications.

Sibley, John (2020) '"Fit as a butcher's dog", UK PM does press ups to show coronavirus recovery', *Reuters*, 28 July. Available from: www.reuters.com/article/us-health-coronavirus-britain-johnson-idCAKBN23Z0FB

Silva, Guillermo Andrés Duque and Higuera, Cristina del Prado (2021) 'Political theology and COVID-19: Agamben's critique of science as a new pandemic religion', *Open Theology*, 7(1): 501–13. https://doi.org/10.1515/opth-2020-0177

Sinnerbrink, Ingrid, Silove, Derrick, Field, Annette, Steel, Zachary and Manicavasagar, Vijaya (1997) 'Compounding of premigration trauma and postmigration stress in asylum seekers', *The Journal of Psychology*, 131(5): 463–70. https://doi.org/10.1080/00223989709603533

Sky News (2020) 'COVID-19: More than 150 arrests as anti-lockdown protesters clash with police in London', 28 November. Available from: www.youtube.com/watch?v=3Dt36h4jqdE

Starmer, Sir Keir (2022) 'Sue Gray Report', *Hansard*, vol 708, col 24, debated 31 January 3.37 pm. Available from: https://hansard.parliament.uk/Commons/2022-01-31/debates/6B412B49-AB7D-4FE3-9F82-B9EAE93FB6AC/SueGrayReport

Stott, Clifford, Radburn, Matthew, Pearson, Geoff, Harrison, Mark, Kyprianides, Arabella and Rowlands, David (2021) 'Police powers and public assemblies: Learning from the Clapham Common "vigil" during the Covid-19 pandemic', SocArXiv. Available from: https://osf.io/preprints/socarxiv/7jcsr

Stumpf, Juliet (2006) 'The crimmigration crisis: Immigrants, crime, and sovereign power', *American University Law Review*, 56(2): 367–420.

Suleman, Mehrunisha, Sonthalia, Shreya, Webb, Caitlin, Tinson, Adam, Kane, Martina, Finch, David and Bibby, Jo (2021) *Unequal Pandemic, Fairer Recovery: The COVID-19 Impact Inquiry Report*, The Health Foundation, July. Available from: www.health.org. uk/publications/reports/unequal-pandemic-fairer-recovery

Sun, The (2020) 'Police officer punched in scuffles outside Downing Street at Black Lives Matter protest in London', *The Sun*, Available from: www.youtube.com/watch?v=rQpm5a4y5XE

Sun, The (2021) 'Anti lockdown protesters clash with cops on the originally intended "Freedom Day"', 21 June. Available from: www.youtube.com/watch?v=cLxutu_3r_E&t=4s

Synnott, Anthony (2002) *The Body Social: Symbolism, Self and Society*, London: Routledge.

Taylor-Broadbent, Jayne (2022a) Tweet, 1 February. Available from: https://twitter.com/SkyNews/status/1488457168131141632

Taylor-Broadbent, Jayne (2022b) Tweet, 21 February. https://twitter.com/MarkOneinFour/status/1516701343196618756?s=20&t=XR2y-WSo5lfRUuFyv6iANw

Taylor-Broadbent, Jayne (2022c) Tweet, 3 March. https://twitter.com/MarkOneinFour/status/1517137937401450498?t=D0CuzrxSlU-OQAZfoUrTzg&s=19

Taylor, Diane (2021) 'Asylum seeker brings case against Covid "curfew" at London hotel', *The Guardian* 19 February. Available from: www.theguardian.com/uk-news/2021/feb/19/asylum-seeker-brings-case-against-covid-curfew-at-london-hotel

Tollerton, David (2022) *Covid-19 Remembrance and Reflection: Lessons from the Past and Attitudes in the Present*. University of Exeter and Arts and Humanities Research Council. Available from: https://humanities.exeter.ac.uk/media/universityofexeter/collegeofhumanities/documents/COVID-19_Remembrance_and_Reflection_Lessons_from_the_Past_and_Attitudes_in_the_Present.pdf

Troyer, John (2020) '"I was completely unprepared": Confronting my sister's death', *The Guardian*, 24 March. Available from: www.theguardian.com/society/2020/mar/24/growing-up-in-a-funeral-home-couldnt-prepare-me-for-my-sisters-death

Tsilivakou, Jenny (2021) 'Death in a Glasgow hotel: The last years of Badreddin Bosh', *Al Jazeera*, 26 June. Available from: www.aljazeera.com/features/2021/6/26/death-in-a-glasgow-hotel-the-last-years-of-badreddin-bosh

UK Visas and Immigration (2022a) 'Immigration and protection data: Q4 2021.' Available from: www.gov.uk/government/publications/immigration-and-protection-data-q4-2021

UK Visas and Immigration (2022b) 'Information booklet about your asylum application.' Available from: www.gov.uk/government/publications/information-leaflet-for-asylum-applications/information-booklet-about-your-asylum-application

University of Nebraska Press (2022) *Survivance: Narratives of Native Presence*. Available from: www.nebraskapress.unl.edu/nebraska-paperback/9780803210837 [Accessed 1 October 2022].

Vallance, Sir Patrick (2020) 'Coronavirus: Health Committee questions Government Chief Scientific Adviser and NHS England', UK Parliament Health Committee, 17 March. Available from: www.youtube.com/watch?v=ytnWsp4-gHE

Van Rythoven, Eric (2020) 'What's wrong with the war metaphor', *The Duck of Minerva*, 5 April. Available from: www.duckofminerva.com/2020/04/whats-wrong-with-the-war-metaphor.html

Vizenor, Gerald (ed) (2008) *Survivance: Narratives of Native Presence*, Lincoln, NE: University of Nebraska Press.

Walter, Tony (1996) 'A new model of grief: Bereavement and biography', *Mortality*, 1(1): 7–25. doi:10.1080/713685822.

Walters, Simon (2021) 'Boris Johnson: "Let the bodies pile high in their thousands"', *Daily Mail*, 25 April. Available from: www.dailymail.co.uk/news/article-9510133/Boris-Johnson-said-bodies-pile-high-order-lockdown-sources-claim.html

Ward, Geoff (2018) 'Living histories of White supremacist policing: Towards transformative justice', *Du Bois Review: Social Science Research on Race*, 15(1): 167–84. https://doi.org/10.1017/S1742058X18000139

Wearmouth, Rachel (2021) 'Boris Johnson accused of making Covid wall visit "under cover of darkness"', *Huffington Post*, 29 April. Available from: www.huffingtonpost.co.uk/entry/boris-johnson-insincere-memorial_uk_608a72eae4b046202703f82c

Wells, Celia (1995) *Negotiating Tragedy: Law and Disasters*, London: Sweet & Maxwell.

Wernimont, Jacqueline (2022) 'Pandemic death counts are numbing. There is another way to process', *WIRED Ideas* [Blog], 21 July. Available from: www.wired.com/story/covid19-data-visceralization-death-statistics

West, Karen, Rumble, Hannah, Shaw, Rachel, Cameron, Ailsa and Roleston, Caity (2022) 'Diarised reflections on COVID-19 and bereavement: Disruptions and affordances', *Illness, Crisis & Loss*. doi:10.1177/10541373211044069.

Westerleigh Group (2020) 'Covid-19 memorial gardens to be created at Westerleigh's 34 crematoria', *Westerleigh News* [Blog], 1 June. Available from: www.westerleighgroup.co.uk/blog/post.php?s=2020-06-01-covid-19-memorial-gardens-to-be-created-at-westerleighs-34-crematoria

Winter, Jay (1995) *Sites of Memory, Sites of Mourning: The Great War in European Cultural History*, Cambridge: Cambridge University Press.

Wynne Jones, Ros (2022) 'Guerrilla act of memorial began 180,000-strong Covid Wall – It must become permanent', *Daily Mirror*, 24 March. Available from: www.mirror.co.uk/news/uk-news/guerrilla-act-memorial-began-180000-26550275

Yarrington, Matthew D. (2010) 'Lived Islam in Bangladesh: Contemporary religious discourse between Ahl-i-Hadith, "Hanafis" and authoritative texts, with special reference to *al-barzakh*', PhD thesis, University of Edinburgh. Available from: https://era.ed.ac.uk/handle/1842/5690?show=full

Yeats, William Butler (1920) 'The Second Coming', *The Nation* (London), 6 November. Available from: www.poetryfoundation.org/poems/43290/the-second-coming

Yellow Hearts to Remember- Covid 19 (2022) Facebook group. Available from: www.facebook.com/groups/262593888277834

Young, James E. (1993) *The Texture of Memory: Holocaust Memorials and Meaning*, New Haven, CT: Yale University Press.

Index

A

Abdul-Latif, Amna 48–50, 54, 55, 59–60, 65–7, 70–1
African community 50, 61–2, 80
Afzal, Nazir 234
Agamben, Giorgio 144, 152–3
ageism 102, 104, 115
Aguilar, Paloma 236
Ahearne, Gemma 79
Ahmed Iqbal Ullah Education Trust (AIUET) 43–74
Ahmed Iqbal Ullah RACE (Race Archives and Community Engagement) Centre 8, 43–74
Ahmed, Sara 82, 90–1
Akhtar, Smina 161
'all in this together/same boat' 54, 64, 204–5, 265, 299
All-Party Parliamentary Group on Democracy and the Constitution 134–5
#allstoriesareinmportant 44
ambiguous loss 26–7, 33, 40
American Journal of Emergency Medicine 295
Amnesty International 103, 104
Ananna (organisation) *see* Islam, Safina
Anatomical Pathology Technologists (APT) *see* mortuaries
Anne Frank Trust *see* Abdul-Latif, Amna
anti-lockdown protests 127–8
Anumol, Dipali 9, 75–6
Aquarius community centre 61, 69–70

Aradau, Claudia 161
assisted living residents and grief 10, 103–17
  grievability of older lives 105
  peer support 112–14
  recollectivising bereavement 109–12
  research process of study 106–7
  shared grief over multiple losses 107–9
  and wider family 114–15
Association of Anatomical Pathology Technologists (AAPT) 197–8, 198–9
asylum seekers 12, 160–75
  civil death concept 171
  claims in progress 173
  confinement continuum 161
  crimmigration 163
  delays in system 162–3
  frequent moves 164, 166–7, 171, 173
  housing 161, 163–9, 172, 173, 174
  housing during the pandemic 166–9, 173, 174–5
  impact of pandemic 169–75
  internet access 168–9
  lack of power 170–1
  loss of identity 170–1
  policies of control 172
  Section 95 & 98 support 164, 167
  and structural violence 173–4
  UK asylum system 161–3
  women 51–2, 56–7, 62–3, 164–6
atmospheric walls 9, 90–1

B

Badreddin Abdallah Adam Bosh 12, 160–1, 174
Bajaj, Simar-Singh 6
Bajec, Manca 12, 154–9
Bangladeshi communities
   funerals 206, 209, 213–18
   women 47, 68–9
Barahona de Brito, Alexandra 236
Barr, Damian 204
BBC 34, 38, 92, 131–2, 167–8
Bedworth, Warwickshire 16
Beiner, Guy 238
Benjamin, Walter 149–52
bereavement *see* assisted living
      residents and grief; death(s);
      funerals; grief; memorials/
      memorialisation
Bereavement Supporter Project 106
Best, David 16
'Better Health' strategy 99
Bhatia, Monish 172
Bhatia, Shekha 97
Bilton, Richard 34
births 61
Black, Asian and Global Majority
      experiences 43–74
   access to hospital 80
   Black Lives Matter 32, 64–5,
     130–2, 134–5, 236, 294
   current situation 62–7
   death(s) 32, 54, 58–62, 65, 73–4,
     80, 205–6, 209–18, 293–5
   disposable lives 58–62, 73–4
   initial responses to pandemic
     45–52
   key workers 78–9
   necropolitics 84–6
   policing of 131, 140, 153
   and policy makers 67–70, 73
   preparedness for next pandemic
     70–2
   systemic discrimination 293–4
   unequal pandemic 31–2, 52–7,
     293–5, 298
   see also asylum seekers; Muslim
     communities

Black Lives Matter 32, 64–5, 236, 294
   policing the protests 130–2, 134–5
Blanchot, Maurice 35
body politics 10, 77–101
   alternative response 100–1
   atmospheric walls 90–1
   depersonalisation of victims 84
   fighting the virus 92–100
   necropolitics 84–6
   and political leaders 94–5
   protection from COVID-19 79
   shielding 79
   'taking it on the chin' 81–92
Booth, Robert 234
Boss, Pauline 26
Bradley, Gracie Mae 11, 121–2
Brand, Dionne 86
Breakspear Crematorium 191, 192, 194
breathing 18, 98
Brexit 92
Bristol 132, 134–5, 236
Brown, Jennifer 129
Brown, Mark 14–15, 179–83
Bryant, Sue 7–8, 19
burials 84, 207, 208–11, 213, 215, 216
   see also funerals
Butler, Judith 16, 83, 237

C

Canning, Victoria 173
care homes
   deaths 81
   impact of isolation 104
   patients discharged into 103–4
   visiting 31, 103
   see also assisted living residents and
     grief
Carney, Sue 36
cemeteries 13–14, 16, 206–11
CeMi research project 206
Centre for Ageing Better 104
Centre for Death and Society,
     University of Bath 13, 185
Channel 4 News 29

Chertsey, Surrey 87–8
Chinese community 47–8, 53–4,
58–9, 64, 71
Church of England 83–4
Civil Contingencies Act 2004 267,
273, 274
civil death concept 171
Clapham Common vigil 11, 89,
128–30, 133–4
clapping for carers 62, 95, 109, 196
Clarke, Martin 31
Clearsprings Ready Homes 168
Coleman, Rita 18–19, 265
Coles, Eve 286, 288–9
colonialism 85, 236, 294
Colston, Edward 132, 236
commemoration *see* memorials/
memorialisation
common humanity 293
Community Risk Registers 268
confinement continuum 161
connective memory 239
conspiracy theorists 127
Conte, Giuseppe 96
Coronavirus Act 2020 83, 89, 189,
269, 274, 285
see also legal education
coroners 83, 195
Cortvriend, Amy 4, 12, 160–75
counter-memorials 34
Couzens, Wayne 89
Cover, Robert 149
Covid-19 Bereaved Families for Justice
16, 35, 232–5, 243–5, 248, 260
origins 255–7
COVID-19 collecting project *see*
Robson, Jo
Coward, Ruth 31
cremations/crematoria 14, 16, 30, 83,
207, 208
Breakspear Crematorium 191, 192,
194
see also funerals
Creutzfeldt-Jakob disease 241–2
crimmigration 163
Cruse Bereavement Care 106
Cummings, Dominic 84, 92

D

Daily Mail 84, 244–5
Danto, Arthur 236
de Londras, Fiona 144
Dean, Robert D. 94
death certificates 29–30, 83, 186, 189,
210, 215, 283, 285
death toll 24, 29, 32, 33, 87, 90, 281,
283
death(s) 24–41
absent rituals 25–31, 36–7, 58–9,
60, 61–2, 65, 204–18
Black, Asian and Global Majority
experiences 32, 54, 58–62, 65,
73–4, 80, 205–6, 209–18, 293–5
certification of 29–30, 83, 186,
189, 210, 215, 283, 285
data quality 29, 281
and deprivation 80–1, 205–6, 293–5
enforced isolation 30–1, 36–7, 60,
188, 213–14
experiences of 25–33
gendering 92–100
Government compensation 81
horrific manner of 30
necropolitics 84–6
number of 24, 29, 32, 33, 87, 90,
281, 283
other than COVID 88
political impact of 33–9
and 'pre-existing' condition 31, 81,
96, 104
preparation of the body 209,
211–12, 213–14
registration of 187, 189, 190, 210,
215, 285
uneven distribution of 24, 32, 40,
54, 80–1, 205–6, 213, 293–5
visiting the dying 30–1, 36–7, 188,
205, 213–14
see also assisted living residents and
grief; funerals; grief; memorials/
memorialisation; mortuaries
delivery drivers 60, 78–9, 203
della Porta, Donatella 124
Department of Health and Social Care
29–30, 269, 270

deprivation, and impact of COVID-19 80–1, 205–6, 293–5

Derbyshire Police 150

Derrida, Jacques 150

Dingwall, Robert 281

Disaster Action 30

disaster management *see* emergency planning/planners

disasters and trauma 33

Disclosure report 167–8

Dodd, Vikram 132

Dodsworth, Laura 30–1

Domestic Abuse Bill 63

domestic violence 48, 56, 63, 100, 295

   see also violence against women and girls

double-loop learning 288–9

Dulce et Decorum Est (Owen) 28

Duncan Smith, Iain 98–9

Dundee City Council 209–10

Dundee, funeral service providers 206–12

Dundee Muslim Cemetery Trust 209–12

Dunn, Tom Newton 29

Dying Declaration (Nair) 11, 137–8

Dynamic Support Greater Manchester *see* Edouke Riley, Yvonne

E

Easthope, Lucy 17–18, 30–1, 38–9, 100, 279–90

Edinburgh, Muslim funerals 206, 215–16

Edkins, Jenny 8, 24–41

Edouke Riley, Yvonne 45–6, 52–3, 60–2, 69–70

education

   Black, Asian and Global Majority experiences 51, 74

   homeschooling 96–7

   students in lockdown 144

Elizabeth Blackwell Institute, University of Bristol 106

Elizabeth II, Queen 96

emergency planning/planners 17–18, 194, 199–200, 266–75, 279–90

   challenges of 280

   government's attitude to 269–71, 285

   hope for the future 284

   and inequalities 280–1

   Influenza Pandemic Preparedness Strategy 270

   law during the pandemic 285

   learning from COVID-19 270–3, 281, 285–90

   managing expectations 282–4

   and moving on 287–8

   necessity for lockdowns 269–70

   origins of 266–7

   pandemic exercises 194, 270, 280, 285

   risk based approach 268–9

   role of 267–8, 279–80, 285–6

   terrorist attacks 272

   urgent priorities 273–5

emergency powers 274, 285

emotional viral load 206

employment

   disparities between rich and poor 298

   financial support schemes 48–9, 59, 73, 80, 203, 295, 298

   migrant workers 57, 62–3, 298

   working from home 59, 73, 79, 87, 203

   see also key workers

End Violence Against Women (EVAW) coalition 130

endoskeleton of the world 86

enforced disappearances 26–7, 28–9, 31–2, 39

Epstein, Rabbi Daniel 233–4

Erll, Astrid 238–9

Eshalomi, Florence 234

European Convention on Human Rights (ECHR) 151–2

Everard, Sarah 11, 89, 121–2, 128–30, 133–4

Exercise Cygnus 194

ExtraCare Charitable Trust 10, 105–17

F

Facebook groups 49
Famosaya, Paul 11, 123–36
Fatai, Kazeem 234
'fighting the virus' 15, 92–100
film projection on Houses of
    Parliament 256
financial support schemes 48–9, 59,
    73, 80, 203, 295, 298
fines 89, 142, 143, 144, 150, 269,
    298
    Partygate 235, 245, 246, 250, 296
First World War 15, 28, 236, 238
Fisher, Pip 175
Floyd, George 11, 18, 32, 130–1,
    294
food, asylum seekers 165–66, 167–8
food banks and deliveries 45, 49–50,
    66, 79
    culturally appropriate 50, 53, 55
Foucault, Michel 84
Fowler, Ian 233, 243, 255, 258
Fowler, Matt 232–3, 243, 244, 255,
    256, 258
Friends of the Wall 17, 233, 248–9,
    259–61
frontline workers see key workers
funeral directors 13, 187, 190, 198,
    207–8, 216–17
funerals 13–14, 202–18
    assisted living residents 111
    burials 84, 207, 208–11, 213, 215,
    216
    cemeteries 13–14, 16, 206–11
    costs of 215–16
    crematoria 14, 16, 30, 83, 207, 208
    direct/unattended 207–8
    early days of pandemic 189–90
    funeral directors 13, 187, 190, 198,
    207–8, 216–17
    impact of pandemic on service
    providers 206–12, 218
    religious/faith requirements 14, 65,
    206–18
    restrictions 83–4, 189–90, 202–18
    see also death(s); grief; memorials/
    memorialisation

G

G20 protests 125
gender
    deaths from COVID-19 58, 93,
    206
    gendering of the pandemic 10,
    92–100
    men's wellbeing group 54
    see also men; women
gender-based violence see violence
    against women and girls
Gentleman, Amelia 141,
    145–9
ghusl 209, 211–12
Gillis, John R. 237
Gilmore, Joanna 125
Glasgow
    asylum seekers 160–1, 167, 171,
    172, 174
    memorials 16
Go Ahead, Tell Me (Coleman)
    265
Goffman, Erving 170–1
Gold Jennings Solicitors 168
González-Enríquez, Carmen
    236
Good Morning Britain 130
Good Things Foundation 47
Goodall, Lewis 38
Goodman, Jo 242, 243, 255, 256
Goodman, Stuart 242, 255
Gove, Michael 94–5
government guidance 11, 140, 141,
    142–6
Gramsci, Antonio 298
Grant, Tim 37
Gray, Sue 36, 37–8, 245, 247
Grayson, John 166
greenspace scotland 16
grief
    grievability 83
    Reckoning with Grief (Twitter
    threads) 179–83
    see also assisted living residents
    and grief; death(s); funerals;
    memorials/memorialisation
Guardian, The 132, 146, 234

H

Hall, Fran 17, 233, 243, 248–9, 252–61
Hamdany, Mahwish 278
Hamdany, Mehreen 18, 276–7
Han, Yuna 40
Hancock, Matt 269
hate crime 48
healthcare workers 7–8, 23
    deaths 60, 81
    heroism narrative 34
    lack of respect 294
    realities of a COVID-19 ward 97–8
heroism narrative 15, 27, 28, 34
Higuera, Cristina del Prado 152, 153
HIV/AIDs memorialisation 237–8
Hogan, Matthew 18, 266–75
Holgate J 133
Home Office 63
    and asylum seekers 51–2, 160–75
    hostile environment 51–2, 63, 145–9, 161, 163, 170, 174
    Windrush scandal 146–8
homeschooling 96–7
Honeycombe-Foster, Matt 95
Honigsbaum, Mark 15, 16–17, 232–50
Horvath, Miranda 129
Hoskins, Andrew 239
hospitals
    Black, Asian and Global Majority experiences 80
    catching COVID-19 in 242, 246
    discharge into care homes 103–4
    Johnson, Boris, treated in 79, 94–5
    lack of equipment 60
    Nightingale Hospitals 83, 197–8, 270
    realities of a COVID-19 ward 97–8
    refused access to 80
    visiting restrictions 30–1, 36, 187, 188, 214
    youth workers in 291
    see also healthcare workers; mortuaries
Hossein-Pour, Anahita 92
hostile environment 51–2, 63, 145–9, 161, 163, 170, 174

House, Danielle 14, 202–18
House of Commons Select Committee 167
Howard, Mark 40–1
Human BSE 241–2
human rights
    and discharge into care homes 103
    and state officials' use of the law 140–52

I

I have a wall in front of all my windows (Bajec) 12, 154–9
immigration see asylum seekers; Windrush scandal
Immigration Act 1971 145
Immigration Act 2014 145–7
Immigration and Asylum Act 1999 163
immigration officials 140–1, 146–8, 168
immigration removal centres (IRCs) 161, 163
Inayatullah, Naeem 32
India 137–8
influenza pandemic (1918–19) 15, 16, 34, 237, 238
Influenza Pandemic Preparedness Strategy 270
intimate loss 26, 33
Iredale, Lara-Rose 14, 30, 184–200
Islam see Muslim communities
Islam, Farjana 14, 202–18
Islam, Safina 8–9, 43–5, 46–7, 52, 55, 58, 62, 63, 65, 67, 68–9, 70, 72–4
Italy 96
ITV 81–2

J

Jayaseelan, Rajesh 34
Jenkins, Ciaran 29
Joanna Gilmore 125
Johnson, Boris
    character references 97, 98–9
    declares 'freedom' from the coronavirus 248

fighting the virus rhetoric 92–3, 235, 249

first lockdown announcement 78

has COVID-19 79, 94–5, 97, 99

'let the bodies pile high' 84, 244–5, 247

National Covid Memorial Wall 233, 235, 243, 244–5, 250

Partygate 11, 38, 235, 245–6, 247–8, 296

physical fitness of 99

shaking hands 98

strategy of 249

on *This Morning* 81–2

Johnson, Stanley 97

Joint Committee on Human Rights (JCHR) 140, 142–4, 148–9, 150, 151

Jones, Fay 129–30

Jones, Marie 37

Joyce, Peter 125, 134

judicial review 168

K

Kennedy, John F. 94

Kernick, Gill 275

key workers 7–8, 23

betrayal of 27, 59–60, 62–3

Black, Asian and Global Majority experiences 78–9

body politics 78–9, 93

clapping for carers 62, 95, 109, 196

commemoration 34

deaths of 34, 58, 60, 80, 81

funeral service providers 206–12

health risks 203

heroism narrative 34

importance of 294

masculinised labour 78–9, 93

portrayal of 27, 34

Khan, Sadiq 129, 234

Kirkup, James 163, 170

Klein, Naomi 292, 297

Knight, Sam 233

knowledge-based public order policing 124, 126, 132–6

Knowles, Oliver ('Olly') 256

Kuenssberg, Laura 99

L

Labour Party 25, 36, 37–8

Lammy, David 131

law-breaking *see* fines; legal education; Partygate; policing of protests

law(s) *see* legal education

learning from the pandemic 70–2, 270–3, 281, 285–90, 291–3, 297–9

Led By Donkeys 16, 35, 221–31, 243, 256–8

legal education 139–53

law during the pandemic 139–41, 284–5

legal violence and natural violence 148–53

state officials' use of the law 141–9, 150–3

Lenin, Vladimir 297

LGBT rights 237–8

Li Wenliang 241

Lindqvist, Sven 297

local resilience forums 267, 269, 273–4

Lock, Daniella 144

London

Muslim funerals 215, 217

protests 127–30, 131–2, 133–4

Lumière Tarot 9, 75–6

Lynn, Vera 96

M

Maddrell, Avril 14, 90, 116, 202–18

Mail on Sunday 99

'MAMILs' (middle-aged men in lycra) 88–9

Manchester

Black, Asian and Global Majority experiences 43–74

Manchester City Council 45–6

see also Abdul-Latif, Amna

Manhire, Toby 38

Mannergren Selimovic, Johanna 26, 33, 39–40, 40

Manzoor-Khan, Suhaiymah 18
Martin, Herbert Woodward 17, 251
Mason, Rowena 79, 98
May 8th, 2020 (Thompson) 42
May, Theresa 163, 170
Mbembe, Achille 84–5
McLays Guest House, Glasgow 172
Mears 167, 172, 174
memorials/memorialisation 15–17
    assisted living residents 111–12
    connective memory 239
    contested nature of 34
    in the digital world 238–9
    and grievability 83
    lack of pre-mediation 238
    and memory 236–7
    and narrative-telling 34–5
    and power 236–7
    of previous pandemics 237–8
    shifting politics of 236–9
    social forgetting 238
    uncommemoration 83
    visibility of 38–41
    see also National Covid Memorial
      Wall
memory work 16, 237
men
    criminalised young Black men 140,
      153
    deaths from COVID-19 58, 93,
      206
    masculinised portrayal of virus
      92–100
    'MAMILs' (middle-aged men in
      lycra) 88–9
    well-being group 54
Mendick, Robert 98
mental health
    asylum seekers 12, 57, 160–1,
      169–74
    Black, Asian and Global Majority
      experiences 48, 50, 54, 57, 61,
      74
    older people 104
middle classes 79, 88–90, 91
Migrant Help 174
migrant workers 57, 62–3, 298

militarisation of the pandemic 15, 34,
    92–100, 235, 249
Miller, Daniel 116
Milne, Amber 94–5
mortuaries 14, 184–200
    deceased's property 186–7, 188–9
    early days of pandemic 185–6,
      189–90
    emergency facilities 191–2, 193–4
    emergency planning/planners 194,
      199–200
    impact of pandemic on staff 194–8
    lack of capacity 190–2
    paperwork 190
    process in 'normal' times 186–7
    staff in the spotlight 198
Mulveen, Jacky 295
Muslim communities
    asylum seekers 167–8
    food banks and deliveries 50
    funerals 14, 65, 206, 209–12,
      213–18
    ghusl 209, 211–12
Mustapha, Jennifer 1–3, 4, 9, 19
Mutual Aid Groups 49–50
*My impending adventure, a story for
    another day* (Ssentongo) 14, 201

N

Nair, Anjana 11, 137–8
National AIDS Memorial Quilt (US)
    237–8
National Audit Office 272
National Covid Memorial Wall
    16–17, 34, 35, 39–40, 232–50,
    252–61
    fading paint 259
    Friends of the Wall 17, 233, 248–9,
      259–61
    graffiti 259
    Led By Donkeys photo story
      221–31
    maintenance/restoration of 233,
      248–9, 259–61
    media reports 234, 245–6, 253,
      254, 258
    opening ceremony 254

origins 232–3, 242–5, 252–4,
255–8
petition for permanency 248
political nature of 233–4, 235, 249,
259
walking and rewalking 239–50
Welby, Justin (Archbishop of
Canterbury) 233–4
as work in progress 250
National Lottery Community Fund
106
National Risk Register 268, 279
Nationalities and Borders Bill 63
necropolitics 84–6
Network for Police Monitoring 132
New Zealand Red Cross 289
Newsnight 38
NHS *see* healthcare workers; hospitals
Nightingale Hospitals 83, 197–8, 270
non-governmental organisations
(NGOs) 168, 175
Northamptonshire's Chief Constable
143
Nuila, Ricardo 97–8

O
obesity 99
Observer, The 257
Olbeh, Adnan 160–1, 172
older people *see* ageism; assisted living
residents and grief; care homes
Omicron variant 90
opinion polls 25, 36
Orwell, George 296
Oswin, Nathan 244
Our World in Data 295
Owen, Wilfred 28

P
Pandemic Easter (Martin) 17, 251
Panorama 34
Parrot, Fiona 116
Partygate 35–6, 235, 245–6, 247–8,
296
public reaction 25, 36–8, 180, 183,
235, 248
Patel, Priti 131, 134

Patterson, Laura 31
personal protective equipment (PPE)
31, 81, 272, 285
Philp, Chris 168
police/policing
interpretation of the law 11–12,
143, 144, 148–9, 150
regulated and unregulated violence
148–9
see also policing of protests
policing of protests 123–36
anti-lockdown protests 127–8
Black Lives Matter protests 130–2,
134–5
Clapham Common vigil 89, 121–2,
128–30, 133–4
historically 124–6
knowledge-based public order
policing 124, 126, 134
policing styles 124–5
understanding pandemic policing
132–6
policy makers, Black, Asian and Global
Majority experiences 67–70, 73
Politico Poll of Polls 25
Pollock Park, Glasgow 16
post-mortems 184, 186, 192–3, 195,
197
poverty 80–1, 205–6, 293–5
'pre-existing' health conditions 31, 81,
96, 104
press conferences 24, 29, 35–6, 249
privilege 55, 59–60, 73, 79, 87–90,
91
proning 98
protests
Black Lives Matter 32, 64–5,
130–2, 134–5, 236, 294
group types 134–5
see also policing of protests
PTSD (post-traumatic stress disorder)
28
public anger/reaction 33–4, 39–41
Partygate 25, 36–8, 180, 183, 235,
248
see also National Covid Memorial
Wall; policing of protests

Public Health Act 1984 274
Public Health England 173
public inquiry
    calls for 255–6, 282
    draft terms of reference 248
    effectiveness of 38–9, 282–4, 286
    protracted nature of 282–3
Purnell, Kandida 9–10, 77–101
Purnell, Sonia 98

R
Raab, Dominic 95
race/racism *see* Black, Asian and
    Global Majority experiences
Reckoning with Grief (Twitter
    threads) 179–83
Reicher, Stephen 124, 125–6, 133,
    134, 135
Reiner, Robert 124
resilience *see* emergency planning/
    planners
Reynolds, Martin 36, 245
risk management *see* emergency
    planning/planners
Robson, Jo 46, 63–5
Rose, Will 256
Rosen, Michael 10, 36, 102
rule-breaking *see* fines; legal
    education; Partygate; policing of
    protests
rule of law 139–40, 141, 143, 149
Rumble, Hannah 10, 103–17

S
Sabbagh, Dan 79, 132
sacrifice narrative 15, 27, 28, 34, 235,
    298, 299
Sadri, James 256
Safety4Sisters *see* Sharma, Sandhya
Sanchez Taylor, Jacqueline 32
'Sanctuary' (memorial) 16
Schafheutle, Karen 36
Schofield, Kevin 95
Schofield, Phillip 81–2
Sharma, Sandhya 50–2, 56–7, 62–3,
    68, 71–2
Shaw, Neil 99

Sheptycki, James 125
shielding 53–4, 79
Sibley, John 99
Silva, Guillermo Andrés Duque 152,
    153
slavery 85, 132, 236
social forgetting 238
soldiers, and grievability 83
Spanish flu pandemic 15, 16, 34, 237,
    238
Ssentongo, Irene Naikaali 14, 201
Starmer, Keir 37–8, 234, 247, 253
state of emergency 145–6, 152–3
statue of Edward Colston 132, 236
Steele, Circle 47–8, 53–4, 58–9, 67–8,
    71
Stevenson, Patsy 130
Stewart, Ben 256
Stratton, Allegra 35–6
students in lockdown 144
Suleman, Mehrunisha 80–1
Surrey 86–8
survivance 290
systemic discrimination 44, 293–4

T
'take it on the chin' 81–92
Tarot cards 9, 75–6
Taylor-Broadbent, Jayne 246–8
Taylor, John 167
Tazzioli, Martina 161
teachable moments 291–2
terrorism 160, 236, 272
This Morning 81–2
Thompson, Marvin 8, 42
Thompson, Tracey 37
Time magazine 295
total institution concept 170–1
traumatic loss 27–31, 33, 40–1
travel restrictions 143, 166, 204–5,
    270
Troyer, John 13, 185
Trump, Donald 96
trust in government 295–6
Tuitt, Patricia 11–12, 38, 139–53,
    284–5
Twain, Mark 297

U

UK Office for National Statistics
(ONS) 29, 80, 93, 213
UN Convention Relating to the Status
of Refugees 161–2
UN High Commissioner for Refugees
(UNHCR) 162
UN Women 295
unattended funerals 207–8
uncommemoration 83
United States
domestic violence 295
Floyd, George 11, 18, 32, 130–1,
294
Kennedy, John F. 94
memorials 236, 237–8
mortality/morbidity rates 293,
296
policing of coronavirus orders 298
university officials 144
Unlawful Gathering (Bradley) 11,
121–2

V

vaccines 6, 90, 295
Vallance, Patrick 33
Vassy, Carine 281
Vietnam War veterans 28
violence
and the law 148–9, 148–53
structural violence against asylum
seekers 173–4'
see also policing of protests
violence against women and girls 48,
50–2, 56–7, 62–3, 129–30, 295
policy makers 68
Virginia Water, Surrey 86–7
Vizenor, Gerald 290

W

Wai Yin Society *see* Steele, Circle
Waiting to Exhale (Hamdany) 276–7
Walters, Simon 84
Waples, Louise 37
war memorials 236
War on Terror 83
Warby LJ 133

wartime terminology 15, 34, 92–100,
235, 249
Welby, Justin 233–4
Wellcome Trust Institutional Strategic
Support Fund 106
Wells, Celia 282
Wernimont, Jacqueline 29
West, Karen 10, 103–17
Westerleigh Group 16
When This Is Over (Mustapha) 1–3,
4, 9, 19
Williams, Kayla 80
Willoughby, Holly 81–2
Wilson, Eric 42
Windrush scandal 11–12, 140–1,
145–9
Winnett, Robert 163, 170
women
asylum seekers 51–2, 56–7, 62–3,
164–6
Black, Asian and Global Majority
experiences 47, 48, 51–2, 56–7,
61, 62–3, 68–9, 164–6
confidence in the police 130
gendering of the pandemic 10,
92–100
lockdowns 90
Sarah Everard vigil 89, 121–2,
128–30, 133–4
violence against women and
girls 48, 50–2, 56–7, 62–3, 68,
129–30, 295
Women's Empowerment and
Recovery Educators (WE:ARE)
295
working from home 59, 73, 79, 87,
203
World Health Organization (WHO)
127
Wuhan whistleblower 241
Wynne Jones, Ros 233

Y

Yancy, George 16, 237
Yeats, William Butler 40
Yorke, Harry 98
Younge, Gary 19, 291–300